MY POETICS

My Poetics

MAUREEN N. MCLANE

The University of Chicago Press
Chicago & London

The University of Chicago Press, Chicago 60637
The University of Chicago Press, Ltd., London
© 2024 by Maureen N. McLane
All rights reserved. No part of this book may be used or reproduced in any manner whatsoever without written permission, except in the case of brief quotations in critical articles and reviews. For more information, contact the University of Chicago Press, 1427 East 60th Street, Chicago, IL 60637.
Published 2024
Printed in the United States of America

33 32 31 30 29 28 27 26 25 24   1 2 3 4 5

ISBN-13: 978-0-226-83038-4 (cloth)
ISBN-13: 978-0-226-83264-7 (paper)
ISBN-13: 978-0-226-83265-4 (e-book)
DOI: https://doi.org/10.7208/chicago/9780226832654.001.0001

CIP data to come

♾ This paper meets the requirements of ANSI/NISO Z39.48-1992 (Permanence of Paper).

Contents

Proem in the Form of a Q&A	oo
A Note to the Reader	oo
"OK Let's Go"	oo
1 * *Conditional/Poetics*	1
"see you've already forgotten"	oo
"Preferences"	oo
"They Were Always Thinking"	oo
2 * *Compositional/Poetics*	oo
"Haunt"	oo
"Crows"	oo
"Weeds"	oo
"Trees"	oo
"Taking a Walk in the Woods after Having Taken a Walk in the Woods with You"	oo
3 * *Notational/Poetics*	oo
"notational/sufficiency…"	oo

4 * *Rhyme/Poetics*   oo

5 * *Choratopical/Poetics*   oo
   "Moonrise"   oo

Acknowledgments   oo
   "envoi"   oo
Notes   oo
Bibliography   oo
Index   oo

Proem in the Form of a Q&A

Why poetics?

> My purpose here is to advance into
> the sense of the weather.[1]

And?

> What I have to
> offer here is nothing revolutionary.[2]

So what is this?

> I am not writing anything that anyone has requested of me or
> is waiting on, not a poetics essay or any other sort of essay, not
> a roundtable response, not interview responses, not writing

---

[1] Lisa Robertson, *The Weather*.
[2] Juliana Spahr, "Transitory, Momentary," in *That Winter the Wolf Came*.

prompts for younger writers, not my thoughts about critical theory or popular songs.[3]

And yet, poetics?

I was fully aware of the risks involved, that any plausible poetics would be shattered, like a shop window, flickering and jagged, all of the wire exposed and sending sharp twists and reversible jolts into whatever it was I was trying to explain or talk about.[4]

And/But, poetics?

It's not that I want to say that poetry is disconnected from having something to say; it's just that everything I want to say eludes me.[5]

And so?

We might could make
a plan, *make something out of
apparently nothing.*[6]

And so?

I made this up from nothing.
It's not myself I sing,
or love, or anything
    that has a source.

---

3   Anne Boyer, "Not Writing," in *Garments against Women*.
4   Sean Bonney, "Letter against Sickness," in *Letters against the Firmament*.
5   Fred Moten, "It's not that I want to say," in *The Service Porch*.
6   Tonya Foster, "High Court," in *A Swarm of Bees in High Court*.

PROEM IN THE FORM OF A Q&A

> I dreamed these words while riding
> on my horse.[7]

What was your first encounter with poetry?

> 'Twas brillig and the slithy toves
> did gyre and gimble in the wabe.[8]

And then?

> You'd notice it
> at grass level, when you're a child.[9]

And then?

> ... free to excavate and interrogate definition, the first labor was to sweep away the pernicious idea of poetry as embroidery for women.[10]

And then?

> I said the difference is complicated
> And she said yes is it it is
> Or she said it is is it.[11]

---

7 Devin Johnston, "Nothing Song," in *Traveler*.
8 Lewis Carroll, "Jabberwocky," in *Jabberwocky and Other Nonsense*.
9 Anthony (Vahni) Capildeo, "For Love of Things Invisible," in *Like a Tree, Walking*.
10 Susan Howe, *My Emily Dickinson*.
11 Gertrude Stein, *Stanzas in Meditation*, part III, stanza II.

PROEM IN THE FORM OF A Q&A

And then?

> I realized then that, by trying to write emotional anecdotes, I was striving to become the kind of poet that I "should be" rather than the kind of poet that I "could be." I decided then that I would dedicate my complete, literary practice to nothing but a whole array of formalistic innovations.[12]

And then?

> Starting as
> a humble poet I
> quickly climbed to the
> top of my profession
> assuming a position of
> leadership and honor.[13]

And then?

> Then I gave it up
> I gave up thinking that the song I heard was the song of the world
> I gave up lyric, gave up reverie, I gave up aesthesis—
> I left my notebook on the park bench open with its pages riffling
>   I kept my head down[14]

And now?

---

12 Christian Bök, "The Xenotext Experiment."
13 Eileen Myles, "An American Poem," in *Not Me*.
14 Christopher Nealon, "Last Glimpse," in *The Shore*.

PROEM IN THE FORM OF A Q&A

> I must make 4000 Lines of one bare circumstance and fill them with Poetry.[15]

But what is poetry?

> Define definition.[16]

What is poetry?

> The difference is spreading.[17]

What is poetry?

> It is easier to think what Poetry should be than to write it.[18]

What is poetry?

> It can be exhausted by no theory and only a divinatory criticism would dare try to
> characterize its ideal.[19]

Why poetry?

> The world is not enough.[20]

---

15 John Keats, Letter to Benjamin Bailey, 8 October 1817, in *Letters of John Keats*.
16 Howe, *My Emily Dickinson*.
17 Stein, *Tender Buttons*.
18 Keats, Letter to John Taylor, 27 February 1818, in *Letters of John Keats*.
19 Friedrich Schlegel, Athenaeum Fragment 116, in *Philosophical Fragments*, trans. Peter Firchow.
20 Ariana Reines, "The World Is Not Enough."

PROEM IN THE FORM OF A Q&A

Why poetry?

Il y a assurément un autre monde, mais il est dans celui-ci.[21]

Why poetry?

we are each other's
business:[22]

Why poetry?

... because in this time song holds loss.[23]

Why poetry?

Poetry sheds no tears "such as Angels weep," but natural and human tears; she can boast of no celestial Ichor that distinguishes her vital juices from those of prose; the same human blood circulates through the veins of them both.[24]

Come again?

Oh, an incurable humanist you are.[25]

Why poetry?

---

21 Quoted in Paul Éluard, "Physique de la Poésie," in *Oeuvres completes*, vol. 1.
22 Gwendolyn Brooks, "Paul Robeson," in *The Essential Gwendolyn Brooks*.
23 Spahr, "Transitory, Momentary."
24 William Wordsworth, preface to *Lyrical Ballads*.
25 Regina Spektor, "Loveology," in *Home, Before and After*.

She heard the death bells knellin'.[26]

And?

The immortal Mind craves objects that endure.[27]

And?

Of all things of thought, poetry is closest to thought, and a poem is less a thing than any other work of art.[28]

And?

Poetry, whose material is language, is perhaps the most human and least worldly of the arts,
the one in which the end product remains closest to the thought that inspired it.[29]

Why poetry?

It alone is infinite, just as it alone is free.[30]

Really?

As if the soul could

---

26 "Barbara Allen" (Child Ballad No. 84).
27 Wordsworth, "Those words were uttered as in pensive mood," in *Poems in Two Volumes*.
28 Hannah Arendt, *The Human Condition*.
29 Arendt, *The Human Condition*.
30 Schlegel, Athenaeum Fragment 116, in *Philosophical Fragments*.

be singled out from the cells,
from the room's clutter.[31]

And poetry?

Poetry = the practice of subtlety in a barbaric world.[32]

And? Huh?

We Barbarians.[33]

Poetry?

Poetry achieves renewable acts of noticing.[34]

And poetry?

Maybe poetry
is what happens on the bus between wanting and having.[35]

And?

           remember
you can have what you ask for, ask for
everything.[36]

---

31 Tonya Foster, "Bullet/in," in *A Swarm of Bees in High Court*.
32 Roland Barthes, *The Preparation of the Novel*, trans. Kate Briggs.
33 We Barbarians, https://webarbarians.com/.
34 Capildeo, "Interview with Vahni Capildeo by Zannab Sheikh."
35 Moten, "It's not that I want to say."
36 Diane di Prima, "Revolutionary Letter No. 19," in *Revolutionary Letters*.

PROEM IN THE FORM OF A Q&A

And?

> The cultivation of poetry is never more to be desired than at periods when, from an excess of the selfish and calculating principle, the accumulation of the materials of external life exceed the quantity of the power of assimilating them to the internal laws of human nature.[37]

Whither poetry?

> It should forever be becoming and never be perfected.[38]

Not Poetry, but poetries?

>   I salute
> that various field.[39]

Whither poetics?

> The death of literature, and its survival in the poem.[40]

Do you have a poetics?

> I am an extinct species, speaking an extinct language.[41]

And?

---

37 Percy Bysshe Shelley, "A Defence of Poetry."
38 Schlegel, Athenaeum Fragment 116, in *Philosophical Fragments*.
39 James Schuyler, "Salute," in *Collected Poems*.
40 Antoine Compagnon, "Roland Barthes's Novel," trans. Rosalind Krauss.
41 Denis Hollier, "On Literature Considered as a Dead Language."

PROEM IN THE FORM OF A Q&A

"i" wants to be a man like marjorie perloff, helen hennessy vendler, boris tomashevsky.[42]

Whither poetics?

A lot of it is just trying to figure out how to say something.[43]

And again, poetics?

By "poetics" I mean, in the widest sense, the discursive and figural parameters of the imagination—the terms in which the poem imagines its subject, figures its thought, thinks its figures.[44]

And?

Poetics is the continuation of poetry by other means.[45]

And?

The great silence is full of noises. And that's what I mean when I talk about poetics.[46]

Whither poetics?

---

42 Olena Kalytiak Davis, "The Lyric 'I' Drives to Pick up Her Children from School: A Poem in the Postconfessional Mode," in *The Poem She Didn't Write*.
43 Moten, "B 4."
44 Laura M. Slatkin, introduction to *The Power of Thetis and Selected Essays*.
45 Charles Bernstein, *A Poetics*.
46 Bonney, "Letter against the Firmament," in *Letters against the Firmament*.

PROEM IN THE FORM OF A Q&A

    O the wind and rain ... O the dreadful wind and rain.[47]

And you?

    I have learned how to behave
    Living like a jar for certain preserved insights that unscrolled
    upon a slender banner, the
          gentlest
    Form of scholarship glossing only delicately an unfolding
    situation that cannot be taught,
          only experienced, rising among a faint and turning mist
    Off the surface of the river[48]

Notes to self?

    Continue your annotations, continue your questionings.[49]

Final thoughts?

    America I'm putting my queer shoulder to the wheel.[50]

---

47 "The Wind and Rain," a version of "The Twa Sisters," Child Ballad No. 10.
48 Reines, "The World Is Not Enough."
49 Walt Whitman, "Song of Myself," section 38, in *Poetry and Prose*.
50 Allen Ginsberg, "America," in *Selected Poems, 1947–1995*.

To the Reader

This book might have been called *Some Poetics*, or *A Poetics* (hat tip to Charles Bernstein[1]): for a long while it was called *Open Questions*, which suggests the assaying rather than conclusory spirit of the venture. In that same spirit I might have called the book *Divagations*, adopting a term from Ezra Pound (see, e.g., his *Pavannes and Divagations*): "divagation" connotes a digression, a wandering itinerary, even perhaps a raving. This book is not a raving, nor even terribly digressive, though I do hope it offers a diverting, productive errancy amidst and through its central chapters and several interludes. It seems worthwhile to set out briefly some of the aims and preoccupations here and to signpost in advance some aspects of the itinerary.

My Poetics arises out of work and thought over the past decade. Testing what might be shadowed forth in and through poetics,

---

1 Charles Bernstein, *A Poetics* (Cambridge, MA: Harvard University Press, 1992).

the book offers a series of encounters with poems and modelings of poetry. Among its tutelary spirits are Hannah Arendt (on the human condition); Percy Bysshe Shelley (on conditionality, subjunctivity, figuration, instrumentality); Roland Barthes (on the notational, that "minimal act of writing"); Bruno Latour (on "compositionism"); and other writers and poets, from Bashō to Wallace Stevens to Gertrude Stein to W. S. Graham, Fred Wah, Tonya Foster, Claudia Rankine, John Ashbery, Ariana Reines, Anne Boyer, Bhanu Kapil, and Juliana Spahr. Other tutelary spirits include the weather (the wind, the rain) and poetic mood in all senses. Traditional balladry offers another crucial resource for poetic thinking here — balladry a rich zone of *poiesis* that eludes, or complicates, more standard literary-critical preoccupations with authorship, historicity, reception, formalization.

My Poetics arises from many years of reading, teaching, writing, and conversing about Anglophone poetries, 1750ish till now; it's inflected too by my long-standing immersion in Romantic-era poems and predicaments. It arises as well from my commitments as a poet, and the ways these have manifested in poems, books, essays; the book is also enriched by many conversations and friendships, with the dead as well as the living. And here my previous book of experimental criticism/memoir *My Poets* (2012) is also relevant: *My Poetics* pursues matters of poetry and poetics in a perhaps more scholarly and theoretical key than that earlier book (this book has endnotes!), but it hopes to welcome readers with general and not only specialist interests and training. The "my" here is an invitation, an acknowledgment, and a wager — that "my poetics" might be shared with you, perhaps challenged by you, developed and revised with "you" in mind. ("I stop somewhere waiting for you." — Whitman) The book aims to sponsor a ramifying inquiry and enactment—of attention, exegesis, meditation, and provocation, offered sometimes through extended readings, at other times via divagations, juxtapositions, refrainings, and even, occasionally, verse.

Among the core concerns here: why poetry, and whither? How have poems shaped and responded to our condition and conditioning, as historically and biodynamically conditioned sentient creatures? How do poems hold open spaces and generate modes for thinking, and how are they themselves speculative instruments of and for thought? What is the relation of poetry to its surround, its environment, "the" environment? How might a specific poem, or ballad, activate such a constellation? How might balladry point to a "field theory" of poetics? How does rhyme help us measure out, sound out thought? What of a poetry not dependent on inspiration (a poetry of "finding," and not of "making up")? And what of poetries invested in "the notational," and others committed to "projects" (as many contemporary poets are, as Wordsworth was in his *Prelude*, as Shelley was throughout his life)?

My Poetics explores how poems and poetic projects variously "think what we are doing" (cf. Arendt); how poems register, sense, and shape their conditions; and how poetics (as a discourse on poetry) might participate in and shape this ongoing relationship between poems and readers. Among many influences, my thinking is informed by ecocritical and romanticist scholarship. This poeti-critical orientation shapes the preoccupations of this book, including its interest in the variables and parameters conditioning *poiesis* and in the ways some poetry (balladry in particular) might offer models for the "redistribution of agencies" some critics have called for—a refusal to center, as it were, the human. *My Poetics* explores how poems *think* as they *do*, as they move, register, rhyme, unfold, refold, resound. Aeolian harps, ballad fiddles, and other poetic instruments make their appearance, as this book takes seriously Shelley's proposition in "A Defence of Poetry" that "Man [sic] is an instrument"—but not only an instrument. Each chapter offers a conceptual or thematic node, anchoring us in a space of poetic consideration. (Readers might want to know that the first chapter is perhaps the densest, and that things become more aerated going forward. It's also worth saying that the chapters do not necessarily depend on one another, so feel free to skip around. Not that you needed permission.) The works in view range from romantic-era odes and hymns to traditional balladry to haikus and haibuns to contemporary poetries in English. Most chapters include, end with, or are followed by a poem or poetic interval (by me, to be clear). This element of the book carries forth a kind of low-key poetic autotheory, poeticritical making in another key.

But even to attempt to lay out what this book is "about" is in part a betrayal of its spirit—for the book is skeptical of ready accounts of poetic "aboutness" (on this, see any number of works on poetry as—at least sometimes—nonpropositional and nonreferential).[2]

---

2   Among many discussions, one might see Theodor W. Adorno, "On Lyric Poetry and Society," in *Notes to Literature*, vol. 1, ed. Rolf Tiedemann, trans. Shierry Weber Nicholsen (New York: Columbia University Press, 1991), 37–54. Adorno suggests that in modernity, the "contradiction between poetic and communicative language reached an extreme" (44). Or see Paul de Man on "the crisis . . . of representation in lyric poetry in the nineteenth and twentieth centuries," which crisis he sees as internal to (and perpetual in) poetry, not as an index of historical development or of "modernity." De Man, "Lyric and Modernity," in *Blindness and Insight: Essays in the Rhetoric of Contemporary Criticism* (Minneapolis: University of Minnesota Press, 1983), 182. For further reflections on the nonpropositional and nonrepresentational commitments of

TO THE READER

My Poetics offers a way to be with (and in) poems and poetics rather than a clarion call for (or against) X or Y. It aims to be companionable, but it is also a book actively worrying, and stress-testing, various questions, texts, and horizons. This is at times a restless book; maybe it's not restless enough. I have had to curb the impulse to write a palinode after every chapter. But, as Blake said, "Enough! or Too much!"

∞

WHY I WRITE SUCH GOOD BOOKS[3]

Over the years, interviewers and students and some friends have asked how I "reconcile" poetic and critical ventures; this question is both important and in some ways unanswerable. I don't reconcile anything. It seems to me that there are many modes out there in the universe, stations that one can tune into or discover; this is one way I tend to view writing and thinking and reading across modes and genres. (Jack Spicer: "the poet is a radio." Choose your media metaphor.) Also, FWIW: I reject any a priori opposition between analytic and so-called creative dimensions, between lyric (or poetry) and critique. (Hello Horace; hello Pope; hello Shelley; hello Baudelaire; hello Lisa Robertson, Anne Carson, Denise Riley, Ben Lerner, Boyer, Rankine, Bernstein, inter alia.) Not that it isn't useful at times to discriminate among "powers" or "faculties"—as romantic poets did and as philosophers and

---

some poetry, see Anahid Nersessian, *The Calamity Form: On Poetry and Social Life* (Chicago: University of Chicago Press, 2020).

3 See the title of chapter 3 of Friedrich Nietzsche, *Ecce Homo: How to Become What You Are*, trans. Duncan Large (Oxford and New York: Oxford University Press, 2007).

critics have long done; not that there aren't different kinds of audiences for works traveling under different banners. Not that specialist discourses and specific genres don't persist amidst what Lauren Berlant called "genre flail" and the emergence of so-called genreless art.[4] Some are given (encouraged? paid?) to write in one mode, some in two or three, some range across genres, some blow up what they see as the prison house of genre. This seems to me a matter of disposition, ability, and opportunity (and do I need to say class? habitus? privilege?) and seems something to be discovered, if possible, and not willed or policed.

To turn things a bit differently: I detest the anti-intellectualism that travels under cover of "professionalism" in some official precincts of poetry, and I detest almost as much the benign contempt or sentimental regard academics and critics can have for "creative writers." And yet it is true that one's life energies are limited; that extended immersion in certain communities (including universities) or ways of thinking and writing (scholarly as well as essayistic and poetic) can't but shape what you do. Life in and adjacent to academic institutions raises the possibility that one could end up like poor sad Coleridge, lamenting in his "Dejection" ode that his commitment to "abstruse research" killed off his "shaping spirit of Imagination."

Regarding that "shaping spirit": it is true that some poems seem— even are!—phenomena occasioned by forces insusceptible of analysis; and yes, as Wordsworth wrote, "we murder to dissect." And yes, "the poem must resist the intelligence / Almost successfully"

---

[4] Lauren Berlant, "Genre Flailing," *Capacious: Journal for Emerging Affect Inquiry* 1 (2): 2018: 156–162; http://capaciousjournal.com/article/genre-flailing/.

(Stevens, "Man Carrying Thing." Note: *almost*; I myself am happy that some poems I care about resist my intelligence wholly and successfully). And yes, batter my heart, and O the mind, mind has mountains, my quietness has a man in it, full well I know that she is there, and where there is personal liking we go.[5] But there is a difference between myth and mystification, and between the stunning mysterious fiat of the achieved work and the manufacturing of poeticity. On some days the same work might seem to partake of both (as I can sometimes think regarding some of H.D.'s work, H.D. whom I love; ditto Keats). At the end of the day, with poetics as with poetry, things are proved on the pulse, as Keats wrote, and you just go on your nerve, as Frank O'Hara wrote. Yet pulses and nerves are shaped bodily things—socialized, communally attuned, sometimes antagonistically developed, creaturely conditioned.

Anne Carson is one writer famously reluctant to call herself a poet; she prefers to gloss herself as a person who makes things. "Poet-critic" is a term that gives me hives, but that may be a resistance worth probing further. Not now. "There are things that are important beyond all this fiddle" (Marianne Moore).

And perhaps it is true that, in the end, *Poetry can only be criticized by way of poetry* (Friedrich Schlegel).

Music it for yourself, William Carlos Williams wrote.

My Poetics: "It is weather, and it is for friendship" (Lisa Robertson). And it is for Laura. And it is for you.

---

[5] A salute to (respectively) John Donne, Gerard Manley Hopkins, Frank O'Hara, Gertrude Stein, and Marianne Moore.

TO THE READER

OK Let's Go

Let's go to Dawn School
and learn again to begin

oh something different
from repetition

Let's go to the morning
and watch the sun smudge

every bankrupt idea
of nature "you can't write about

anymore" said my friend
the photographer "except

as science"
Let's enroll ourselves

in the school of the sky
where knowing

how to know
and unknow is everything

we'll come to know
under what they once thought

was the dome of the world[6]

---

6 Maureen N. McLane, "OK Let's Go," in *Some Say* (New York: Farrar, Straus & Giroux, 2016), 5–6.

* I *
Conditional/Poetics

There is a phrase that has haunted me for years—Hannah Arendt's "to think what we are doing."[1]

For after all: "The condition of the human species at the present hour is critical and alarming" (William Godwin).[2]

For after all: "We are living through two catastrophes of thought, neither of which needed to be. The first is the sheer devastation of climate change. . . . At the same time that we are thinking and failing to think about our new world with old categories the 'we' that thinks is collapsing" (Liane Carlson).[3]

For after all: "Understanding the Anthropocene . . . necessitates not only new periodizing approaches . . . but a reckoning with what the *unmaking* of these longstanding definitions means for the possibility of historical thought itself" (Margaret Ronda).[4]

For after all: "The current planetary crisis of climate change or global warming elicits a variety of responses in individuals, groups, and governments, ranging from denial, disconnect, and indifference to a spirit of engagement and activism of varying kinds and degrees. These responses saturate our sense of the now" (Dipesh Chakrabarty).[5]

For after all: "Life is, generally speaking, a blessing independent of a future state" (Thomas Robert Malthus).[6]

For after all: "Then, what is Life?" (Percy Bysshe Shelley).[7]

∞

When in 1958 Arendt enjoined us in *The Human Condition* "to think what we are doing," she had in mind both the atom bomb and space exploration as the immanent horizon of crisis and transformation. She was also taking aim, here and elsewhere, at the reduction of the activity of thought to—indeed, its replacement by—"science," "know-how," merely instrumental reason.[8] The freedom and precarity of thought were both assumed in Arendt's injunction.

To think what we are doing.
Many of those I know do nothing else, and they are such beautiful thinkers.

Yet one confronts here the possible inefficacy of thought, and another kind of melancholia.

Though this is perhaps premature and a well-worn path to the forest of quietism. And it is worth being skeptical of what Fred Moten calls, in his trenchant essay on Arendt, "the cult of intelligence."[9]

Have I, like the philosopher of religion Liane Carlson, lost faith in thinking?

Is this a contemporary resounding of the Keatsian diagnosis, *Where but to think is to be full of sorrow*—
Or of Coleridge's effort "not to think of what I needs must feel"?[10]
O for a life of sensations rather than of thoughts! (Keats).

There was a time when meadow, grove, and stream,
The earth, and every common sight,
        To me did seem
        Apparell'd in celestial light,
The glory and the freshness of a dream.
It is not now as it hath been of yore;—
        WILLIAM WORDSWORTH, "Ode: Intimations of Immortality from Recollections of Early Childhood"[11]

There was a time when people were extremely exercised by binaries, and whether one could think outside or beyond them.

That was another time.

There was a revival among some scholars of medieval theology, a revival of Aristotle, of Lucretius, a return to Marx, another return to Marx, a new political theology that chimed frighteningly with the old.

There were new aesthetic categories and there was a revivification of the old: the sublime returned as the imagined mind began to fail before the hyperobjects it could not grasp yet could not but posit. It was as if no one could imagine their minds not failing.

Enough! or Too much! (William Blake.)[12]

A very old and lively man said to me early in the new century: ah, I am glad I will be dead before all this prevails.

"Perhaps this can be a poem about how I think about the future. It can be a poem of servile innocence. Since I do not 'think' about the future" (Lucy Ives).[13]

Can this be a poem, can this be a chapter, about how I think about the future?

Do I think about the future?
Do I think?
I remember the future. I remember poet Joe Brainard's classic work *I Remember*.
I remember futures past.[14]
I remember the past's future.
I remember Jerome McGann's chapter in *The Romantic Ideology: A Critical Investigation*: "Shelley's Poetry: The Judgment of the Future."[15]
I remember Louis Althusser: "The Future Lasts a Long Time." I remember Althusser's "L'avenir dure longtemps" is also translated as "The Future Lasts Forever."[16] Forever? A Long Time? The Future?

I remember that in 2011 the Geological Society of America entitled its annual meeting "Archean to Anthropocene: The Past Is the Key to the Future."[17]

Is the past the key to the future? This is the crux of the modern conception of revolution, as Arendt among others has explored. See her *On Revolution*.[18]

Is the past the key to the future?

This is the crux of the reproduction of production, as well as the reproduction of reproduction.

I remember Shelley: "One comes behind, / Who aye the future to the past will bind— / Necessity"! (*Laon and Cythna*, canto 9, XXVII).[19]

I remember the ruse of necessitarianism.

I remember that Shelley's revolutionary heroine Cythna salutes "the future, a broad sunrise" (*Laon and Cythna*, canto 9, XXV).

Yet I remember that his despairing revolutionaries also invoke "the homeless future's wintry grove" (*Laon and Cythna*, canto 9, XX).

I remember the revolution.

I remember several revolutions.

I remember the End of History.

I remember Francis Fukuyama's essay.[20] I remember 1989: the Berlin Wall, the Fall, I remember Tiananmen and June 4th and 9/11 and all the hot dates some of which you too may remember.

I remember the end of the Future.

I remember Shelley and "the gigantic shadows which futurity casts on the present."[21]

I remember Bruno Latour: "The French language, for once richer than English, differentiates '*le futur*' from '*l'avenir*.' In French,

I could say that the Moderns had '*un futur*' but never '*un avenir*.'"²²
I remember *Four Futures: Life after Capitalism*, by Peter Frase.²³
I remember Lee Edelman calling stringently for "No Future."²⁴
I remember Julia Jarcho quoting José Esteban Muñoz's rebuttal: "The present is not enough. It is impoverished and toxic."²⁵
I remember Latour's "Compositionist Manifesto": "Instead of a future of no future, why not try to see if we could not have a prospect at last?"²⁶
I remember Gertrude Stein: "Not to the future but to the fuchsia."²⁷

∞

Early in the new millennium, Alan Weisman offered a vision of "the world without us" (i.e., humans). Bill McKibben has registered since the late 1980s the imminent horror of "nothing but us"—"the end of nature," man become geophysical force, nothing not touched, not transformed, not damaged by the forces unleashed by extractive industrial processes.²⁸

Tell me, "Where can a lady reside" (Lisa Robertson)?²⁹

I want to reside in a place somewhere between the World Without Us and Nothing But Us, between thought experiment and apocalypse. I want to resist the overwhelming catastrophism of a flattened determinism, to open a space between the logic of the condition and the logic of determination. I want to station us between the etymologic of condition as *con-dicere*, co-saying, stipulation, proviso, antecedent circumstance, and the etymologic of determination as the prefixing or causing of limits, the bringing to an end, decision.³⁰ Between condition as the prevailing state of the weather, ground, sea, or atmosphere at a particular time, and determination as a catastrophic calculus and teleologic.³¹ I want to station us between, as it were, the weather and the climate, between the multiple parameters of the atmosphere (weather) and the statistical averaging thereof over decades (climate).³² Poetry is one peculiar instrument for registering this oscillation, for as NASA reminds us, "the difference between weather and climate is a measure of time," and among many things poems can do is to give time a particular linguistic measure: the time in and the time of the poem.³³ I want to invoke the poem as a measuring and sounding instrument, as a conditioned and conditioning instrument, and as a speculative instrument. (Consider the first *Oxford English Dictionary* definition of "instrument": "1. An object, device, or apparatus designed or used for a particular purpose or task." And further: "1. c. A device or apparatus for registering, measuring, or recording a physical quantity, property, or phenomenon."³⁴) I want to register what conditioning sounds like in poems, what modes it might take up, what elemental parameters a poem might assume or probe.

But again: "conditioning"? the "conditional"? Why these terms? I invoke the "conditional" as a way to register the complex relations among grammatical modes, philosophical concerns, and environmental preoccupations in poems. ("If Winter comes, can Spring be far behind?" So Shelley ends his "Ode to the West Wind," with a question in the conditional mode.) A "conditional" inquiry into poetics allows us to move from the broadest horizons of entanglement/crisis to "the human condition" (as in Arendt) to poetic formalizations of grammar and mode (the "conditional mode"): or rather, the "conditional" holds the space where these domains might be loosely coordinated. To think what we are doing, under and toward what conditions; to explore how poems register and test their conditions, not least through a speculative, conditional mode.

What conditions the human? In *The Climate of History in a Planetary Age*, Dipesh Chakrabarty invokes "conditions (such as the temperature zone in which the planet exists) that work like boundary parameters of human existence."[35] In *The Human Condition*, Arendt lists among "the conditions of human existence" "life itself, natality and mortality, worldliness, plurality, and the earth."[36] ("Natality": the condition of having-been-born, and more broadly, the capacity to initiate, for the new to come into the world; "plurality": the condition of being one-among-others.) More recently, John Durham Peters has observed that "the human condition is recursive: it is a conditional condition: our actions change the conditions they act in, especially since they change us."[37] (This "conditional condition" aligns with some biologists' interest in "codetermination," in complex, recursively shaping co-influences.[38]) Marx's version of recursivity, of codetermination, offers a nightmarish amplification: "Men make their own history, but they do not make it as they please; they do not make it under self-selected circumstances, but under circumstances existing already, given and transmitted from the past. The tradition of all dead generations weighs like a nightmare on the brains of the living."[39] If "capitalism" is one name for undead "tradition," the Anthropocene suggests another horizon for congealed "circumstances."

To think what we are doing.

And, or: poetry?

In *The Human Condition*, Arendt specifically noted the proximity of poetry to "the thought that inspired it."[40] She further observed, "Of all things of thought, poetry is closest to thought, and a poem is less a thing than any other work of art."[41]

Enter, again, Shelley—and a peculiar "thing of thought," his "Hymn to Intellectual Beauty." This strange and compelling poem is a bravura inquiry into the conditions of thought in and against our given world. The poem begins thus:

The awful shadow of some unseen Power
    Floats tho' unseen amongst us,—visiting
    This various world with as inconstant wing
As summer winds that creep from flower to flower.—
Like moonbeams that behind some piny mountain shower,
    It visits with inconstant glance
    Each human heart and countenance;
Like hues and harmonies of evening,—
    Like clouds in starlight widely spread,—
    Like memory of music fled,—
    Like aught that for its grace may be
Dear, and yet dearer for its mystery.

stanza 1, lines 1–12[42]

One registers in this first stanza Shelley's ostentatious negations and the proliferations of similes, the unseen power twice glossed as unseen and yet also twice hailed, the enunciatory leveraging itself over the visible. However "unseen," Intellectual Beauty manifests itself in visual and auditory similes ("Like moonbeams . . ."; "Like hues and harmonies of evening"; "Like memory of music fled").

Shelley conspicuously tropes the operations of Intellectual

Beauty by accenting its medial, motile, flowing logopoiea and dispersive acoustic. Intellectual Beauty moves and floats; it visits; it is provisionally materialized in thought through spectacular nested similes—"visiting / This various world with as inconstant wing / As summer winds that creep from flower to flower—" (stanza 1, lines 2–4), the motion of its power (a kind of naturalized paraclete) become wing likened to the winds animated and animalized as creeping from flower to flower.[43] One notes too the strong seasonal markers here. If it is not clearly summer in the beginning of the poem, there is a summonable summer in the mind of the poem, as Intellectual Beauty moves and visits this various world "with as inconstant wing / as summer winds." And this early salute to winds prefigures Shelley's later focus on winds and Aeolian instrumental processes.

Would anyone today write a "Hymn to Intellectual Beauty"? What was Shelley thinking? What is "Intellectual Beauty?"[44]

Paranoid reading[45]: a beautiful idealism, a compensatory ideational structure, a concept, a personification—that embarrassing and abominated figure, even more embarrassing than flat out anthropomorphism. Intellectual Beauty: a transient ideologeme that—unlike Nature, God, the Soul, or the Sublime—never quite took wing?

Reparative reading: A hymn to a mysterious presence and/or a beautification of mystification; an invocation and evocation of poetic and intellectual power; a peculiar artifact of what Shelley calls later in this poem "human thought or form." Not a category of aesthetic judgment but a pulse, a force, a visitant, the figure of shaping and informing power per se.

The "Hymn to Intellectual Beauty" holds within it a muted elegy for concepts and for a solacing poetry. The poem puts tremendous effort into opening a space of thought through its proliferation of negations (unseen, unseen, unquiet, uncertain, unknown, unlink'd) and its spectacular profusion of figuration. The Hymn later revs up its tropological engine:

Thy light alone—like mist o'er mountains driven,
    Or music by the night-wind sent
    Thro' strings of some still instrument,
    Or moonlight on a midnight stream,
Gives grace and truth to life's unquiet dream.

stanza 3, lines 32–36

This is a strenuous performance of *copia*, as well as a cataloging of alternatives—thus the reigning conjunction "or," coordinating and sequencing the brilliantly rung subclausal clichés of romantic instrumentality.[46]

And regarding *some still instrument*: here Shelley conjures an Aeolian harp, or perhaps a lyre, a stringed instrument that produces musical sounds when a current of air passes through it. Eighteenth-century Britain saw a fashion for Aeolian harps, small instruments you could put on your desk or table. You will find Aeolian harps (and sometimes lyres or lutes) all over romantic-era poetry. More broadly, Aeolianism appears as a governing figure for inspiration and for *poiesis*, from Coleridge's "The Eolian Harp" to his "Dejection" ode to Shelley's "Ode to the West Wind" to his extended meditation in his "Defence of Poetry": "Man is an instrument over which a series of external and internal impressions are driven, like the alternations of an ever-changing wind over an Aeolian lyre, which move it by their motion to ever-changing melody" (511). Aeolianism offers a figure of the poet-as-instrument, as played upon and playing; Aeolianism also more generally indexes (in Shelley's view) the *human* condition, "Man" (*sic*) as an instrument, not only the poet. And indeed, Coleridge scales up this instrumental condition to all nature: "what if all of animated nature / Be but organic Harps diversely framed" ("The Eolian Harp")?

In the "Hymn to Intellectual Beauty," Shelley's passing invocation of "some still instrument" suggests a subtle oscillation between the attribute and the condition of the instrument, between the adjectival sense of "still" (as in, this quiet, unmoving, still instrument) and the adverbial sense of "still" (as *yet*, as in, this instrument that is *still* an instrument, however still). Unspecified, the instrumental action here is apparently Aeolian and definitely nocturnal. And the prepositional relay of its figured music—"music *by* the night-wind sent / *Thro'* strings *of* some still instrument"—exemplifies the logic of the condition, of antecedent circumstances (not *cause*).[47] With "some still instrument," Shelley conjures an Aeolianism as one among several figures of medial recursivity, the amplifying "power" and "light" of Intellectual Beauty playing upon us.

But as it turns out, the hymn is addressed to an absent power, for the Spirit of Beauty has fled:

Spirit of BEAUTY, that doth consecrate
    With thine own hues all thou dost shine upon
    Of human thought or form,—where art thou gone?
Why dost thou pass away and leave our state,
This dim vast vale of tears, vacant and desolate?

stanza 2, lines 13–17[48]

Shelley swiftly pushes back against the very grounds of this questioning:

> Ask why the sunlight not for ever
>   Weaves rainbows o'er yon mountain river,
> Why aught should fail and fade that once is shewn,
>   Why fear and dream and death and birth
>   Cast on the daylight of this earth
>   Such gloom,—why man has such a scope
> For love and hate, despondency and hope?
>
> stanza 2, lines 18–24

The stanza's inquiry pivots sharply toward a critique of the bases of inquiry: you might as well, or as good as, *ask why*: things are as they are; phenomena appear as they do; the human condition is what it is.

This is precisely what Shelley asked! In poem after poem, in essay after essay! — "where art thou gone? / Why dost thou pass away..."; or, from "The Triumph of Life," "Then, what is Life?"[49]

Are these the wrong questions? Are they the right questions? Who is responding to these questions? Another voice *within* the poem? A dialogue of self and soul? Intellectual Beauty itself, conjured out of the urgent air?

A further trapdoor opens—for not only are the poet's urgent questions perhaps wrong or beside the point: this inquiry partakes of a history of unanswered address. These lordly chastising responses we've just heard (e.g., you might as well as ask why) have in fact *never been given*:

CHAPTER ONE

> No voice from some sublimer world hath ever
>   To sage or poet these responses given—
>   Therefore the name of God and ghosts, and Heaven,
> Remain the records of their vain endeavour,
> Frail spells—whose uttered charm might not avail to sever,
>   From all we hear and all we see,
>   Doubt, chance, and mutability.
>
> stanza 3, lines 25–31

Shelley outlines here not only the pathos and durability of "obstinate questionings," as Wordsworth put it in his "Immortality" ode, but also the perhaps irremediable phantasy of a transcendental responsiveness.[50] This stanza offers en route an etiology for poetry (as "frail spell") and religion as ideology: not as false consciousness but as an apostrophic structure, necessarily imaginary names given to real objects of supplication.[51]

This poem makes a speculative wager: it sustains a grand "as if"—*as if* there were Intellectual Beauty. This is a hymn in the optative mode, addressed to a not quite artifactualized idea, which overcodes or, rather, tints with its hues the affective and intellectual origins of ideology, concepts, the very dream of an adequate responsiveness. The poem thus offers both mythopoesis and mythography, mythmaking and an analysis thereof. It offers an array of supernatural categories and an etiology and critique of the same, governed by a further displacement: voilà! Intellectual Beauty!—a not-quite concept (though an Arendtian "thing of thought"), an a posteriori appearing as an a priori, whose function is not quite to answer or even to stay questioning, but to hold open the space of the counterfactual as well as the addressable:

> Love, Hope, and Self-esteem, like clouds depart
>   And come, for some uncertain moments lent.
>   Man were immortal and omnipotent,
> Didst thou, unknown and awful as thou art,
> Keep with thy glorious train firm state within his heart.
>
> stanza 4, lines 37–41

As the poem knows, man is precisely not immortal nor omnipotent: thus the subjunctive. Again, we might recall Arendt on the conditions of human existence, not least mortality. Man were immortal if: the conditional subjunctive.

Here we might consider Shelley as part of a long line of speculative poets, poets invested in what Samuel Delaney calls "subjunctivity" and which Margaret Ronda has animated for recent North American poetries in her article on speculative poetics.[52] Shelley's entire oeuvre is ostentatiously engaged in speculative, often counterfactual, imaginings: from *Laon and Cythna* on the fortunes of revolution to *Prometheus Unbound* (ditto) to "The Triumph of Life." In the "Hymn to Intellectual Beauty," Shelley works modally, though a particular set of modes linguists call *irrealis*: including the optative, conditional, subjunctive, imperative, hortatory. He repeatedly activates the conditional: what is striking is that he activates the conditional subjunctive, not the conditional indicative. His is a mode of hypothetical world-framing—not quite building or even modeling but *moding*.[53]

We might say that Shelley is modulating from the *as*—spectacular likenings—to the *as if*: subjunctive positings. The final modulations of the poem lean into this subjunctivity through the medium of seasonality:

CHAPTER ONE

The day becomes more solemn and serene
    When noon is past—there is a harmony
    In autumn, and a lustre in its sky,
Which thro' the summer is not heard or seen,
As if it could not be, as if it had not been!
    Thus let thy power, which like the truth
    Of nature on my passive youth
Descended, to my onward life supply
    Its calm—to one who worships thee,
    And every form containing thee,
    Whom, SPIRIT fair, thy spells did bind
To fear himself, and love all human kind.

                                   stanza 7, lines 73–84

The poem has unfolded itself (we now realize) within given structures of day and season, temporal modalities here caught in a mode of nuanced skying à la Constable: these implicitly form a lifeweb sustaining and shading aspects of human conditionality—mortality, natality, plurality, earth, and world. One might recall here as well Chakrabarty's invocation of "conditions (such as the temperature zone in which the planet exists) that work like boundary parameters of human existence." Shelley probes the status of such given conditions, of such parameters: how is the given-as-expected held in mind, given form? The what is, the what will be, the present: all are shimmering, shot through with alternate temporal modalities. We confront here a stunning node about autumn, how its light and harmony *are*, are declarable, predicable, rememberable, though absent to the sensorium throughout the summer. The idea of a ruptured seasonality is itself presented in the subjunctive—"As if it [autumn] could not be, as if it had not been!"—an astonishing and complex variation on the later, balder, more famous interrogative probe in Shelley's "Ode to the West Wind": "If Winter comes, can Spring be far behind?"[54]

"As if it could not be, as if it had not been!": here Shelley evokes the path and pathos of incredulity. He also inadvertently charts the historicity of incredulity and the contingency of the subjunctive—the mode of the hypothetical, the counterfactual, the irreal. The counterfactual stations itself in the white mythologies of an earthly order, the supposedly given regulatory orders of the earth, which the poem presents as categories of thought if not sense, and as a mode of binding past to future. The incredulity held by the poem as a counterfactual has moved toward the possible and now even grimly probable: as has been brought painfully home to those who live (as Shelley did) in the soi-disant temperate zones of the Global North, one can fully imagine, one can indeed painfully experience an autumn or a summer or a spring not returning as before. Seasonality no longer offers sure ground for predictability or continuity. Here Shelley staves off the possible impoverishment of the merely present, a devastated and total "eternal now" (to torque a phrase from his poem "Mont Blanc"): an overwhelming present that would obliterate not only the sense but the memory of periodicity.

Is it the work of this poem to hold open the place of some other if not sublimer world? Shelley both invokes and almost cancels the possibility of some sublimer world:

No voice from some sublimer world hath ever
    To sage or poet these responses given

Is it that we have "no world but the world" (to invoke the poet and essayist Anne Boyer?)?[55] Is this partitioning of possible, thinkable worlds—"this various world" versus "some sublimer world"—a finessing of the political, the essence of which Jacques Rancière has specified as *dissensus*, "*two worlds in one*"?[56]

Recall that Shelley's poem invokes in its first stanza "this various world." The Scrope Davies Notebook shows that Shelley had first written "this peopled world"—a phrase aligning intriguingly with "this peopled earth," which he later invoked in *Prometheus Unbound*, II.4.[57] There is a lot of peopling in Shelley, as in the zones "*Peopled* with unimaginable shapes" in *Prometheus Unbound* (IV.244),[58] which figure I take to be an impalpable index of Malthusian populations.[59] The peopled world as a given, the condition of plurality in Arendt's terms, of being one among others; "of being numerous," as George Oppen put it; of ante/antipolitical sociality, in Fred Moten's terms: all this is something Shelley was often quite weak on, though Mary Shelley was brilliant on.[60] It is a characteristic Shelleyan revision, this, from "this peopled world" to "this various world." It is characteristic as well that this hymn of massive sublimation, this call upon Intellectual Beauty as a spirit of liberation, figures the world, and not actual people, as enslaved. The phantoms he calls upon

> . . . know that never joy illum'd my brow
>   Unlink'd with hope that thou wouldst free
>   This world from its dark slavery

Here one encounters one of the crucial aporias of Shelley's political imagination, its premature abstracting from historical and material specificity, its swerve from the problem of violence, its repeated dramaturgy of singular, exceptional, often incestuous revolutionary heroes and heroines.

Whether hailing a peopled or various world, Shelley is offering in this poem not so much world-building as an inquiry into the parameters of world-building. So: from this various world—this world of multiplicity and inconstancy—to a phantasmatic sublimer world? to various worlds? to the multiverse?[61]

For after all, as the poet Ariana Reines has written, "The World Is Not Enough":

Sometimes I think this entire culture five thousand years was just a rehearsal for the wrong apocalypse[62]

What would the right apocalypse be?

What is the apocalypse we deserve?

What is the apocalypse we get?
Is this a Calvinist question?

I remember thinking that our prevailing apocalypticism is ethically compromised and mentally stunting. I remember there are of course good reasons.

Some will tell you the alphabet was a secret math
Some will say our speech was a bovine eructation
A kind of polluting fertilization
Ferreting out of the air
A weird palazzo of the air
An edifice of clouds and hierarchies of heaven
Down whose rutted facade slides the sun

CHAPTER ONE

Like a bright medicinal ointment
So our world might be glanced off of
As a beam of white light would, hitting a clean medical instrument
Instrument of what?[63]

Instrument of what?

This passage offers an extraordinary neo-Shelleyan exposition of beautifully and frankly rancid making, of barely there artifactualization—a weird palazzo made out of the air itself transformed by our speech, Latinate cow belches, bovine eructations that in their very contamination produce cracked Italianate architectures, barely materialized structures that become the surface and substance of the always already acculturated atmosphere, here indexed by clouds and hierarchies of heavens. This is a *poiesis*, a making out of the air, itself briefly figured as an animal logic of "ferreting." This elaborate conceit involves us in an emergent structured atmosphere: the world emerges as a surface along which the sun slides, the contact medicinal and palpable. There is something elaborately, metonymically slippery here, with gross ecstatic contact the key element of this world-building. This is a merrily heterodox *poiesis* of abjection and contamination, of polluted animal and elemental atmospherics. What strikes me in this poem is the emphasis on parameters, the air itself a ground for, and medium of, imagining and materialization.

Reines gives us an Aeolianism of the carbon cycle, a cycle we know is transforming; an atmosphere made and differentially conditioned by co- and interspecies breathing, belching, the factory farming in the hinterlands of the poem. The residual theological diction here—e.g., hierarchies of heaven—registers a transcendental domain Reines for one will not abjure. What is this world that is not enough? What to say about it? Some will tell you this, some will tell you that. Reines's catalog of interpretative possibilities encompasses occult knowledges and esoteric codes—the alphabet as secret math—as well as parameters for life and making.

But again: instrument of what?

Bovine eructations?

The west wind?

... Be thou, Spirit fierce,
My spirit! Be thou me, impetuous one!
SHELLEY, "Ode to the West Wind"[64]

Nothing?

Today the mind is not part of the weather.
Today the air is clear of everything.
It has no knowledge except of nothingness
WALLACE STEVENS, "A Clear Day and No Memories"[65]

The air, the wind, the world?

Here one could go further down a serious romantic-period wormhole, that much elaborated zone of romantic ventilation, its tropologics of winds and breezes, its effortful searching for correspondence between Mind and Nature, its inquiries into "correspondent breezes" (cf. Wordsworth's *Prelude*) and Aeolian vexations (cf. Coleridge's "Dejection" ode), the aspirational coordination of inner and outer weather, as Robert Frost later put it.[66] More recent scholarship has revived and complicated this nexus.[67] And crucially, when assessing the instrumental logics of worldmaking—instrument of what? for whom? toward what?—it is impossible not to think of conditioned breathing, contaminated and precarious breathing, violently snuffed-out breathing, the biopolitics of wind, breath, force, the laboring of bodies, the crushing of instruments.[68]

∞

I remember that I have been wanting in this chapter to keep open and turn differently the question of parameters, elements, winds, and poetic conditioning. I remember a decidedly non-Aeolian instrument, and a ballad parable of instrumentality, the ballad known variously as "The Twa Sisters," "The Cruel Sister," "Child Ballad No. 10," and "The Wind and Rain."[69] This murder ballad is a classic love-and-kinship-gone-wrong song, two sisters vying over a lover—variously a miller, sailor, or other young man who courts the elder but secretly prizes the younger The elder in a jealous fit pushes the younger into the river, where she drowns, floats, and ultimately provides some good ballad fodder in many senses. The ballad concludes with a fiddler (or harper in other versions) making of the dead girl's breastbone a fiddle (or a harp), stringing the instrument with her long yellow hair, and bowing it with a bow made of her long fingerbones. Other more macabre versions of the ballad have the suitor and elder sister in league, the suitor stealing the rings from the dead girl's hands; the miller is ultimately hanged and the elder sister is burned at the stake.

Most versions devote several verses to this making of an instrument: this is a ballad strikingly oriented to what Roman Jakobson would call the metapoetic function. The ballad points, then, to a kind of ballad recycling, a kind of composting, offering a grimly dispassionate etiology for ballad instruments. A constant in most versions of this ballad is the creating of the instrument out of dead, inorganic, yet—within the world of the ballad—very recently alive human female matter. What is also notable: the ballad introduces the fiddler/maker of instruments as a figure orthogonal to what we might have thought was the main story—he simply comes along the road, sees the bones a-lying there on the riverbank, and begins the work (as Arendt might say) of *homo faber*.

The fiddle (or harp) that emerges in the ballad is an instrument made by another, for another, the fiddler (or harper or miller) coming *after* and upon the matter, the human female *materia* now inorganic matter—yet still residually female: her long yellow hair, her long finger bones, her little breastbone. (This is a ballad some scholars have classified as belonging to the international tale type of "the singing bone."[70]) Here we have an instrument as deferred protagonist, an instrument as fashioned opportunity, as affordance.

But affordance for what? The variants of "The Twa Sisters" give us several answers, exploiting the many possibilities of instrumental conditioning and/as codetermination—in terms of both the etiology of instruments and their possible repertoires. For in several versions the player (harper or fiddler) has a repertoire of tunes to hand, through which he variously plays out the dead sister's farewells and final accusation. In "Child Ballad No. 10," version B, for example,

CHAPTER ONE

The first tune he did play and sing,
Was, "Farewell to my father the king."

The nextin tune that he playd syne,
Was, "Farewell to my mother the queen."

The lasten tune that he playd then,
Was, "Wae to my sister, fair Ellen."[71]

The invocation of nameable and citable tunes here (and in other variants) suggests that these tunes ("Farewell to my father the king," etc.) must precede and accompany, and perhaps condition, the events this specific ballad narrates.[72] (It's worth noting that successful ballad tunes were often repurposed with new wordings, and that broadside ballads were often printed with such directives as "To the Tune of 'Flying Fame,'" or "To the Tune of 'Chevy Chase.'") The harper comes upon the matter, so to speak, with a prepared (and socialized, musicalized) mind. And further: we see that the events of the ballad are perhaps neither the origin of these cited tunes nor their singular content (or message). In the world of this ballad, repertoires emerge as an activated reserve, a summonable and citable and refunctionable resource.

Quite another instrumental logic emerges in version C: here, the harper, having fabricated the instrument, sets it down before the court such that it can "play alone," by itself, a kind of automated program music avant la lettre:

He brought it to her father's hall,
And there was the court assembled all

He laid this harp upon a stone,
And straight it began to play alone.

"O yonder sits my father, the king,
And yonder sits my mother, the queen."

"And yonder stands my brother Hugh,
And by him my William, sweet and true."

But the last tune that the harp playd then,
Was "Woe to my sister, false Helen!"[73]

What exactly is the harp playing "alone"? Not direct verbal "content" but melodic matter, which itself implicitly carries verbal content. Here the harp's strings themselves, and the tunes themselves—not any verbalizations or pluckings by the harper—channel the dead girl's acknowledgments and curse. The tunes carry the verbal content, ambiently and automatically generated—which of course is exactly what happens in a communal musical culture, as tunes call to mind particular lyrics, and as the invoking of lyrical scraps or song titles can generate the tunes themselves. ("Amazing Grace." "Auld Lang Syne." "Happy Birthday." "Jingle Bells." "Break My Soul.") We have here not a player piano (to speak anachronistically) but a player harp, culturally programmed and specifically harnessed to this emplotment. Version C gives us, then, not an Aeolian harp, passively sounding as the wind strikes its strings, but a particularly determined and conditioned harp. If Shelley invoked "music by the night-wind sent / Thro' strings of some still instrument," this harp on a stone "straight . . . began to play alone," occasioned not by ambient variable winds but as if by narratological-musical magic. This version offers, one might say, a historical-material parable of automated instruments.[74]

One needn't sift through every version of "The Twa Sisters" to register its richness as a complex model for, and diagnosis of, conditioned and conditional making, of instrumentality per se: though the versions put pressure on that very "per se," because what we see, ranging across the case of "The Twa Sisters," is that there are many instrumental conditionings, determinations, and futurities held by this ballad. Yet most versions notably highlight the recursivity of singing and of making, of the "conditional condition" (cf. John Durham Peters). As a brief survey of these variants suggests, the "conditional condition" is not a single or determinate one: the instrument, the condition of emerging *as* a recognizable or playable instrument, and the repertoires and uses thereof are variously and complexly codetermined.

But perhaps this isn't saying very much. Perhaps we could look again at recursivity as a binding constraint, as blockage and not only as affordance, as antagonism. For in one particularly striking version of the ballad—"The Wind and Rain"—the instrument is also, for its user or player, an impediment, a forcing tool, a strongly conditioning and even determining apparatus. The fiddle, once fabricated from the once-living body, can play *only one tune*:

And he made a little fiddle of her little breastbone
O the wind and rain
He made a fiddle [little] fiddle of her breastbone, cried
O the dreadful wind and rain

But the only tune that the fiddle would play
O the wind and rain

The only tune that the fiddle would play was
O the dreadful wind and rain[75]

The ballad variant "The Wind and Rain" suggests, pace Marshall McLuhan, that not only is the medium not the message, the message here determines the medium: the fiddler cannot play just any tune on this instrument but can play only this one tune: "the *only* tune that the fiddle would play was *O the wind and rain*" (emphasis added). With its fighting kin and its strikingly transformed and ultimately determinative refrain, we might read this version as a media allegory—a tale of two kindred strains, jealous of each other, words and tunes vying to win the same instrumental, medial triumph.

This is how I used to think of this ballad variant. I have also considered "The Wind and Rain" as offering an instrumental parable of the revenge of the instrument on its player—which could figure for us the revenge of balladry on a monomaniacal, mono-medial account of literature: O the wind and rain. This is a striking shift from the revenge logic in other versions, wherein the dead girl curses the sister, who is sometimes hanged. "The Wind and Rain" suggests something else, in a more philosophical key: the revenge of the instrument on a blinkered utilitarianism, an instrumentality of means trumped by the instrument's own ends. (The fiddler may have musical plans, but the instrument has its own.) Following this line of thought, we might think of this variant as a parable against mere or mono-instrumentality.

If in "The Wind and Rain" the fiddle can play only one tune, in other versions—including its earliest attested version in print—the fiddler/instrument plays (as we have seen) several specific tunes. "The Wind and Rain" asks us to consider recursivity not simply through thematics or narration or the assumed iterability of ballad singing but through the very logic of refraining itself: here we can move from etiology (a logic of explanation and causation) to refrain—to refrain as a marking of parameter and condition. In "The Wind and Rain," the refrain—typically regarded as nonsensical filler, fol-de-rol-de-rol-ish stuff, or bits of merely local detail—becomes the crucial message of the ballad: the refrain is suddenly semanticized, its refraining atmospherics suddenly focalized. *O the wind and rain*: an exclamation, apostrophe, elemental deixis, a specification?—a phrase whose source, sounding, effects, and affects are themselves mobile and multiple.

Recall that in "The Wind and Rain" the fiddler coming upon the bones cries *O the wind and rain*; that the instrument ultimately sounds only this tune, *O the wind and rain*; that any ballad singer co-cries, ventriloquizes, or is possessed by *O the dreadful wind and rain*. The recursivity here points to the wind and rain (both a notional tune and atmospheric conditions) as *prior to* this ballad story, and as taken up by and in this story. As it recurs, the refrain resounds and permutes: *O the wind and rain, O the dreadful wind and rain*. The refrain becomes a placeholder, a timekeeper, and also an elemental diagnosis of parameters, of atmospheric conditions. As Celeste Langan and John Hollander remind us, a refrain is both a binding and a breaking, a breaking into song, and a repetition with a difference.[76] A once-common term for refrain was "burden": here the refrain carries the burden of parameters, the "boundary parameters of human existence" (Chakrabarty), the conditions for making, singing, loving, dying, for taking up or becoming instruments at all.

O the wind and rain: the refrain indexes elemental media, or perhaps what John Durham Peters calls sky media and oceanic media.[77] Or rather, the refrain registers disturbances and flows with these. The refrain sounds out the way an environment becomes palpable, sensible: *O the wind and rain*. These are, in this ballad, *conditions for poiesis*, not merely elemental media. The ballad refrains, that is, not "O the air and water," not "O the sky and sea," but "O the wind and rain": brief, transitory, yet iterable phenomenalizations of the elements, motion and substance made perceptible to an implied sensorium that a notional human collective still shares.

By this point you will undoubtedly have noticed the slight extension of the refrain in its second phrasing—how "O the wind and rain" becomes "O the dreadful wind and rain," this dilation happening in each verse, a dreadful clockwork. To whom is that wind and rain dreadful—the dead girl? the miller? the murderous sister? an unspecified and omniscient narrator/singer? the audience, perhaps moved by pity and terror? Perhaps any, perhaps all. The refrain is a contingently focalizable utterance; the refraining also floats beyond focalized utterance. The refraining here points to the status of refrain/repetition *as* difference, as emergent differentiation, as well as an accumulation of reverberation. The ballad also implicitly registers how humans take the weather personally, anthropocentrically: O the *dreadful* wind and rain.

So: the ballad channels the wind and rain, as harnessed to human pathologies, kinship structures, notional circuits of justice, bad romance; yet the ballad also sounds out the wind and rain independent of these. We have here a wind hailed not as an anthropocentric correspondent breeze, nor even as a disjunctive breeze, but as a citable variable in the intermittently yet regularly dreadful conjunction of wind and rain. "The Wind and Rain" presences both the wind and the rain and keeps these elements (and their disturbances and flows) as accompanying, if not decisively conditioning, human life. "The Wind and Rain" is both *this* tune and, as the wind and the rain, the a priori of any tune, a vocalization of elementality and atmospheric conditions, contributory flows toward the weather, both the aftermath and the prequel to a notionally endlessly iterable ballad. This ballad offers, then, not a kind of weather forecasting—as in "Sir Patrick Spens" ("I feir a deadlie storme")—nor even weather reporting ("an the wind blew loud / an gurly grew the sea")[78] but a specifying of atmospheric conditions as among the "boundary parameters of human existence."

The refrain itself, in its various transcriptions and mediations, hovers between an exclamation and a vocative, between an undirected vocalization and an apostrophe—between "Oh the wind and rain" and "O the wind and rain." (There is an additional complexity in that some versions specify a comma after the "Oh" or "O": e.g., "Oh, the wind and rain."[79]) One could possibly make too much hay out of such differences, though scholars have long teased out the profound implications of the merest marks in Wordsworth's lyrics—see, for example, readings of the line (and punctuation of) "and oh! / The difference to me" in "She Dwelt among the Untrodden Ways" (1798).[80] Yet unlike print-based, authored, copyrighted poetries, balladry—sometimes printed, sometimes not, multiply mediated in transmission and performance—has a variable relation to fixity, recombination, and authority. My passing point here is that ballads in their variability and multiformity—in print and on the web as well as in performance, in manuscript, in broadsides, in anthologies—allow for and even promote such oscillation and comparative suspension. And in the case of "The Wind and Rain," the refraining attests to the recursive, conditioning horizon of the wind and rain as *variable* elements, sometimes hailed, sometimes channeled, sometimes phenomenalized, always atmospheric, always possible parameters for and in this ballad.

Another way to approach this territory might be to ask, Is it raining in "The Wind and Rain"? Possibly, but not necessarily. It would seem not. The ballad holds the *sounding* of the wind and rain, the singability/thinkability of the wind and rain, the burden and refraining of the wind and rain, the interrupting and binding by the wind and rain—interruption and binding the double work of refrain: to break and to bind.[81] Consider the difference between this refrained wind and rain and the wind/rain/storm complex in Coleridge's "Dejection" ode, a poem that times its enunciation against an approaching "coming on of rain and squally blast," which by its penultimate stanza has arrived.[82] And further, just as we saw in several "Child" versions (with their citation of notional tunes, e.g., "Wae to my sister, Fair Ellen"), "The Wind and Rain" may be understood as a tune already circulating, already known in this ballad world—as we see when in "The Wind and Rain" the refrain modulates from an apparently unspecified iterative, atmospheric utterance to a suddenly specific speech act, when the fiddler (happening upon the dead girl) "cried *O the wind and rain*" and then "cried *O the dreadful wind and rain.*" This raises the intriguing possibility that the ballad cites, or presents itself as citing, a tune known as either or both "O the Wind and Rain" and "O the dreadful Wind and Rain." These are the kinds of suspensions and reverberances balladry specializes in.

Moreover, the complex recursivity of the refraining here—of the "body" of the phrase ("O the wind and rain")—highlights the recursive instrumentalization of the dead sister's body.[83] It might well be the fiddler is always already reciting, or prepared to recite, "O the wind and rain," even as the ballad compulsively refrains it. Yet "The Wind and Rain" does put great emphasis on what seems to come as a surprise to the fiddler, the sudden "gotcha" revelation that "the only tune that the fiddle could play / was *O the wind and rain*": an instrumental comeuppance, his notional repertoire reduced to degree zero. (We might also read this as a gendered resistance or payback: who exactly is whose instrument?) "The Wind and Rain" is notable in that in this version the fabricated instrument does not accuse the sister, nor does it acknowledge the parents, beloveds, or any other human-all-too-human figure: this version foregrounds the metapoetic function, the message become code. Here there is one overcoding message and the message is *O the wind and rain*, the message become code (weather-as-atmospheric-condition).

So again: Instrument of what? Recall that, among its several definitions for "instrument," the *Oxford English Dictionary* glosses it as "a device or apparatus for registering, measuring, or recording a physical quantity, property, or phenomenon."[84] The ballad variant "The Wind and Rain" offers a way to register, measure, and record the space between determination and condition—between the fated a priori of the only tune soundable on *this* instrument and the conditions governing, and affordances available via, any instrument.

And yet, and further: what I just called the fated a priori of the only tune is shown precisely to be unfated, aleatory, a taking-place, a surprise. "The Wind and Rain" offers an etiology not only of instruments but of tunes, poems, stories, of emplotment itself. In all versions, "The Twa Sisters" offers an emplotted instrument, and in some versions (as we've seen) the tune feeds back directly into human-all-too-human plots and affairs, the tune (or strings) accusing one sister of murdering the other: "Wae to my sister, fair Ellen." The variants themselves point to several instrumental directionalities and futurities.

In "The Wind and Rain," the instrument also indexes what Louis Althusser called "the underground current of the materialism of the encounter"[85]: the way "necessity" should be understood as the retroactive becoming-necessary of contingency, how necessity is always a backformation to explain the given, Heidegger's *es gibt*, Althusser's fait accompli, Wittgenstein's world, everything that is the case, the case reopened in Althusser and in this ballad to encompass both occurrence and chance—the making of this ballad instrument, for example, arising out of the chance passing-by of the fiddler, the apparent determination of the instrument's tune an *effect* of that conjuncture, not a necessary a priori. Althusser tracks a materialism through which there is a giving form to the effects of an encounter: the fiddler gives fiddle-form to the dead girl's body parts, which he encounters by chance: "and along there came a fiddler."[86] The ballad presents a complex case, as both occurrence and chance: within the world of the ballad, the dead sister's body parts provide the material cause, the fiddler the maker and thus efficient cause, the idea/design/plan of a fiddle (or harp) the formal cause, the tune and refrain internal final cause. Yet ballad recursivity confounds teleology and neat Aristotelian modeling, for its nature is reiterative, its conjunctions repeatedly contingent, its givenness provisional and always signaling what might have been otherwise, amidst a manifest logic of fatality. The ballad itself offers a meditation on its—and any ballad's—making, and sounds out the territory between a conditioned instrument (common to all variants) versus a determined and determining instrument (that in "The Wind and Rain"). And after all, the fiddler who comes upon the bones "cried *O the wind and rain*": an index of an already-known ballad, a circulating tune, a prepared mind, a program for *homo faber*, ready to gather up a body and to *break it into song*: "breaking into song" the very title of Hollander's essay on refrain. Among many things, "Child Ballad no. 10," "The Twa Sisters," offers in all versions a parable about refraining itself—refraining as "breaking it into parts as well as binding it together,"[87] the dead girl's broken body, its repurposed parts, "bound" into and for a new instrument.

As this ballad attests, and as Althusser (among others) would have us recognize, the given, the *es gibt*, the fait accompli—a ballad, an instrument, a Shelleyan season, capitalism, the Anthropocene—has a history and a historicity, is the effect of (often violent) contingencies which may now seem hard facts but were themselves formed, accomplished, congealed: and, moreover, these might not have been. Well: so what? A materialism of the encounter and a conditional poetics keeps open the space both for speculative futurities and for assessing the contours of the world we're in, precisely because one discerns its aleatory and contingent formation: simultaneously that it is and that it *might not have been*. Harnessing what would seem to be ballad fatalities to speculative futurities (or to aleatory encounters) may seem perverse, but one of the things ballad refraining makes visible/audible is such turning and interrupting through verse, per-verse. And as Althusser notes, that there is a fait accompli is no guarantee of durability:[88] by extension, we might say that the predicable is not sutured to the predictable. And further, the world that is not enough—to invoke Reines—might not have been at all: something perhaps liberating to consider, or perhaps devastating, but significant for thought and action. One registers, that is, the background (or negative space, to use another spatial metaphor) of the aleatory of the *non*-encounter, as well as that of the encounter.[89] Insisting on the *counterfactual and subjunctive*, Althusser (like Shelley) offers an *irreal* horizon of what might have been but also what yet might be.

The question and mode of the instrument—whether Shelley's "still instrument" or the dreadful fiddle of "The Wind and

Rain"—sounds out the complex space between condition and determination. The ballad strongly marks the instrument's conditionality (instrument of what for what by whom). Indeed, the complexities of the instrument in these cases allow us to register the doubleness in "condition" itself, as involved in antecedence but also in the circumstances of the now—the conjunction we call "the now," as if "the now" weren't also the mark of a conjuncture.

So again: instrument of what?

In her poem "The World Is Not Enough," Reines offers one answer to this question, and does so via an intriguing, demanding Aeolianism, proffering the poet-as-conditioned-instrument:

You have to be the sound of the world
Flowing through you and you have
Like a pointer on a delicate dial
To be made to tremble even by the sound
Of a sobbing child many hundreds of miles away
Which is a sound you have never exactly heard
But you have. And you can hear it. And the flame
That burned off the ears of a koala
Only one, and Anacaona
Moving
Moving
Anacaona moving underground[90]

Do you have to be the sound of the world? Is this now, is this ever, is this always the poet's project, task, vocation—registering (for example in this passage) terror, massacres, the cries of caged children, lethal fires in Australia, the inferno of climate change, the undersong of history, Anacoana the Taíno cacique, woman leader of Xaragúa (in present-day Haiti), slain by the Spanish in 1504; do you have to be the sound of the world?

This final movement in Reines's poem reads as an attempt at poetic self-conditioning amidst duress, a casting of a spell on the poet-as-conditioned-instrument: hers is a tough Aeolianism.[91] Do you have to be the sound of the world flowing through you? What world? Shelley's "various world"? His proposed and almost canceled "sublimer world"? "The very world, which is the world / Of all of us" (Wordsworth, *Prelude*, X.725–26)?[92] That other world which is supposedly within this one?

I remember Christopher Nealon's "Last Glimpse" from *The Shore*:

Then I gave it up
I gave up thinking that the song I heard was the song of the world
I gave up lyric, gave up reverie, I gave up aesthesis—
I left my notebook on the park bench open with its pages riffling
    I kept my head down
I said ok fine Elon Musk is the most important person on the planet
I did not read "Ozymandias"
But like that monument I started to crumble[93]

Oh but could we should we "give up thinking that the song [we] heard was the song of the world"?

From Reines's "sound of the world" to Nealon's "song of the world": in this shift from sound to song we can register a movement from the perceived to the shaped, from sensory vibration to artifactualized reverberance. Or rather, with these two poems before us, perhaps we can register the subtle emergence of a threshold of formalization—the condensation of atmospheric conditions in general into *these conditions*, a phenomenalization we might call wind or rain.

Nealon invokes the crumbling of the monument, not least the monument of the reified lyric "I," as well as that of that compact monument, Shelley's sonnet (itself a famous savaging of monumental imperial presumption, whether Napoleonic or Pharaonic—or, indeed, Hanoverian). An extraordinary and economical relay, this, pointing to a legacy of poetics as it internalizes historiography and confronts world-historical claims. (This conjuncture of poetry and world-historical liberation was, after all, Shelley's prophetic métier: see his "Defence of Poetry.") In Nealon's renunciation, this seeming palinode, the ruin itself further ruined in this "last glimpse," the poet and the poem step out into the weather of the now in and of history:

You no longer need to know the end of the story
You no longer dread the great devaluation
  No ziggurats collapsing
  No cities on a plain
You shake yourself, head high like a horse,
And step out into all the rain that's ever rained.
        NEALON, "Last Glimpse"[94]

The poem is conditioned, we might say, by residual Ozymandian problematics, while registering emergent, underdetermined textures: you no longer need to know the end of the story. The totalizations of world history, of the spirit of the age, are invoked and not quite set aside, fleet ironies and topical nods (Elon Musk, etc.) notwithstanding. This is a shaping via conditions, not determination as teleology; yet a notional whole if not a totalization is proffered—all the rain that's ever rained: not only the rain of the now, the sensible rain, o the wind and rain, but the notionally total rain, the refrainable rain, and perhaps the Epicurean or Lucretian rain of matter and its swerves in the void, the Althusserian "'materialism'... of the rain," the rain that raineth every day, all that rain that's ever rained...

see you've already forgotten

see you've already forgotten
    the rain
in the cumulus courting
    the sun
it won't block—forgotten
    the pull
of the moon just past full
    is affecting
the waves. The song
    of the cardinal
flaring the hemlock so long
    ago rang out
so long ago nothing belongs
    to that rain
gone so long you've almost
    forgotten
how long ago rained down
    the rain[95]

CHAPTER ONE

Preferences

we would have liked the moon
unshrouded, declaring itself
in August, but we'll take
the vagrant yellow barely visible
amidst thick clouds

we would have liked the rain
sufficient to revive the ferns,
the farmers' fields, the well, the hay
otherwise lost, animals parched

even the hurricane failed
to provide

one leans into seasons
as if they were imperishable

as if the earth revolved the same
as ever, dumb core shrouded
by cooler layers and a sky
itself divided into sheltering parts

I am not drunk
as I write this
by which I mean type this
I am at most slightly buzzed
by a Jamaican rum

a Turner night sky
become an Ofili blueblack
a night sky that doesn't yet reign
in video games or porn

everyone wants clean sheets
amidst the stones and holes[96]

CHAPTER ONE

They Were Always Thinking

they were always thinking
about the weather
as if they were farmers . . .

the cedars grew taller
each year till they would grow
no further—

a finished sky, a plane
gliding above the still cedars

this was the end of thinking
the trees arrested in an undying blue

the weather forever
the same as if painted[97]

* 2 *
Compositional/Poetics

> ... downe in yonder greene field ...
> —"The Three Ravens"

> I salute
> that various field.
> —JAMES SCHUYLER, "Salute"

From the conditional to the compositional: but what do I mean by a "compositional" axis of poetic inquiry? For poets and composers, the compositional might evoke thoughts of composing, of making, arranging, wordsmithing, tunesmithing, *poiesis* itself. For botanists, the compositional might conjure the plant family Compositae (also known as Asteraceae, a vast group including daisies, asters, sunflowers). For some readers, the compositional might call to mind philosopher and sociologist Bruno Latour's notion of "compositionism," viz. his "Attempt at a 'Compositionist Manifesto'" (2010): "It is time to compose—in all the meanings of the word, including to compose with, that is to compromise, to care, to move slowly, with caution and precaution."[1] We might think of "the compositional" as registering those aspects of poetry that aim "to compose with"—with other works, people, materials (animate and inanimate), what have you. Poetry emerges as that various compositional field—as holding and enacting relations among animal, vegetal, and mineral elements we might not yet have fully reckoned with. Poetry in this compositional light emerges as an archive for sensing and perceiving these relations.

Among his many sallies, Latour observes in a footnote to his manifesto, "The redistribution of agencies is the right purview of literature studies."[2] Compositionism, then, might be one name for this mode of literature studies—alert to ecological entanglement, pluralizing and redistributing "agencies." Compositionism might also designate what literature—or some poetry—has long undertaken. Latour's compositionism notably aligns with some recent reflections on poetics—as when Marjorie Levinson draws on political theorist William E. Connolly, "defining agency as distributive across a wide spectrum of life forms, including the inanimate ensembles woven into our everyday routines."[3] Or when Susan Manning (in her posthumous *The Poetics of Character*) proposed an analytic of "correspondence"—in her lexicon, a conceptual category allowing for the mapping of anachronic networks of rhetorical and ethical relations—and called for an "affective poetics based on principles of analogy."[4] Among other things, "compositionism" offers routes to take seriously challenges to anthropocentrism (including that unslayable dragon, "pathetic fallacy") without throwing out the anthropomorphizing baby with the anthropocentric bathwater.

Latour excavated and critiqued the division between human and nonhuman subjects he saw as central to "the Modernist Constitution," circa 1600 to yesterday, and he polemically endorsed a kind of neo-animism the regime of modern science has long scorned.[5] Here and elsewhere his work chimes with posthumanist, ecocritical, Anthropocenically minded critics—from Timothy Morton on "the mesh" to Jane Bennett on "vibrant matter" to

Margaret Ronda on "great acceleration poetics" at "nature's end" to Anahid Nersessian on "the calamity form" to Ada Smailbegović on "the poetics of liveliness" to Levinson's reactivation of Spinoza alongside new morphogenetic modeling.[6] Rather than plunging further into new or old materialisms, ecocriticisms, folds, spheres, meshes, entanglements, or hyperobjects (inter alia), I would like to explore the compositional more modestly in a poetico-botanical key, taking plants as one crucial node for thinking about horizons for *poiesis*—both the making of poems and the theorizing of them. For as certainly as literature has long redistributed agencies, often violently, along planty lines—from Ovid's metamorphoses to Shelley's "old root" that "was once Rousseau" in his "Triumph of Life"—plants have long been significant players in the fatally vivifying game of anthropomorphism and trope: not for nothing does Ruskin begin his reflections "On the Pathetic Fallacy" with the matter of a blue gentian.[7]

Yet now that we seem to have arrived at a post-natural, post-human/ist, post-historical moment, it is worth wondering: are we post-plant? I would say that in many ways I am pre-plant.

But, you may well say, your entire lifeworld depends upon your interactions, overt and covert, with plants: you eat them, you wear them, you breathe them, you touch them, arrange them, pluck them, smell them, ingest them! You are indeed a plant codependent!

Pressed thus, one might want to consider the plant unconscious—a phenomenon not so complex perhaps as what Fredric Jameson called years ago the political unconscious but not unrelated. (Might plants have a politics? Might minerals? Or consider the granting of legal personality to the Whanganui River in New Zealand.[8]) Plants have always been good to think with and good to think through; I would further suggest that plants have been thinking poetry for a long while—and continue to. And so I want to consider poetry as a mode of what the philosopher Michael Marder has called "plant-thinking":

> "Plant-thinking" refers, in the same breath, to (1) the non-cognitive, non-ideational, and non-imagistic mode of thinking proper to plants (hence, what I call "thinking without the head"); (2) our thinking about plants; (3) how human thinking is, to some extent, de-humanized and rendered plant-like, altered by its encounter with the vegetal world; and finally, (4) the ongoing symbiotic relation between this transfigured thinking and the existence of plants.[9]

I will suspend the question of whether plants "think" and will attend rather to Marder's options 2 and 4, pursuing "our thinking about plants" and the "transfigured thinking" that might emerge, compositionally, symbiotically, when we think with poetry's plants.[10] Marder draws inspiration in part from Gilles Deleuze and Félix Guattari, who in *A Thousand Plateaus* commanded us: "Follow the plants"![11] And one hears echoes of Deleuze and Guattari's call for a "rhizomatic" thinking over and against "arborescent" thought—excessively rooted and hierarchized. And perhaps rhizomes offer one compositionist model for the composing and receiving of poems. Alive to the roots of and in language, one might stumble upon new linkages and new futurities: rhizomes in the tree, the composite in the apparently singular specimen, a plant within and without the self, the plant in the poem, the poet in the plant.[12]

So let us follow the plants. Consider Louise Glück's poem "The Red Poppy," spoken in the voice of the flower, which modulates toward a striking apostrophe:

... Oh my brothers and sisters,
were you like me once, long ago,
before you were human? Did you
permit yourselves
to open once, who would never
open again? Because in truth
I am speaking now
the way you do. I speak
because I am shattered.[13]

Note the reverse-engineered logic here, such that the plant is imagined as addressing the humans. Here we have dramatized not anthropomorphism but plant-o-morphism, phytomorphism, the plant imaging the human as plant: a plant's human-thinking (so to speak), dependent on, corresponding with, human plant-thinking. One could also say, of course, that such a poem conducts a classic naturalizing move, naturalization "the reversal of anthropomorphism" (as Paul de Man observed), yet profoundly and anthropocentrically collusive with it.[14]

Or consider this outrageously bathetic venture in species projection, my poem "OK Fern":

OK fern
I'm your apprentice
I can now tell you

apart from your
darker sister ferns
whose intricate ridges

overlay your more
regular triangled fans.
Tell me what to do

with my life.¹⁵

Now, rather than defend my, or Glück's, or any number of potentially problematic, appropriatively planty poems, I would like to move from the language of critique to that of composition: for not only is there no way out of sympathetic (or antipathetic) projection, it may be that this is precisely the required medium for an acknowledgment of common life. Or rather, we might say that what's been called "the pathetic fallacy" registers not so much the human expropriation of the animate—or even the inanimate—world but rather an implicit recognition and mapping of the interdependence thereof.

Indeed, despite Sidney Burris's flagging "the overall weariness of the concept in contemp. usage" in *The Princeton Encyclopedia of Poetry and Poetics*, "pathetic fallacy" seems newly robust especially in critical and theoretical discourse.¹⁶ That the pathetic fallacy might carry in any literary instance its own complex ideologics does not tell us in advance its political or ecocritical charge—though it may register an epistemic a priori. Levinson, for example, aims to rehabilitate the pathetic fallacy, rejecting the charge of "subjectivism" and "anthropocentrism."¹⁷ Latour makes a similar point, mordantly observing that those ("naturalists," "reductionists," blighted "modernists") who attack anthropomorphism are themselves anthropocentric: "An extraordinary feat: making, for purely anthropocentric reasons, the accusation of being anthropomorphic into a deadly weapon!"¹⁸ It can seem that everyone these days is defending anthropomorphic moves from the charge of anthropocentrism.

The planty poems thus far invoked have been, arguably, lyric poems. I would like now to consider two ballads as specimens of exemplary plant poetics: for, insofar as traditional ballads allow us to rethink organic and inorganic ecologies and economies, they put pressure on a premature or exclusive lyricization of the pathetic fallacy, and they offer another archive for compositionism. Balladry offers an especially rich resource for thinking character, rhetoric, and sympathy; ballads offer too a counterpressure to those fallacies often hooked to or constellated around the literary—e.g., the intentional, the biographical, and yes, the pathetic. One can bracket, for example, questions of authorial intent without doing violence to the typically unauthored or anonymously authored work of traditional balladry; one can test, too, whether ballads are as reliant on, or generative of, pathetic fallacies as lyric has notoriously been. As narrative poems, ballads are precisely not lyrics, though perhaps by now they are inevitably "lyricized" in ways we have been taught to be alert to and skeptical of.[19] Also: ballads are not literary, or not only literary—they are transmedial, tunes as well as texts, notionally floating on the tongues of the people, in print, and via the bits and bytes of the web. Balladry ingathers a corpus both historical and transhistorical, variously and contingently nationalized and regionalized in ballad collections yet at times prenational, postnational, transatlantic, and indeed translinguistic, when approached with a longer comparative historical horizon in view.[20] Finally, in its lateral networks, its transhistorical reverberance, its spatialization of horizons for comparison, balladry offers a compositionist complement to, and complication of, the historicizations we might also wish to pursue.

CHAPTER TWO

My ballad specimens first appear in the written record in the seventeenth century. "The Three Ravens" first appeared in print in 1611, in Thomas Ravenscroft's songbook *Melismata: Musicall Phansies. Fitting the Court, Citie, and Countrey Humours*.[21] "The Three Ravens," and its Scottish counterpart "The Twa Corbies," are also known—since Francis James Child's compendium—as "Child 26."[22] Featuring the ballad in his *Ancient Songs* of 1790, the English antiquarian Joseph Ritson observed that this ballad, though published in the early seventeenth century, surely went back much further in oral tradition—an observation with which Bertrand Bronson later agreed in his *Traditional Tunes of the English and Scottish Popular Ballads*. Over the centuries we find these balladized birds variously nationalized and localized: in one "Child" variant, three ravens lament a dead knight in Lincolnshire; in James Reed's *Border Ballads*, twa corbies croak hungrily over a dead knight in the Middle Marches of Scotland; and in its transatlantic migration, raucous American crows often caw over a dead horse (the horse having replaced the dead knight in some versions). The gregarious birds continue to seek out their food, alternately pitying or exulting over the dead creature which lies "downe in yonder greene field" (in England), "behint yon auld fail dyke" (in Scotland), or "on yonders plain" (in the US).[23] The three ravens of the English ballad sit on a tree, confer on where to take breakfast, and note the knight lying on the field. The birds then offer an elegy (or "dirge," as Ritson called it) for this knight, enumerating his faithful attendants: hawk, hound, leman (the beloved, sometimes a "fallow doe," other times a gravid lady). The ballad closes with a benediction: "God send euery gentleman / Such haukes, such hounds, and such a leman."[24] Breakfast seems to have been forgotten. Or perhaps the diversion from implied hunger to a mode of elegy is a kind of apotropaic incantation against the desecration of the corpse—for in "The Twa Corbies," the surveying birds plan ultimately to "pike [peck] out" the dead knight's "bonnie blue een."

"The Three Ravens" could be glossed as an intriguing specimen of avian poetics—birdsong affiliated with yet distinct from human song, in this case, elegy. Approaching this ballad with a planty consciousness, one notes as well its richness of plant materials—most notably the tree on which the ravens sit and the green field on which the knight lies. As important as the nouns here—tree, field—is their phrasal, adverbial, prepositional locale: the ravens sit "on a tree"; the knight lies "downe in yonder greene field." Syntax here implicitly maps a field and (pre)positions within it. The tree and the field would seem to be generic locales, indeed the epitome of generic location.

One might think of Wordsworth's "Ode: Intimations of Immortality":

> —But there's a Tree, of many one,
A single Field which I have look'd upon,
Both of them speak of something that is gone:
    The Pansy at my feet
    Doth the same tale repeat:
Whither is fled the visionary gleam?
Where is it now, the glory and the dream?[25]

Within the world of this ode, we don't know which *kind* of tree Wordsworth looked upon, or which specific field. We get a little bit more specificity with the flower, that flagrantly tale-telling pansy, that flower of thought, that *pensée*: but is this plant-thinking, in Marder's terms, or Wordsworth ventriloquizing plants? How would we know? Why do we care? What is important in Wordsworth, however much the plant word is here mustered through and by a dejected consciousness, is that the plant world—field and tree and pansy—implicitly precedes and coexists with this particular moment of consciousness and subjective reflection. And while Wordsworth's poem may seem to be one of the high-water marks of romantic projection, it is worth noting that it is also an anatomy of such an anthropomorphizing logic: the pathetic fallacy is here both activated and analyzed.

Both tree and field speak of "something that is gone." What is elided here is the indirect object: to whom do the tree and field speak? Presumably, to Wordsworth, but perhaps also to each other, and to themselves, and to any electrochemical receptor: to paraphrase Wittgenstein, if a tree (or pansy) could talk, would we understand it? Wordsworth's ode suggests, possibly, yes. This also allows us to rethink John Stuart Mill's (in)famous account of lyric as not heard but overheard: at this moment in the ode, we may be not so much overhearing Wordsworth's lyric effusions as (over)hearing through Wordsworth the speech of a tree, a field, and a pansy. Lyric enunciation moves along weird axes: if the pansy's testimony has seemed to some readers a registration of Wordworthian dejection, his spiritual collapse, or—in other readers' accounts—a marker of his disappointed hopes in the French Revolution, that tale-telling pansy also tells another, albeit the same, tale[26]: the fading of the glory and dreams of the pansy—the perishable flower, the flower of thought; an ecologically inflected lament.

I make this brief and partial turn to Wordsworth in the spirit of a compositionist criticism: in activating one archive of historical poetics (romanticism) alongside a transhistorical poetics (the ballad), I abstract each from their historicity into order to serve as responses to Latour's compositionalist provocation.[27] To consider ballads alongside lyrics, romantic or contemporary, is to clarify, and hopefully pluralize, certain points of comparison. In "The Three Ravens," as opposed to Wordsworthian or Glückian or any number of poetic ventures, the tree and field are not summoned to do the job of human speech or to sustain the work of human responsiveness; they mediate no consciousness, carry no affect, transmit no lessons. If any nonhuman figures do that in this ballad, it is the ravens, or whoever else might be the ghostly speaker of the last lines of the poem: "God send euery gentleman / Such haukes, such hounds, and such a leman."

Our usually unexamined animalism (a proxy humanism, perhaps) frames and inflects our reading and emphases of such ballads: certainly it has until recently biased mine. With this ballad, that is, it is easy to miss the tree for the ravens, easy to miss the green field for the knight. Tree and field are not, it would seem, the subjects or agents of the poem: they are, however, its infrastructure and its support, a condition encoded in those grammatical figures of positionality and relationality, the "prepositional," the adverbial and adjectival phrase: "There were three rauens sat *on* a tree . . ."; "*Downe in* yonder greene field . . ."[28]

I want to suggest that the appearance and mobilization of the plant world in this poem exemplifies what we might call plant prepositionality. This is not to relegate the plant field to the realm of "support" or to a Heideggerian ground but rather to suggest how balladry maps the interactive mobile relations of the mineral, vegetal, and human world. For the notionally but not exclusively human world, the common space sung by balladry presupposes a greeny thing, a green field—a green wood, perhaps, to invoke that liminal space so often traversed in balladry, by lovers, thieves, and Robin Hood. Black is the color of my true love's hair, but green is the field of the possible earthly space of a common air.

With this greeny field more vividly in mind, one begins to see a new horizon for thinking through something that has always compelled me about this ballad yet had remained (at least to me) obscure: the status of the refrain—"Downe a downe, hay down, hay downe."[29] When one sings or listens to this song, the status of "down" becomes more than a fol-de-rol-ish placeholder, more than something to fill time or perhaps mindlessly to tune out (cf. a terse *OED* entry for "down, *adv*.": "Used in ballad refrains, without appreciable meaning"[30]). In listening or singing, one starts to notice the sonic and temporal weight given to this "downe a downe," and to note its dispersal and punctual return throughout the poem. The trajectory of the poem is encapsulated in its first two lines:

There were three rauens sat on a tree,
    Downe a downe, hay down, hay downe

original orthography

From the animals above to the knight below, we are moving, throughout, *downe a downe, hay down, hay downe*. We have a trajectory and a field. The entire motion of this poem is, we might say, "downward to darkness, on extended wings."[31] If the knight is at first down in yonder green field, he is, by the poem's end, buried before the prime, *in* the ground, no longer *on* the ground. The poem is both a grounding and a sounding. Its refrain might be seen, fancifully, as a species of diverted apostrophe—the refrain hails no human or animal but "down," the condition of moving, of being, down, itself: Hey down! One might also hear in this a hailing of the field itself, if one recalls that a "down (*n*.)" can specify "an open expanse of elevated land . . . serving chiefly for pasturage."[32] And a further philological sounding suggests the refrain might be heard as a recurring self-address, refrain as self-reflexive apostrophe: for as the *OED* also informs us, "down" specifies "the burden of a song."[33]

For all their trees, downs, and green fields, ballads don't talk about "nature." Ballads would seem to agree with Latour that "nature is not a thing, a domain, a realm, an ontological territory."[34] Ballads in this way manifest a compositionist spirit—they carry forward into our moment a prenaturalism or multinaturalism: a refusal to partition the world into human and nonhuman, under the sign of a reified capital-"N" Nature. Ballads rarely invoke the "plant" kingdom per se: they rather invoke type and specimen, genus and species: a tree, a green field, an oak, a rose, a briar. And this brings me to my next ballad specimen, "Barbara Allen."

"Barbara Allen" (or "Allan") is another ballad that appears in the written record by the seventeenth century, in Samuel Pepys's journal, but probably circulated long before that; it continues to find new interpreters, as any quick glance at YouTube attests.[35] A "romantic ballad," in Walter Scott's taxonomy, it features the story of hard-hearted Barbara Allen, who spurns the sick man (sometimes named Sweet William) who loves her; she then hears of his death and soon dies herself, apparently in a burst of erotic remorse.[36] Aside from this notably undermotivated plotting—a special feature which balladry shares with Shakespeare—a plant-minded reader or listener will note again the recurrence of planty motifs. The ballad opens with a seasonality marked by and in plants as well as other ordering systems, like the calendar:

All in the merry month of May,
When green buds they were swellin'
Sweet William on his death-bed lay,
For love of Barb'ra Allen.

And it is interesting that older variants retain the larger logic of planty seasonality and preserve an attendant pathetic fallacy: "It fell about the Martinmastime / When the green leaves were a-fallin'." If ballad love can swell with the "sweet buds" in May, or mock in their vitality the ailing hero, the hero here "falls" in love in Martinmas time, amidst "fallin'" leaves.[37] The ballad variants tend to conserve seasonality per se and the affective analogy (whether conjoint or disjoint) between humans and plants: what matters is their compositioning, their co-dwelling and entanglement in the poetic field.

Regarding the matter of plant composition: a stanza of particular interest is the fifth, which resonates with the green field already encountered in "The Three Ravens." Having left Sweet William's room, Barbara Allen

. . . walked out through the green green fields
She heard the death bells knellin'—
And every stroke it seemed to say
Hard-hearted Barbara Allen.

Such lines distill what we might call a "field theory of poetry": the "green green fields" here are traversed both by Barbara and by liturgically organized sound, the death bells. Again, as in "The Three Ravens," we note that the green field is moved *through*, that the field is grammatically an object of a preposition, a precondition of her movement, and a signifier of both location and motion. With its interest in an emergent field acoustically shaped by movements through it, "Barbara Allen," like "The Three Ravens," aligns intriguingly with biologists Gerry Webster and Brian Goodwin's "field theory of form."[38] This green green field is neither static nor a reified, geometrized space. It is rather called into being precisely as a relational field, the field appearing only as, only because, she walked *through* it.

From the point of view of the ballad's plants, the human protagonists, Barbara Allen and Sweet William, are just means to planty ends: "they" (presumably the townspeople) bury them in the old churchyard; the rose and briar emerge from their respective graves; these grow up the church wall "until they could grow no higher" and then tie themselves in "a true lover's knot." The flagrant acculturation of plant meanings here (lover's knot and all) should not obscure the core plant means and motions which the ballad can't but record: all along we thought this was a song about vexed lovers, when perhaps it was a song about aspiring plants.

What we have here is a kind of ballad composting, a compositioning—a composting-via-balladry.[39] Despite the ballad's momentum and the human rage for metaphorization-as-meaning, we should resist a premature identification of rose and briar with the dead human subjects, their blighted love transfigured and transformed into motile plants, saturated with their own cultural connotations. Rose and briar are not necessarily figures for Barbara Allen and Sweet William, that is, nor are they metamorphoses (or naturalizations) of them. To insist on this would be to accede prematurely to the humanist attempt to resexualize and conserve ballad matter in one direction.

It is more productive to think of this as a ballad mapping a network of relations unfolding in time, along several orders of time and modes of being. What would seem to be the planty telos of "Barbara Allen" looks from another vantage to be a classic case of ballad networking: the rose-and-briar stanza is one of several so-called "floating stanzas" in balladry—stanzas that move among ballads, fitting in as easily with one ballad as with some others. The concluding rose-and-briar stanza shows up in, e.g.,

"Fair Margaret and Sweet William" and "Lord Thomas and Fair Annet," neither of which is reducible to one of the many variants of "Barbara Allen." Such floating stanzas are characteristic of a ballad economy in which types and tropes are conserved and recycled, plots repeated and subtly varied, often without much singularity or specificity.

Viewed in this way, one could also say that balladry reveals and reenacts more generally an ecology of interacting animate and inanimate matter; of human, animal and vegetal life; of the mineral realities of the rocks of the churchyard wall and the death bells; as well as the subterranean rhizomatic life of graveyards, fields, and ballad grounds. These interactions are of course hierarchized and focalized: yet ballads offer an archive for thinking across an anthropocentric poetics and horizon of pathos. With its provisional resolution in the rose-and-briar floating stanza, "Barbara Allen" intriguingly cuts across a species a priori, that assumed "givenness of the essence of the human" that Barbara Johnson, for one, argues subtends anthropomorphism.[40] The "presupposable" human is what traditional balladry both assumes and undoes. Sweet William (the dying and then dead man) does not quite align with Sweet William, the plant; and from another angle we might say that "Barbara Allen" entangles far more than Barbara Allen (human protagonist) and merely human destinies. The ballad toys with and troubles personification and offers en route a fascinating inquiry into the logic of names.

The very existence of a ballad character like Sweet William—the name of a flower as well as that of a lovesick young man—raises questions about the relations among anthropomorphism, personification, prosopopoeia, and metamorphosis. One could say that Sweet William is always already both the lover of Barbara Allen and a plant. He is perennially both. From the point of view of the plant circuitry mapped in "Barbara Allen," Sweet William was always already a specimen tending toward plant-becoming—whether by having a rose grow from his heart or in inhabiting, inflorescing his being through his floral name. Yet it is striking that in their posthumous persistence or traces, in their plant postpositions and adjacencies, so to speak, Sweet William and Barbara Allen do not neatly function as provisional vehicles for red rose and briar.

They buried her in the old churchyard
Sweet William he was nigh her
And from his heart grew a red, red rose
And from her heart a briar.

That is: from Sweet William's heart does not grow Sweet William. Such a displacement, such a refusal of an identitarian monologic, suggests in its very figural mobility what Deleuze and Guattari called "wisdom of the plants"—a non-identitarian relational logic. The narrative sequencing, this tracking of a material transubstantiation that is not quite consubstantial, shows how ballads might resist the violently anthropomorphic pedagogy de Man suggested was the work of lyric. Such a ballad suggests that personification doesn't work in any straightforward way, and that, more strikingly, anthropomorphism doesn't either.

Ballads are filled with characters, such that their names often designate the ballad itself: Barbara Allen, Fair Margaret and Sweet William, Lord Randal. These characters need not be human: see the Three Ravens, the Twa Corbies, the Elfin Knight. Their characters are emplotted, entangled, enmeshed, but rarely psychologized. They navigate intriguingly the relations between name, personification, character, and prosopopoeia. Ballads expose, resist, and ceaselessly, performatively iterate what Alain Badiou has called "the pure utterance of the arbitrariness of a proper name."[41] Ballads make a wager on the iterability and the contingent yet non-arbitrariness of the proper name. As Levinson has argued, "Not all nouns can sponsor poetry, only a noun whose meaning is or has become entailed by its name."[42] Ballads entailed by their names show how specific proper nouns can indeed sponsor an ongoing poetry. Barbara Allen will always be a Barbara Allen, if—as the ballad has it—her name be Barbara Allen.

The matter of the proper name, and the name of (the) matter, is compulsively iterated throughout. As the anonymous, yet topographically grounded, narrator announces: "Her name was Barbara Allen." The servant goes to her at William's bidding, "cried Master bids you go to him / If your name be Barbara Allen." Barbara Allen—provisionally, conditionally Barbara Allen—answers to the subjunctive, confirms en route its proposition, and is subsequently apostrophized by the bells, granted a seeming epithet, her provisionally proper name: "hard-hearted Barbara Allen" (or "cruel Barbara Allen," inter alia). Ringing variations on "Barbara Allen," the ballad proposes, tests, and refines the name, occluding it finally in the branching out into other planty life. Barbara Allen ends up the grounds for, if not identical with, Briar (Rose).

This is one aspect of what I am calling a compositionist poetics, a poetics that registers what balladry reminds us—that poems, like people, thoughts, plants, and ballads themselves, are co-composed, are made and unmade together in a contingent networking of the animate and inanimate. From the perspective of ballad plants and fields, humans are resources for co-living; from the perspective of balladry, any given ballad is a node in an ongoing, ramifying feedback loop. In this sense ballads partake of Marder's "plant-thinking" and follow what Deleuze and Guattari hailed as "the wisdom of the plants: even when they have roots, there is always an outside where they form a rhizome with something else—with the wind, an animal, human beings."[43]

Balladry follows "the wisdom of the plants"—ceaselessly forming rhizomes "with something else—with the wind, an animal, human beings." With ravens, corbies, Barbara Allen, a dead knight, a green field, the wind that "sall blaw for evermair" (in "The Twa Corbies"). Any ballad, any poem, is potentially (as Deleuze and Guattari wrote of "the rhizome") "in the middle, between things, interbeing, *intermezzo*."[44] No ballad is a beginning, none an ending: ballads are always in medias res, interbeings, en route to another ballad, another version, performance, or iteration. Any reading or singing of a ballad is a singing or reading or listening of the same which is not the same: a complex and plural evocation, simultaneously a haunting, a presencing, and a futuring. Any given ballad may entangle us, enmesh us, wittingly and unwittingly, in all versions and performances of that ballad: we emerge provisionally as listeners onto the field through which we and the ballad move, contingently co-composed.

Now, all of this can seem another pretty (or sad) tale, a conservationist metonymizing of ballad characters into plants and back across time, through various ballad iterations, a compositionist ballad poetics become a glorious composting of the human saved by its recognitions of various alterities and redistributed agencies. Indeed, this is one limitation of a compositionist poetics (or ethics) without politics, historical specificity, or—dare one say it—ideological critique. What I aim to do here, as I hope is clear, is not to save poetry from the bad conscience of its fallacies, pathetic and otherwise, or from its murderously humanist army of tropes, nor do I aim in the end even to rehabilitate these fallacies and ontopoetic operations but, rather and more modestly, to suggest how some poems have long held within them potentialities we might have felt but not yet named. Latour suggests that literary study might explore "the redistribution of agencies";[45] with a compositionist lens, we might also undertake a redistribution of possible perception and sensation. I wonder too whether this might open us to something like a prehermeneutic stance, a peculiarly sensuous askesis of deferring interpretation, not quite (or not only) an embrace of surface reading but a registering of the possibility of other, or multiple, grids for supposedly, merely, *noticing*: the tree under the ravens, the emergent field though which (a) ballad character walks.

For certainly, in some (if not all) modes of reading, and in some (if not all) modes of listening, we take ourselves as "composable-with." It is worth considering further how poems might diagnose and not only enact the relations among pathetic fallacies and anthropomorphism. "Barbara Allen" offers en route a stunning anatomy of the workings of the pathetic fallacy. Consider again the fifth stanza:

She walked out through the green green fields
She heard the death bells knellin'
And every stroke it seemed to say
"Hard-hearted Barbara Allen."

Those speaking bells toll for Sweet William but also, it would seem, for Barbara Allen: the acculturated, shaped, architected metal apostrophizes the suddenly stricken girl. Here we see dramatized the pathetic fallacy as mortal contagion, as a sudden seeming saying, the inorganic acquiring a (double) voice—as "death knell" (communally perceived, a cultural given) and as a new, additional diagnosis: "hard-hearted Barbara Allen."

Are the bells acquiring, or being lent, a voice? And if so (and if either), by whom? Here the projective logic of the pathetic fallacy appears and ramifies. One might recall Ruskin's "main point . . . respecting the pathetic fallacy,—that so far as it *is* a fallacy, it is always the sign of a morbid state of mind, and comparatively of a weak one."[46] Whether Barbara Allen is morbid-minded, the ballad does not say; the ballad itself dispassionately carries the bells' seeming saying, and relentlessly pursues its mortal logic. The ballad raises questions of orientation and direction—questions always activated by apostrophe—and the temporalities of both. "Every stroke it seemed to say": to whom? To Barbara Allen, it would seem, and implicitly perhaps to us. Here we are not quite overhearing lyric address (as in Mill), nor are we clearly operating in what Jonathan Culler has long argued is the basic apostrophic structure of lyric[47]: we rather confront here the dramatic structure of apostrophe itself, its a priori—under what conditions one takes oneself as an addressee (however inadvertent) of a message.

What does one do with an apostrophe? How does one take speaking bells? Barbara Allen takes the bells' saying as a diagnosis and moves on to prognosis: "I'll die for him tomorrow." Within the world of the ballad, Barbara Allen is an accurate prognosticator: Sweet William is in fact dying; she does die tomorrow. And then the plants take over, seemingly emplotted by and yet defiant of a pathetic fallacy that would culminate in a metamorphosis and a fixed, tellingly proper name.

But again: those plants. Do the rose and briar tie a "true lover's knot," or is it that the townsfolk see it thus? Is this figuration an example of a pathetic fallacy, communally sustained? How would we know? The report of the final stanzas comes to us via a notional first person, but we have long been moved securely into the third-person communal report of the town: it is so, the ballad says, not "it seems so to me" (the subjectivism Ruskin enjoined against). One could argue that a ballad such as "Barbara Allen," with its native-informant narrator and account of how "they buried her in the old churchyard," distributes the pathetic fallacy more generally across a generically human plane: pointing to a subtler yet persistent anthropocentrism. In critical discourse, "pathetic fallacy" has typically indexed a form of subjectivism (as in Ruskin) or an anthropocentric anthropomorphism masquerading as trope (as in de Man). It has often been attributed to artists—"the tendency of poets and painters to imbue the natural world with human feeling"[48]—yet also opens more broadly onto questions of anthropomorphism and personification as operations of mind, and whether there is any difference between them: questions Paul de Man infamously addressed and Barbara Johnson later returned to, concluding: "Anthropomorphism, unlike personification, depends on the givenness of the essence of the human; the mingling of personifications on the same footing as 'real' agents threatens to make the uncertainty about what humanness is come to consciousness."[49] Anthropomorphism, on this view, is indeed an anthropocentrism. Yet anthropomorphism "after personification" (as it were) might be in this sense something else: an anthropomorphism dethroned as master "figure of being," one ontology among others.[50]

As I have suggested, "Barbara Allen" unfurls this distinction between anthropomorphic and personifying operations. De Man observed years ago that "'anthropomorphism' is not just a trope but an identification on the level of substance."[51] Ballad composting both invites and thwarts that identification. A ballad like "Barbara Allen," moreover, temporalizes such "identifications"—whether anthropomorphic or naturalizing. Personification is itself composted with the ballad, Sweet William not Sweet William. This is not (only) to find in balladry a posthumanist archive but rather an archive—a ramifying corpus? resources for contingent performance?—of compositionist and historical resonance.

Let us recall Latour's declaration: "It is time to compose—in all the meanings of the word, including to compose with, that is to compromise, to care, to move slowly, with caution and precaution."[52] Sure. Yet what is required "to compose with" or (to continue the Deleuzian/Guattarian figuration) "to form a rhizome with something else"? Proximity, not least: and here balladry helps to outline the pleasures and dangers, and the preconditions and afterlives, of de/compositionism. "Barbara Allen," and indeed "The Three Ravens" and numerous other ballads, station themselves on the hinge of death: before it, after it, beyond it, next to it, digging graves, sprouting plants, burying knights, tending plots. They are preoccupied with the penetrability and permeability of the human, the becoming-dead of their human characters, all the while carrying forward alternate plant livelinesses; these ballads also point to the inorganic within the organic, the proximity of these domains become their fatality. One notes a simultaneous preoccupation with and aversion to corporeal-material phase change, as when the birds of "The Three Ravens" approvingly note of the dead knight, "His haukes they flie so eagerly, / There's no fowle dare come him nie." From a ritual or anthropological (or ethological) angle, one could say that these ballads are preoccupied with how to manage dead bodies and their imminent material indifferentiation. And thus the loyal animal attendants holding off the threatened depredations of *other* animals pave the way for the fallow doe, the leman, a good burial, an elegizing, a benediction.

In these ballads, then, one encounters both the power and the directionality of what Gertrude Stein called the "most nextily," and what traditionary balladry tends to call the "nigh."[53] "Nigh" is, as the *Oxford English Dictionary* tells us, a verb both transitive and intransitive; it can function as well as adverb, preposition, adjective, and noun.[54] "Nighing," one approaches the contingency, materiality, and sociality of the compositional.

Let us recall crucial verses from both "The Three Ravens" and "Barbara Allen." From "The Three Ravens":

His hauks they fly so eagerly,
    Downe a downe, hay down, hay downe
There's no fowle dare him come him **nie**.
    With a downe
Downe there comes a fallow doe,
As great with yong as might she goe.
    With a downe, derrie, derrie, derrie downe, downe.[55]

And from "Barbara Allen":

So slowly, slowly got she up,
And slowly she went **nigh** him,
But all she said as she passed his bed
Was "Young man, I think you're dying!"

And later:

They buried her in the old churchyard
Sweet William he was **nigh** her
And from his heart grew a red, red rose
From her heart a briar.

To nigh is to approximate, to come close, or to come close enough for a possibly transformative contact—to come into a relation capable of co-composition or decomposition. To nigh is not necessarily to be in contact per se but is a tending toward, a "kyndely enclynyng," as Chaucer might put it (see his "House of Fame," l. 734). Nighing is inclination-in-motion. The nigh signals imminent mobility, motility, or change—typically encoded as touch but equally imaginable as any imminent contact. (Stein: "next to be blender, next to between, next to between in intend intender. In tender."[56]) To come nigh, to nigh, to be nigh, is in balladry a condition of imminent identitarian collapse: the nigh in these moments marks the threshold *before* phase change, before metonymy or metaphorization, before transfer and the catalytic bearing-across.

In "The Three Ravens" (and "The Twa Corbies" as well), we encounter a knight about to become not-a-knight, a fresh body tending toward carrion, a potentially preyed-upon corpse. In "Barbara Allen," we encounter, with Barbara Allen *nigh* him, a still live Sweet William about to die; we see the dead bodies of lovers de-/re-composed into plants *nigh* enough to form a true lover's knot (both their endlessly deferred yet endlessly iterated connection and the great knot/not of the lovers' "no"). To preserve the knight, carrion birds must not come nigh him; the fallow doe can and does indeed come nigh him, pick him up, and bury him. One hears the nigh in "knight" and the everlasting night in "knight." We note that Barbara Allen comes nigh Sweet William, speaks, and soon dies: nighing, coming close, approximating, here yields both a diagnosis and a prognosis: "Young man, I think you're dying!" Nighing implicitly becomes as well the occasion of contamination and transfer, Barbara Allen's own death now prepared. Sweet William, buried *nigh* Barbara Allen, creates with her plot (in all senses of plot) the occasion for plant entwining, ballad composting. To be nigh or to nigh is to be available for composting and compositioning. It is precisely not to be single in the field, of many, one—though I would argue, as already intimated, that Wordsworth's "Ode: Intimations of Immortality" offers its own brilliant inquiry into the preconditions for composting and compositioning, and that his ode diagnoses the resistance to such. To be nigh is not to be single or singular; it is to sense oneself or to sense itself as already other.

In these ballads, nighing marks not least a proximity to death, to the afterlives of human deaths, or, more precisely, to indifferentiation. "Let the dead bury the dead," says Latour, quoting Jesus.[57] And perhaps the twa corbies would agree. In "The Twa Corbies" (as noted), the birds do not elegize the knight, nor do they hail his loyal attendants: instead they gleefully note that the hawks, hounds, and leman are faithless, and they propose to swoop down upon the dead knight and "pike out his bonny blue een." There is much to say about the creepy torque of this song, but let us attend to its final stanza:

"Mony a one for him makes mane,
But nane sall ken where he is gane;
Oer his white banes, when they are bare,
The wind sall blaw for evermair."[58]

Beyond culture, beyond elegy and the making of moans for the dead, there are the mineral realities of bare bones, and the persistence of that wind which "sall blaw for evermair." This turn to the everlasting wind evokes the oldest trope for respiration, inspiration, sentience, and insentience; this turn also conjures, perhaps, a phantasmatic horizon of a wind pre- and post-trope. The dispersal of corpses and corpuses into the wind: here traditional poetry offers a premodern antihumanist *poiesis* which might align with and chasten our own supposedly post-critique enforced climate-mindedness.

But/and also: in the alternatives of the elegizing ravens and the gleefully scavenging corbies, we find possible images (defunct? dead as the knight? compostable?) of ourselves as readers—humanist guardians vs. antihumanist skeptics; aestheticizing tenders of tradition vs. incisive paranoiacs; posthumanist witnesses or scavengers, depending on disposition. The balladized birds are, it must be said, close readers; what is required in any variant is their proximity, their coming nigh the matter. So in addition to a posthumanist postnatural ecocriticism, or a chastened formalism, or a poetic historicism, we might remind ourselves—via ballad wind and bones—of a prehumanist elementalism, which poetry also channels, not least in ballads, and which might productively goad us and temper us, adjust and remake "us."

Or might not.

CHAPTER TWO

Haunt

There are too many cedars here
    hiding the sun hovering
        over the dead
    the lakes won't wash away
& the ghosts the locals talk of
        are their memories
      singing and shifting unbidden *I heard it*
      last night *I saw it*
    on the staircase
testimony weaving its own
      shimmering cloth
we wear to keep ourselves warm
      & to spare the others
        our nakedness
—better not to have heard
      the stories
    the dead children
lunatic mothers gimlet-
    eyed servants and
absentee lairds
the old murder ballads in Scotland
    depend on
there's a dead soldier on auld fail dyke
    on yonder greene plain
    a knight centuries ago
there's a dead woman in the river
dead baby in the cradle
    there's a dead soldier in the desert

Compositional/Poetics

  & three crows wonder over and over
        whether to cry out
              an elegy
        or to sit on his breastbone and pike out
              his bonnie blue een[59]

Crows

whining not crawing
the sociable murderous crows

---

today's news thin
predictable grueling alarm
and the small slugs for eating
are plenty

"the mind fails"
"the mind fails"
"hyperobjects"
"the sublime"
it can't happen
to me
nononononono it can't happen to us

---

let's talk and talk and talk
about it so it becomes
warm and toasting as the oven
warming the room
in the witch's house

Compositional/Poetics

why a witch
why not accuse
the obvious ruling goons
or ancestors some propitiate
or whatever force to which you've given a human face

~~~

a crow walks slowly across the mown lawn
a great lawn with clumps of drying grass here and there

these ferns will not outlast the coming heat[60]

Weeds

all day
personifying plants
Evil Nettle
Fascist Weed
boing boing
I do not want you
matter out of place
I rip you out
I favor the desired
the useful to me to me to me!

meanwhile stars doing themselves
in the sky
insouciant celebrity
assholes they don't care
why don't they care
don't they
Cassiopeia angling the sky
open triangles mouths and teeth
of vanity, grief
but where, where is the belt
of Orion and where can we see
the once-in-a-lifetime
comet

I am feeling Babylonian
I am feeling antediluvian
I am thinking Noah

should take us aboard
but we would be extra cargo

there are worlds
and worlds to come

hello! we say
from this one[61]

Trees

Everywhere/today
the irises insisted
on waving their blue flags

Hairy tongued things
with mouths
hanging open

as if to fuck the air

O la la la spring
& dying

the usual song

> "Every flower in a garden/is a sign
> of a complete failure"
> the landscape designer declared

Why not salute the trees
They take a long time to die

& then can die only half way
for a long time

for a long time
be half alive[62]

Taking a Walk in the Woods after Having Taken a Walk in the Woods with You

Now I cannot not see
the blight everywhere[63]

* 3 *
Notational/Poetics

Some years ago I realized that I had felt for some time a lack of inspiration, or rather, a lack of motivation—something different, perhaps—in all kinds of keys: poetic, political, critical, affective. I was and am interested in this lack of inspiration, both personally and impersonally. Perhaps I was suffering from what the critic and theorist Lauren Berlant called "political depression."[1] Perhaps I was suffering from gender. Perhaps this was a matter of electrochemical receptors. Perhaps this was a perfectly fine interval or suspension that was meant simply to be endured or even embraced.

Perhaps the requirement of inspiration is itself the problem, or a problem. Maybe we could follow the poet Fred Wah, who some years ago wrote:

Ikebana

Don't make it up
find it

dead brown pods
a few shiny green leaves period[2]

Wah here offers a mini-statement on poetics, a provocation under the sign of ikebana, the Japanese art of flower arrangement, also known as Kadō (華道, "way of flowers"). Wah's economical poem presents *poiesis* not so much as the work of *homo faber* as the work of an alert scavenger, a finder, a gleaner with a prepared mind, prepared not least by complex traditions of finding and arranging, prepared to see in apparently random materials the basis for a new assemblage: "Don't make it up / find it." And what might "it" be made of? Dead pods, shiny green leaves, an apparently haphazard mix of dead and living matter gathered and arranged, assembled and lightly transformed into an emergent "it," its provisional finality marked wittily by the lexicalized period, that mark of punctuation stopping the finding into the Gestalt of assemblage—

It's worth noting that Wah's "Ikebana"—in its finding and arranging of pods and leaves—swerves from the flower-as-blossom. If the first stanza functions as a kind of note-to-self (or to anyone wrestling with the demands of making vs. "making it up"), the second notates an ingathering of materials, an enactment of assemblage itself, capped by the period, not notated but lexicalized, rendered part of the verbal assemblage, functioning in its fleet emphasis perhaps a bit like the cutting word, *kireji*, of traditional Japanese haiku.[3] In its negative construction and hortatory mode ("Don't make it up / find it"), Wah's poem implicitly offers a counterstatement to a poetics of making-it-up, of imagination, of *fingo, fingere*, of creating, inventing, contriving, and/or feigning. Wah points to a poetry committed to something else, to a provisional sufficiency, artful in its reckoning with and through minimal means, supremely artful nonetheless period.

Wah's poem, its economy and ethos, calls to mind (if only to distinguish itself from) Wallace Stevens's "Anecdote of the Jar," the humble vernacular artifact there taking "dominion everywhere," the poem asserting the power of the homely aesthetic object to transform and tame the heretofore "slovenly wilderness" of Tennessee, now "no longer wild."[4] Stevens's antinomies are not Wah's, nor are his anxieties or claims.

Don't make it up
find it

Or maybe, simply, *note* it.

Wah's poem vibrates in several dimensions, but I register it here as both a notational poem and a poem about notation. The poem invites us to move before or behind the assemblage, the title, the governing concept, the provisional totality of ikebana or poem. And in tracking further a poetics of notation, I will draw on several notational forms, including haiku (the famous seventeen-syllable Japanese poetic form), tanka (another notably brief form, thirty-one syllables), and notes-to-self (perhaps less a form than a practice). The notational in its broadest remit may appear in various forms and places — not least the notebook; it may also be the sign of a disposition, of one inclined (or taught) to take or make notes.[5] Notation for me has ramified along several axes — as a taker of notes, a keeper of notebooks, and a student of others' notational practices, from eighteenth-century antiquarians' headnotes to twentieth-century liner notes to John Cage's and Cecil Taylor's scores to Makoto Ueda's great volume, his anthology of notes on that notational form, the hokku: *Bashō and His Interpreters: Selected Hokku with Commentary* (1992).[6]

My thoughts on the notational have been informed in recent

years by several poets and by the work of Roland Barthes. In reading Barthes's *Preparation of the Novel*—his final two courses of lectures and seminars, 1978–79, 1979–80—I was particularly drawn to his meditations on notation, which he theorizes across his own practice of note taking and more generally across *poiesis*. Here we see one route into a practice and poetics of notation. Or at least I found such in Barthes: for in reading this work, it seemed that I was encountering belatedly an illumination and theorization of my own (and other writers') practices and inclinations. Barthes offered, as it were, a retrospective theorization of writing I had understood, long before reading him, as enmeshed in the possibilities and problems of the notational. (As Rosalind Krauss writes of her own work on Jasper Johns via Barthes, "Who among us has ever prevented our ego from experiencing a new body of work through the lens of our own current projects?"[7])

I'd like to anticipate here that "the notational" is ultimately not reducible to, or captured in, "notation."

In his lectures, Barthes contemplates and celebrates "the minimal act of writing that is Notation."[8] And he further distinguishes what he calls the initial *notula* from the rewritten *nota* in his practice: "notula" designates for him the one word which shall remind him of his "idea" (90).[9] The *notula*, the single jotted word, becomes a kind of key which can unlock the safe of the notation, to be further jotted down, amplified, when Barthes has time. Barthes raises the questions, asking, "What is the *noteworthy*, the *notandum*?" and "*What's the point?*" (192, 94). As he writes elsewhere: "What is noted always appears as being notable."[10] He is, one might say, reanimating Sartre's question, "Why Write?"[11] This subtends the question what to write, make, or compose: a novel? a haiku? a photograph?

Among many things I appreciated in this work was Barthes's

cheerful setting aside of inspiration—"the haiku and any short form that's fascinated by it, all Notation, *lacks inspiration*" (47). His account of the rhetoric and practice of notation partakes of his broader project of rethinking classical rhetoric.[12] Barthes reanimates in his lectures some if not all of the force of *notatio* in Latin rhetoric: as he writes, "In Latin: *Notatio* (the fact of noting down)" (49). For Barthes, *notatio*, the practice, conjures maternity, refuge, interiority (91). Consider "notatio," from "noto," "to mark":

NOTATIO:
notātiō, notātiōnis
noto
noun (f., 3rd declension)

1. A marking, noting
2. The inflicting of disgrace by the *nota censoria*
3. A designation, choice
4. A noticing, observing, observation
5. The designating of the meaning and derivation of a word, etymology
6. The use of letters to denote entire words, a species of short-hand
   from the LEWIS and SHORT *Latin Dictionary*[13]

One might observe the incommensurate relations among these definitions, their slippage from mere marking to juridical censure to an illocutionary choosing to a mere noticing to etymology to writing systems.

The *Oxford English Dictionary* intriguingly tracks the path of "notation" in English, following its postclassical Latin fortunes, and the *OED* specifically marks several aspects of "notation" as obsolete and/or rare since the seventeenth century. There are two senses the *OED* presents as current: no. 3, "A note, an annotation," and no. 6, "The process or method of representing numbers, quantities, relations, etc. by a set or system of signs or symbols, for the purpose of record or analysis; (hence) any such system of signs or symbols."[14] This matter of "system" is further specified in the full entry via math, music, dance, the sciences. Even these two current senses of "notation" point to a paradox: that notation conjures both abbreviation and dilation, both condensation and explanation, a mark sufficient unto itself and a mark specifically harnessed to another system or ideational referent.

Barthes's *notula* might be seen as a kind of note-to-self—an indexical keyword for retrieval of mental files, and for dilation toward the *nota*.

Note to Self (Strandhill)

Freshwater woman—
time to remember the taste of the sea.

MCLANE[15]

And this is where my own unsystematic practice of keeping notebooks, for fifteen or twenty years, links up with others'. One could cite any number of contemporary poets and writers who work with notational forms and practices, such as Harryette Mullen, who explicitly invokes "the notational spirit of this [tanka] tradition" in *Urban Tumbleweed: Notes from a Tanka Diary* (2013)[16]:

Paparazzi snap snoozing celebrities
in stretch limos cruising down Hollywood
Boulevard past anorexic palm trees.

Between train station and high-rises,
he diverts pedestrians, drumming on
plastic buckets and battered metal canisters.[17]

Or consider Fanny Howe, long a practitioner of a poetics of the notebook. As she writes in *Love and I* (2019): "Proof that you lived is that you kept notebooks."[18] (As a friend mordantly observed, notebooks could also offer proof that you had died, or would soon. And here one encounters the question of writing toward and against death, and the status of notebooks as archive, evidence, spolia, realia.)

Or one might reach slightly further back and consider W. S. Graham, whose notebooks have become a newly generative resource for poets and artists. A Scottish poet who lived most of his adult life in Cornwall, Graham was associated with a modernist romantic school, active in the visual as well as poetic arts. 2018 marked the centenary of Graham's birth, and to commemorate this via the multidisciplinary engagement Graham himself undertook, poets Sam Buchan-Watts and Lavinia Singer gleaned some prompts from his notebooks and letters and invited writers and artists to respond in whatever form they thought most suitable: poem, prose, criticism, letter, artwork.[19] What they sent:

To have a question, the construction of which, is as creative as its answer.

. . .

To talk most richly universally the artist talks to himself. — Subject for a poem.

. . .

The "help" the critic should give us in work like this is towards understanding the "language apparatus" which has been constructed.[20]

...

idea — subject — love and myself? What?

...

Nature — where does "nature" stop and non-nature begin?

...

To make a poem about some object in this room.
To see how it will change the object. (The poem short — 10–15 lines. maybe better fairly descriptive visually first of all.)

...

Take down actual speech.

W. S. GRAHAM, "From a 1949 Notebook"[21]

Given this commission, I decided to follow Graham's final injunction, "take down actual speech," which then animated my notebook jottings for many months. What ultimately emerged:

I'm going to tell you a story.
The lane we're going down
goes by another name.
                    Groper's Lane.
That's right. We're in the red light district.
It must have seemed rather avant-garde.
It does so even now.

            I see more
and more people sleeping rough.
Because I always stay in nice hotels
I love brain. I know where your head's at
because mine's been there.

CHAPTER THREE

    It's very hard
for a Japanese person to understand
what will appeal to American readers.

I eat dramatically less
than I did three years ago.

    Where's that heading?
The incinerator.
                    Will you be here for long?
Inglan is a bitch.
                    Isn't he the one
who found your country? discovered it?

It was an experiment.

    How do they decide
which one is the male and which one is the female?

Please proceed to the transfer desk.

    What you fuckin doin?

We are flying through trauma clouds.

                Regardez, Maman!

It's low tide. Let's go collect something.

I have a great crested newt.

I confess I'm nostalgic for the old days
when there was the avant-garde and the establishment and you knew
                          what side you were on.

We may expect to see Paris

        on the right hand side of the aircraft.

I believe in something

but broken bones are stronger bones.

They don't have human rights in Berlin.

                She simply can't talk to the young people
of Lampedusa.
                Why don't you smile?
Give me two minutes.
      Cinque stelle. Cinque stelle.

Someone could have died.
      It was the best possible outcome.

Life is hard why do you have to make it harder.

We are the adults.

Can you erase our messages.[22]

"Take Down Actual Speech" is a cento, a patchwork made of other people's phrases and statements rendered into notes; the poem is made out of notebook gleanings I took down over the course of several months in summer 2018 into the fall and the next winter (see figures 1–5). During that time, I was traveling among several places in Europe, during Brexit anxiety and refugee crises, moving among the various privileged nodes and no-places of late capitalism including airports, museums, trains, and train stations. Graham's note-to-self—"take down actual speech"—particularly resonated because I had long had a habit of jotting down bits of overheard speech, and these bits had sometimes made their way into poems or essays or ongoing conversation. Graham's phrase became an organizing principle for what had been an inchoate practice. I found myself most attuned to others' words and phrases in semipublic places—pubs, train stations, subway cars, airplanes, street crossings. Then too I was struck anew by people's phrases and phrasings—those of friends, those of strangers. That the actual speech I took down was inflected by my own (largely urban, deeply classed, raced, gendered, trans/national) itineraries, alertness, obliviousness, and so on, perhaps hardly needs saying. Ditto which languages I could even register or notate. In the end, a compositional question governed this process: how one moves from jottings to the poem. Or how to move, as Barthes titles the first section of *Preparation of the Novel*, "From Life to the Work."

Poets have long followed (or exploited) this injunction to "take down actual speech": from T. S. Eliot's "Hurry Up Please It's Time" in *The Waste Land* (2022) to Tonya Foster's *Swarm of Bees in High Court* (2015). Foster describes her practice in her afterword, "Notes: Titular Lineages," as in part a collecting of the language of the place, Harlem:

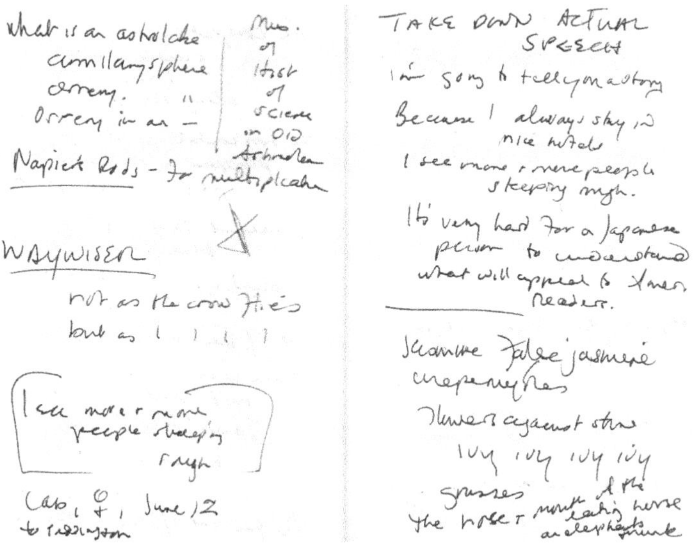

Notational/Poetics

[handwritten notebook pages]

- What is an astrolabe
- armillary sphere
- orrery.   "
- Orrery in an —
- Napier Rods - For multiplication
- Mus. of Hist of Science in Old Ashmolean

WAYWISER
not as the crow flies
but as I [ ] [ ]

I see more + more
people sleeping
rough

Cab, ♀, June 12
to Paddington

Right page:
TAKE DOWN ACTUAL
    SPEECH
I'm going to tell you a story
Because I always stay in
    nice hotels
I see more + more people
    sleeping rough.

It's very hard for a Japanese
    person to understand
what will appeal to Amer.
    Reader.

Jasmine False jasmine
crepe myrtles
flowers against straw
ivy ivy ivy ivy
grasses
the horse's mouth of the
    eating horse
    an elephant trunk

FIGURE 1 • From a notebook, June 2018 ("Take Down Actual Speech," Oxford)

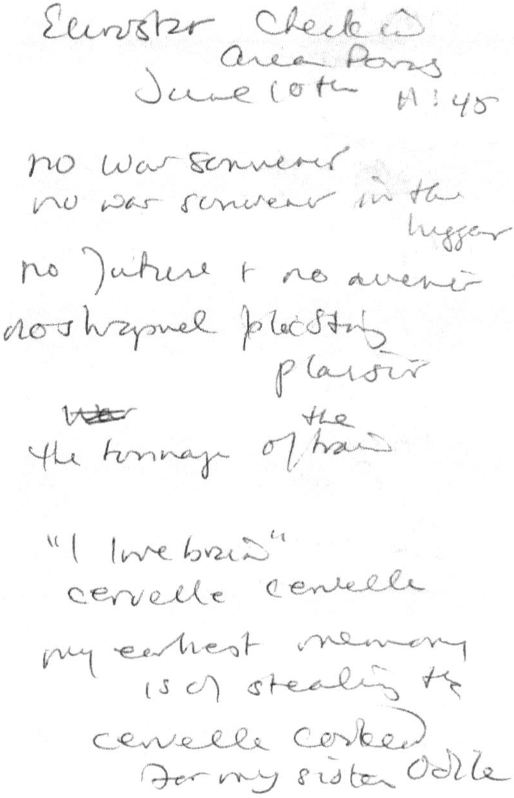

CHAPTER THREE

> Eurostar Checked
> Area Paris
> June 10th H:45
>
> no war souvenir
> no war souvenir in the
> bigger
> no future + no avenir
> no hazmel pleasure
> plaisir
> ~~her~~ the
> the tonnage of train
>
> "I live brain"
> cervelle cervelle
> my earliest memory
> is of stealing the
> cervelle ~~for~~ corked
> for my sister Odile

FIGURE 2 • From a notebook, June 10, 2018 (Eurostar)

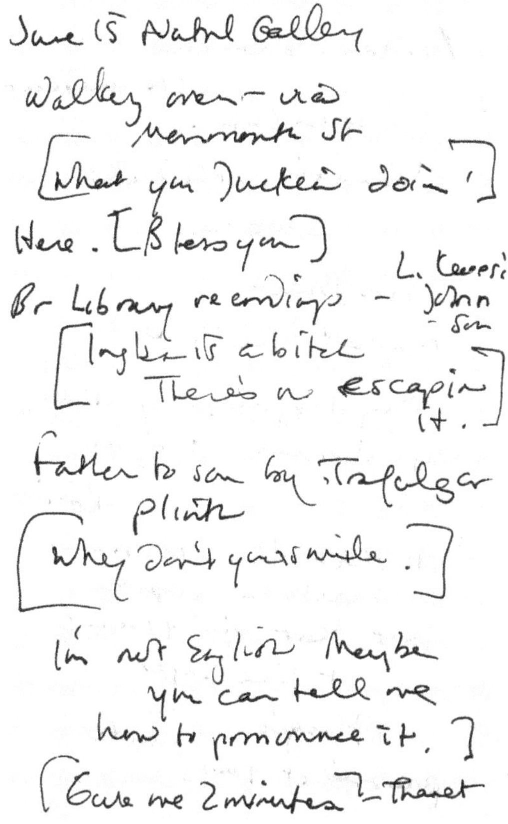

Notational/Poetics

June 15 National Gallery
Walking over — via
    Monmouth St
[What you Duckies doin'?]
Here. [Bless you]
                    L. Lewsi
Br Library recordings — John
                         — Son
[Inglis is a bitch
    There's no escaping
                       it.]
Father to son by Trafalgar
    plinth
[Why don't you smile.]

I'm not English. Maybe
    you can tell me
    how to pronounce it.]
[Give me 2 minutes — Thanet

FIGURE 3 • From a notebook, June 15, 2018 (National Gallery, British Library)

91

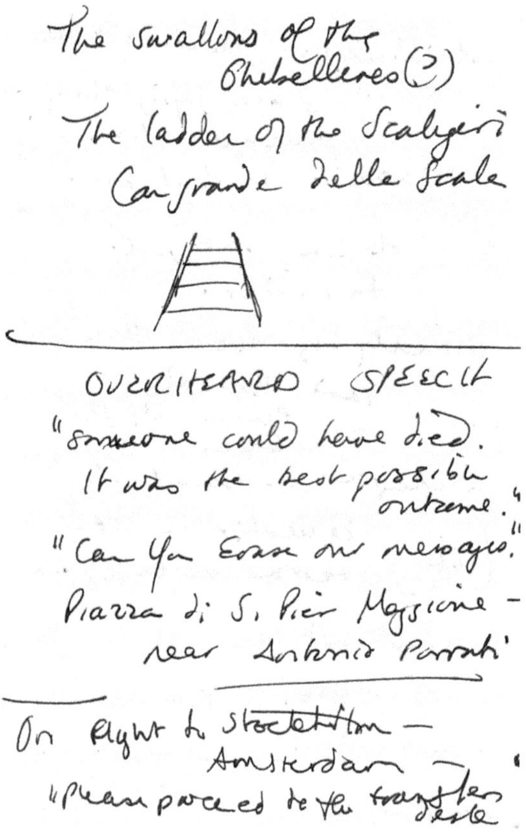

CHAPTER THREE

The swallows of the Chibelleres (?)

The ladder of the Scaligeri
Cangrande delle Scale

OVERHEARD SPEECH
"Someone could have died.
It was the best possible outcome."
"Can you erase our messages."
Piazza di S. Pier Maggiore —
near Antonio Parrati'

On flight to Stockholm —
Amsterdam —
"Please proceed to the transfer desk"

FIGURE 4 • From a notebook, June 2018

Notational/Poetics

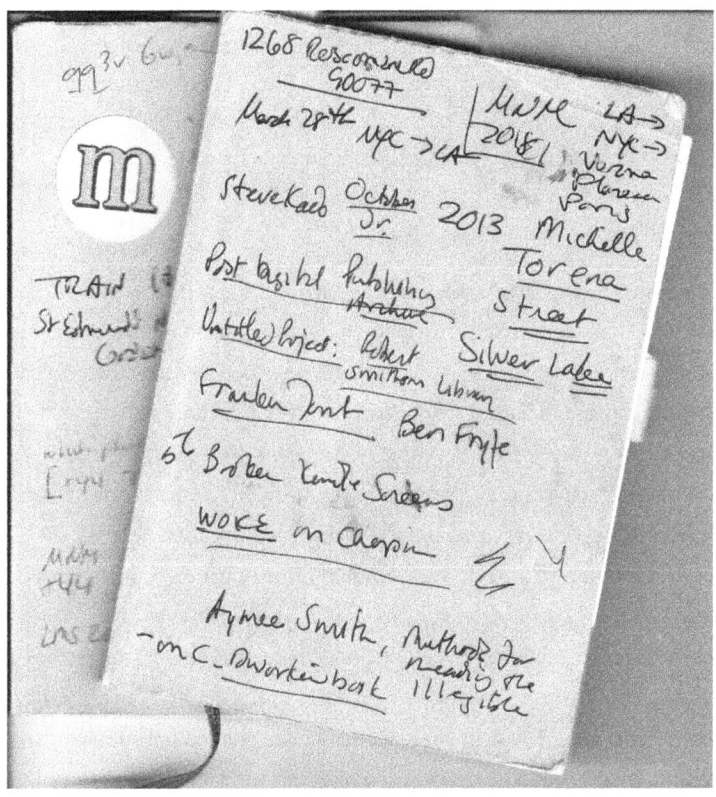

FIGURE 5 * Small brown notebooks, 2018 (LA→NYC→Verona, Florence, Paris)

CHAPTER THREE

> I began to think about and collect the language of the place—the people and things that occupy the place. This is a biography of life in the day of a particular neighborhood. The cameras, bodies, televised portrayals, voices, and doorways of the place demanded a different pronoun for dealing with the multiple as subject and as swarm of actors.[23]

It's not obvious that one would write "a biography of life in the day of a particular neighborhood" via haiku, as Foster partially does—one might think that a novel, or prose poetry, or dramatic monologues, or a short film, might offer a readier vehicle—and it's not obvious either that the taking down of speech or the collecting of language might flow into haiku-ish forms. But this is where Barthes's musings on the notational are instructive.

For one of the great paradoxical illuminating conjunctures of Barthes's *Preparation of the Novel* is that a significant part of it is devoted to the haiku. The haiku distills for Barthes the essence of notation: "the very essence of Notation: the haiku" (19). He further proposes, quoting Maurice Coyaud, that "a haiku 'is simply what happens in a given place, at a given moment'" (52).

Consider Foster:

> We might could make
> a plan, *make something out of*
> *apparently nothing.*
>
> "High Court," 76

Now, for Barthes, "Haiku = exemplary form of the Notation of the Present = minimal act of enunciation, ultrashort form, an atom of a sentence that *notes* (marks, delimits, glorifies, endows with a *fama*), a tiny element of 'real,' present, concomitant life" (23). (One registers en passant that Barthes's sessions, themselves rendered intermittently in a notational form, occasionally use the shorthand notation and symbolic logic of "=," that mark pointing to, and intersecting with, other writing systems, as one of the *OED* definitions of "notation" suggests.) The haiku, then, is linked to the present moment; it is for him the least temporalizing of forms, the most apparently immediate; the most minimal act of enunciation; a noting, illuming, or packaging of an atom of the so-called real.

The haiku is notable in Barthes too because is it above all else deictic, a pointing form, asserting the this-ness of the now-ness of enunciation, the compression of pointing: *that*. "Saying that you can't say: the whole haiku tends toward this — toward '*that*.' There's nothing to say, in short, other than the vertiginous limit of language, the *deictic Neutral*" (80). As he remarks, the haiku distills the spirit of "*That's it!*" and also aligns with "a Zen notion, the *Wu-shi*: 'Nothing special.'" (80). "It could therefore be said: a (good) haiku *sets a bell ringing*" (78).

The appeal of haiku for Barthes, preparing to undertake his notional novel, includes its displacement if not effacement of subjectivity, its commitment to specificity, and its orientation to "circumstants" over referents — its interest in environment, weather, seasonality, implied situation. For regarding subjectivity: in haiku, Barthes claims, "*I* is always a *remainder*" (83).

As if the soul could
be singled out from the cells,
from the room's clutter.

FOSTER, "Bullet/in," 69

As if singled out from the clutter, a residue of the clutter; the Soul, the I *as if* a remainder; the soul as if singled out, as if singlable-out, single-outable. What we have in Barthesian haiku is not so much an asserted subject nor even an implied I but a registering sentience and sensorium. But as Foster's "as if" suggests, this single-outable I is precisely what she complicates throughout her book, pluralizing the "I," distressing too the "we," searching for "a different pronoun for dealing with the multiple as subject and as swarm of actors." As she writes in the concluding lines of her book, "Central to this meditation—'We think, therefore we are t/here, therefore t/here is.'" This offers a striking extension and communalization of the *cogito* but also an accenting of, a presencing of, deixis: the calling forth of the "t/here" as well as, through, and following upon the "we" (122). Foster variously undertakes the specifying, accenting, and vexing of collectivity, partly through a/na/grammatical conjugation; testing the I, the We, and the Other, the *be/e* of being, the finitude of the infinitive, the condition of the conditional:

We might could make
a plan, *make something out of*
apparently nothing.

"We-might" could make
I-am soar/sore, make "I" commit
to be an other.

FOSTER, "High Court," 76

As Foster's tercets suggest, pace Barthes's dream of haiku, we won't get away so quickly from the problematics of subjectification.

Grammatical I
    ons: shit happens, shit be done
        happened, shit be.

Grammatical "I"
says, "Am." "Am. "Let." "Am I?" "I'ma
tell Mama." "I am."

FOSTER, "High Court," 77

And moreover, as "swarm" suggests, Foster won't hold with subjectification as individuation: "Bees are communal, plural, public, unindividuated, corporate, en masse" (121).

"If I was a bird,
I'd shit on you, and Keisha,
Chris, and Giselle too."

If "I" was a bird
instead of an axle-tree,
"we" might could fly.

FOSTER, "High Court," 75

Foster's haikus activate other resonances than Barthes's theorizations suggest, and this should not be surprising: the form (along with its aura) has been adapted, torqued, bent, transformed along many axes, for over a century, in English and many other languages, and indeed in Japan as well.[24] And more broadly, it's also worth remarking here what must be obvious: Barthes's reflections on haiku are highly arguable, not least in their period-style Orientalist remarks on the Void and the Orient.[25]

While Barthes might be wrong about the haiku, he does seem to me on to something about and through notation, and the stake of a minimal act of writing. A poetics arising from or indexing an absence of inspiration, the haiku appears to Barthes as the short form par excellence. I want to make clear here that this interest in a lack of inspiration, this commitment to the notational as sufficient, is not aligned with, say, so-called uncreative or automatic writing but with something else.[26] We might immediately think of several other short forms—the epigram, the epitaph, the aphorism, the riddle, the isolatable couplet, the single-line or single-word poem.[27] In his own musings, Barthes compares haikus in translation against several short-form poems in French (by, e.g., Apollinaire) and finds these poems wanting, vis-à-vis haikuity[28]: for what the haiku carries for Barthes is the promise of nonmoral nonsubjectivized mere noticing, a poetics of the gesture, and of what he calls a paradoxical dialectic of instant memory. The moral or moralizing force of epigrams, the packaged and portable sayings of aphorisms or, indeed, tweets, the cognitive kapows of riddles, the brilliant distillations of these kinds of short forms are not the haiku's business. Haiku offers, in Barthes's telling, another kind of constellation, in which the subject is implied yet not announced; in which the ephemeral is noted yet not monumentalized; in which writing serves less as capture than as release—a gleaning, not a reaping.

I already remarked on the curiosity that a course of lectures on the "preparation of the novel" should first devote itself intently to the haiku. But this points to other aspects of the significance of this form for Barthes—for *The Preparation of the Novel* is itself a testament to a profound trans- and intermedial thinking. His lectures and seminars triangulate the haiku, the novel, and photography, testing the possibilities and interrelations of each. Barthes's haiku is an implicitly intermedial form enmeshed with and against the novel and the photograph, with the haiku's instant memory, deictic gesture, and compression distinct from, and distinguishing the specificity of, the novel's temporal dilation, memorious ongoingness, and meanwhileness vs. the photograph's "this was" vs. the haiku's "here now."

Moreover one finds haiku punctuating Barthes's work at crucial moments—not least in his essay on Eisenstein, "The Third Meaning" (1970): and it is worth noting that this essay is subtitled, "Research **Notes** on Some Eisenstein Stills" (emphasis added).[29] In this essay we discover that haiku becomes the exemplary case of the third, or obtuse, meaning: the obtuse meaning as *accent*.[30] After offering several glosses on the third or obtuse meaning—the signifier without a signified, that which is discontinuous, indifferent to story and to the obvious meaning, as an always depleted or etherized signifier—Barthes arrives at his final gloss:

> Finally, the obtuse meaning can be seen as an *accent*, the very form of an emergence, of a fold (a crease even) marking the heavy layer of informations and significations. If it could be described (a contradiction in terms), it would have exactly the nature of the Japanese *haiku*—anaphoric gesture without significant content, a sort of gash rased of meaning (of desire for meaning). Thus in image V:
>
> > Mouth drawn, eyes shut squinting,
> > Headscarf low over forehead,
> > She weeps.
>
> This accent—the simultaneously emphatic and elliptic character of which has already been mentioned—is not directed towards meaning (as in hysteria), does not theatricalize (Eisensteinian decorativism belongs to another level), does not even indicate an *elsewhere* of meaning (another content, added to the obvious meaning); it outplays meaning—subverts not the content but the whole practice of meaning.

> A new—rare—practice affirmed against a majority practice (that of signification), obtuse meaning appears necessarily as a luxury, an expenditure with no exchange. This luxury does not *yet* belong to today's politics but nevertheless *already* to tomorrow's.[31]

The luxury of obtuse meaning—an expenditure with no exchange, an end run around, and outplaying of, meaning, a defeat of the ceaseless productions of meanings, a luxury for tomorrow's politics: note this invocation yet deferral of a potential political communal luxury, carried by means of haiku. Not only is haiku an exemplary case of, or model for, the obtuse or third meaning, for *signifiance* beyond signification: it offers the very form through which Barthes conducts his annotation. Barthes notably renders his reading of the Eisenstein still in a kind of haiku form—his notation, his annotation, formally and philosophically tending toward the haiku, always already haikuized. "Mouth drawn, eyes shut squinting, / Headscarf low over forehead, / She weeps."[32]

Why the need for such a hermeneutical edifice, third or obtuse meanings fracturing the zone of the signifier? Why the distaste for obvious meaning intermittently pulsing throughout this essay? An understandable loathing of precooked, reified meaning, the prescribed, the overdetermined; a desire to preserve a remainder, something not assimilable to the machinery of critical-theoretical processing and exchange. The obtuse meaning offers a revenge on the presumption of criticism itself: "In short, what the obtuse meaning disturbs, sterilizes, is metalanguage (criticism)."[33] And yet Barthes will still make his obtuse meanings mean, and will develop here a nonce yet portable metalanguage for their possible capture and sharing. As Barthes concedes, the obtuse meaning could be something for you, something for me.

Notational/Poetics

Barthes's haiku carries the promise of an affect that never had to wane as it was never more than barely emergent; of a subject present only by inference, if at all; the promise of an I not as origin but rather as a remainder of notational processes and dispositions: That's It!—a subject precipitated out of the gleaned dynamism of circumstants. Haiku are precipitated out of circumstances, gleaned from the surround: that is why seasonality matters when thinking about haiku, and notation in general, and why the weather matters: these are some crucial ambient conditions for our noticing and more profoundly for the sensorium's subliminal sensation of being alive.

a gull with a shattered wing
ended the spring

∞

a day without rain
I'd almost forgotten
the shape of the sun

[...]

∞

to be calm and still
as the Morandi bottles
on the windowsill

                    from MCLANE, "Notationals/ Songs of a Season III"[34]

CHAPTER THREE

Minimal, notionally evanescent as well as "about" and "around" the evanescent, yet structured in and by time-as-seasonality, the haiku doesn't have to scale: it makes molehills out of mountains, moments out of contingent attentiveness; punctuations of (if not perforations in) the flow of so-called experience. Of haiku one would never write, as Eliot did, that we had the experience but missed the meaning. There is no missing of meaning; the small atom of "the real" (in Barthes's terms) suffices —

Update

what threatened all day
is here — thunder, rain,
and now your text

MCLANE[35]

Barthes's haiku offers a potential remedy for strenuousness, the obligation to do something, make something, inaugurate something, respond.

Furu ike ya   kawazu tobikomu   mizu no oto

BASHŌ

The old pond —
A frog leaps in,
And a splash.

BASHŌ, translated by Makoto Ueda

The old pond —
a frog jumps in,
sound of water.

BASHŌ, translated by Robert Hass

Old pond | frog leap | splash

MCLANE version[36]

But are we obliged to do something? as poets, writers, citizens, denizens, humans?

We might could make
a plan, *make something out of
apparently nothing.*

FOSTER

Ikebana

Don't make it up
find it

dead brown pods
a few shiny green leaves period

WAH

What period are we in? what punctuates our lives?

3.
MARCH
Birdfeeder's
    snow cap

    sliding
        off

4.
Spring
    stood there
        all body

Head
    blown off
        (war)

showed up
    downstream

October
    is the head
        of spring

Birch, sumac
    before
        the blast

LORINE NIEDECKER, "Five Poems"[37]

In his lectures, Barthes invokes: "*Poetry* = practice of subtlety in a barbaric world. Whence the need to fight for poetry *today*: Poetry should be one of our 'Human Rights'; it isn't 'decadent,' it's subversive: subversive and vital" (45–46). These musings on subtlety returned me to the remarks of performance artist and playwright Taylor Mac, in a 2019 interview with Sasha Weiss:

"Subtlety is a privilege," he said. When I asked him what he meant, he explained: "The trend of subtlety in the theater is one of people who didn't have to shout in the streets and do direct-action protest in order to stay alive because the government was refusing to acknowledge the AIDS epidemic. Like, Larry Kramer is not subtle, right? So that's what I mean. Subtlety is a privilege. And so when I go to the theater and I see people being subtle, I'm like: Oh, great, what do you [expletive] want? What are the stakes? What are you risking?"[38]

Here I think Mac is throwing out the subtlety baby with the privileged bathwater. Though fair enough, in terms of theater, "civility," the mandate to keep your mainly white bourgeois audience comfortable, or to disturb it in assimilable ways. Fair enough, in terms of poetry. The bracketed "[expletive]" in the quote above tells you a lot about the policing of "subtlety"—or is it "vulgarity"?—by institutional norms (call it house style). Yet it's worth noting that, in a mediascape and ambient environment of screaming obviousnesses, subtlety is itself sometimes a risk, a delicate stake planted in a damaged field. But there are subtleties and subtleties, no? (See Kara Walker's 2014 installation, *A Subtlety*.)

What Barthes seems to be reaching for in his final lectures, and in such previous work as his essay "The Third Meaning," is a rhetoric and a poetics of the nuance: "This path of the *Nuance* (which started out from the Weather and follows it): so what's at the end? Well, *life*, the sensation of life, the feeling of being alive" (47). Haiku, and more broadly, the path of the nuance, are on the side of life. But what if the "feeling of being alive" is coextensive with duress and pain? "Then, what is Life?" (as Shelley asked).[39] And further, what about wrong life, or a surround or experience of damaged life (to invoke Theodor Adorno)?[40] What if an alertness to "circumstants," to the ambient surround, obliterates nuance? Whither noticing, and notation, then? And what of the obscenity of life mere life as a value? What about noticing death, what about noting the structure of, or the irruption of, what Achille Mbembe calls the necropolitical?[41]

because white men can't
police their imagination
black men are dying[42]

This is the haiku Claudia Rankine wrote in 2014 after visiting Ferguson, Missouri, lines which featured in her book *Citizen* (2014). These lines emerged in the wake of Michael Brown's murder by police officer Darren Wilson and in the midst of intensifying protests. Rankine went to Ferguson to talk to people gathered there. And the haiku arose in part from Rankine's thinking about Wilson's description of Michael Brown as appearing to him as "Hulk Hogan" and as an intimidating "demon."[43]

Here we have a contemporary haiku that defeats the ostensible aims of haiku, according to Barthes: specificity, absence of judgment, avoidance of abstraction. This tercet resists Barthesian haikuity: instead of merely noting, or pointing, or setting a bell ringing, these lines offer quite insistently a diagnosis and a prognosis, a causal logic: "because" X, thus Y. And beyond the formal structure of causation, which would seem inimical to the poetics of the gesture and evanescence, the implicit remedy encoded therein is striking, and abstract: that white men might be able to police their imagination.

Perhaps it's worth saying that upon first reading *Citizen*, my mind snagged on that tercet, which both evokes and evades the haiku. Instantly memorable and memorizable, this tercet—

much quoted, excerptable, memeable—is *diagnostic*. Certainly Rankine's tercet throws into relief several aspects of notationality that Barthes pursued; her haiku puts enormous pressure on his sense of haikuity. This tercet follows upon the memorial page, her epitaphic list of names, the famous and terribly expanding "In Memory" on page 134 of *Citizen*. Rankine's tercet comes next, featured on page 135 in all printings of *Citizen* since the third printing in November 2014. Haiku would seem to be the opposite of epitaph: it is about the fleeting alive, not the memorialized dead; about the writing of or toward the present, not inscribing the past. Rankine's work offers, as it were, a haiku against haiku, a haiku against nuance, evanescence, gesture. Barthes insisted that "no haikus deal in generalities" (50). But here we encounter the politicized deictic, the murderous interpellation, haiku gone both general and diagnostic.

Rankine offers here a brilliant and bleak transvaluation of policing, an epitaph on the situation, of Ferguson and more broadly of the ongoing murders of Black men, women, and children. Her tercet transvalues and displaces policing from the notionally public patrolled and patrollable streets to the always socially structured imaginations of white men, police or not (and, one might say, of police, white or not). And the logic distilled here transvalues the policing elsewhere so rigorously tracked in *Citizen*: the police cars and other police vehicles patrolling the book that patrols them.

Rankine's tercet suggests that there is no outside of policing, and further, that the where of and the subject of policing are always the matter of *struggle*, of the *litigiousness* of the actually political, as Jacques Rancière has argued.[44] Here Rancière's description of the paradox of the political becomes helpful, the paradox by which "politics is the ruling of equals, and the citizen is one who part-takes in ruling and being ruled."⁴⁵ Also relevant is his distinction between "the police" and "politics":

> There are two ways of counting the parts of the community: The first only counts empirical parts—actual groups defined by differences in birth, by different functions, locations, and interests that constitute the social body. The second counts "in addition" a part of the no-part. We will call the first *police* and the second *politics*. (Thesis 6)
>
> Politics is specifically opposed to the police. (Thesis 7)
>
> Consensus is the reduction of politics to the police. (Thesis 10)⁴⁶

We might consider Rankine's haiku as a kind of part-taking ("the citizen is one who part-takes"), a policing against the police, and a refusal to reduce politics to the police.

Rankine's work makes me (re)consider both Barthes's account and her own project. She wrote this haiku, she says, thinking she would write more. She ultimately didn't, or couldn't. This haiku-ish poem, the severe tercet, has a specific function in the dramaturgy of the book. It is excerptable, yes, and it has been, yet it is also enmeshed in *Citizen* and in the making of *Citizen*. I have extracted Rankine's lines from *Citizen*, where she housed them. That one even speaks of Rankine's "haiku" attests to a long and complex history of formal and social abstraction and an extraction—haiku (as already noted) is a fairly recent form, itself an early twentieth-century Japanese term and formalization, an autonomization of the opening *hokku*, which had for centuries launched linked verse, *renga*.⁴⁷ Haiku is, from one angle, an extraction from the older sociality of renga, and from longer hybrid forms like the mixed prose-and-verse form of *haibun* (e.g., Bashō's *Narrow Road to the Deep North*, 1702; or Issa's *The Year of*

My Life, 1819).⁴⁸ For more than a hundred years, "haiku" has also marked a space of complex negotiations among Japanese, French, English, Spanish, and other modernisms and notional modernities, a horizon perhaps best reconceptualized as an emergent, agonistic global condition of modernity.⁴⁹

One might read *Citizen* in many ways: one of which is as a haibun, a mixed form of prose and verse, Bashō's *Narrow Road to the Deep North* perhaps the most famous example. With haibun in mind we are more attuned to what we might call the en-routeness of haiku—its status as an accent that is felt precisely by differentiation from the surround, a surround that in haibun is typically prose narrative but might as easily be other textures of verse or prose or visual art, as in *Citizen*. And Rankine's haiku does in fact work precisely as accent in Barthes's sense, if we recall his remarks in "The Third Meaning": "Finally, the obtuse meaning can be seen as an *accent*, the very form of an emergence, of a fold (a crease even) marking the heavy layer of informations and significations." Its blatantly obvious though puzzling meanings, its oversaturated signifiers, would not seem to align with the elliptical evanescent notational spirit that one had thought haiku carried for Barthes. But as accent, this haiku *marks*, and it marks an unfolding emergence and emergency that is the mixed-genre and intermedial work that is *Citizen*. Here we have not "Meditations in an Emergency," à la Frank O'Hara, but "Notations in and of an Emergency."

And here we might recall again one of the supposedly obsolete senses of "notatio," listed in the *Latin Dictionary*: "the inflicting of disgrace by the *nota censoria*"—marks made by Roman censors against those who committed crimes. In Rankine's tercet, the censuring force of notation is restored to haiku by means of haiku. One might think here of poet and critic Anthony (Vahni)

Capildeo's comment (glossing one of their own poems) that "poetry achieves renewable acts of noticing, here noticing power relations."[50] In lines conspicuously shaped into a notational form, Rankine goes beyond "noticing" to emphasize the diagnostic and censuring dimension of "notation."

Through Rankine's haiku-ish lines we confront the collision of ontopoetic and political operations. And this tercet points as well to additional dimensions of a notational poetics. Here I return to the extraordinary ending of Barthes's essay on "the third meaning," in which he asserts that the film still is precisely not a fragment, that it offers rather "the *inside* of the fragment" (67). The still, Barthes says, allows for both the vertical and horizontal readings Eisenstein called for; moreover, the still constitutes the essence of the filmic:

> The still offers us the *inside* of the fragment.... We must adopt here, with some rehandling, Eisenstein's own formulations, in discussing the new possibilities of audio-visual montage: "... the basic center of gravity ... is shifted to *inside* the fragment, into the elements included within the image itself. *And the center of gravity is no longer the element 'between shots'—the impact, the shock, but the element 'inside the shot'*—the accentuation inside the fragment." (67)

And he further writes, "The still, then, is the fragment of a second text *whose existence never exceeds the fragment*; film and still find themselves in a palimpsest relationship without it being possible to say that one is *on top of* the other or that one is *extracted* from the other" (67). With Rankine in mind, or with Bashō in mind, or with Tonya Foster in mind, one can see too that the haiku in the haibun (or in the mixed or transmedial work) is not a fragment; it is rather the *inside* of a fragment.

I am flagging several things here: first the superposition of and within the haiku itself, its intermedial character, via what Tollof Nelson has called "haiku-technics."[51] I am also flagging what Barthes, following Eisenstein, calls the "inside the shot" aspect of accentuation.[52] But further, I am also noting the residually diegetic aspect of haikuity, which returns, having been apparently banished by deixis. One registers here the restoration of the haiku form to a diegesis, to a narrative (and narratable) world: as in haibun, as in Rankine, as in Foster's *A Swarm of Bees in High Court*, or as in any number of works from recent decades, from Eve Kosofsky Sedgwick's haibun *A Dialogue on Love* to Brian Teare's extraordinary poetic essay–via–haiku "Toxics Release Inventory (Essay on Man)."[53] Whether the itineraries are psychoanalytic (as in Sedgwick) or urban-dystopic (Teare), one discovers that the haiku was perhaps always already—or at least always potentially—diegetic.

Consider haiku, then, as "the inside" of haibun, or of renga, or of "swarm," "dialogue," or "essay," the inside of poetry collections or of longer works. Consider that, as Barthes argued, "the filmic is not the same as the film." So too he says the novelistic is not the same as the novel. We can further observe that the haikuic is not the same as the haiku, and that the notational is not the same as the note—*the notational exceeds the note*. Moreover, via *Citizen*, and also in Foster's *Swarm of Bees*, we can see that the haiku in haibun opens the space for a critical negativity, and for a diagnostic performativity, that the Barthesian haiku would seem to have banished.

We find a further aspect of what Barthes calls "the diegetic horizon" (66) registered in the notes to and around haiku—as in the proliferative commentary around haiku that Makoto Ueda so strikingly anthologized. One observes too the perpetual return of *annotation* around the minimal act of writing that is notation, around the haiku, or famously, around the imagist poem. As Ezra Pound wrote in 1913, regarding his poem "In a Station of the Metro":

> The "one image poem" is a form of super-position, that is to say it is one idea set on top of another. I found it useful in getting out of the impasse in which I had been left by my metro emotion. I wrote a thirty-line poem, and destroyed it because it was what we call work "of second intensity." Six months later I made a poem half that length; a year later I made the following *hokku*-like sentence:—
>
> "The apparition of these faces in the crowd:
> Petals, on a wet, black bough."[54]

Not only is Pound's poem a precipitate of a massive reduction, it is the occasion for apparently endless annotation, by Pound and ensuing commentators. Indeed, Pound's auto-annotations followed as if immediately. But regarding the poem "itself"—the very isolatability of which is under pressure and contingent—we might recall Barthes on such superposition: "The still offers us the inside of the fragment.... The still, then, is the fragment of a second text *whose existence never exceeds the fragment*; film and still find themselves in a palimpsest relationship without it being possible to say that one is *on top of* the other or that one is *extracted* from the other" (67). Pound's poem and his ongoing annotations almost parodically anticipate Barthes's meditations in "The Third Meaning" (themselves indebted to Eisenstein) and in *The Preparation of the Novel*. Pound's poem stations us, as it were, within the surround of the transit station, his colon analogous perhaps to the *kireji*, or cutting word, of Japanese haiku; the registering subject inferred (no "I" announced); the circumstants privileged. (This poetic-theoretico resonance is no surprise, no bug but a feature of the extensive and complex modernist engagement with and through haiku, an often Orientalist haiku-technics and media theory that spans from Ernest Fenollosa and Pound through Barthes and beyond.)

With Pound's proliferating annotations on his notational poem, we see both the return of the note and the en-routeness of *poiesis*, with the instant memory of the notational poem over- and underwritten via notation-as-explanation. This goes back to the ambiguity in "notatio, notationis": a mere marking, or an exfoliation of explanation? The term points to a conceptual dialectic between condensation and dilation (such that *dichten* = *condensare* and/or *dilatare*). One might note too that Pound's poem is *not* one of instant memory or swift notation but is rather the precipitate of an extended processing, reflection, and reduction; or perhaps we might say that what appears to be a poem of instant memory—a conjunction of gesture and noted/notated circumstants—has emerged out of an extraordinarily complex process, an impressing and writing and revising and rethinking heading toward an instant-memory effect.

One arrives here, via Pound, at a haikuic poem via reduction, excision. One arrives here, one might say, at the form of, if not the practice of, the notational.

On the conceptual dialectic in the notational, the unsynthesized reverb of condensation and dilation, perhaps we might be open with John Ashbery to the possibility of a perpetually new spirit:

CHAPTER THREE

I thought that if I could put it all down, that would be one way. And next the thought came to me that to leave all out, would be another, and truer, way.

> clean-washed sea

> > The flowers were.

These are examples of leaving out. But, forget as we will, something soon comes to stand in their place. Not the truth, perhaps, but—yourself. It is you who made this, therefore you are true. But the truth has passed on

> > to divide all.
> > ASHBERY, "The New Spirit"[55]

Jeremy Noel-Tod has read this as a kind of parody of Poundian imagism.[56] I don't quite think so, or I don't think only so. Here, instead of the division between, say, Pound's imagist poem (originally itself thirty lines) and his elaborate note, we encounter a poem offering what we might see as haiku-in-solution, or notation-in-solution. The poem emerges as a precipitate of the you "who made this." I think it specifies and renders soluble precisely this doubleness of the notational, this paradox here registered as two ways—the putting it all down way, versus the leaving it all out way. The minimal act of writing that is notation/haiku, or the total act of writing that is the aspirational novel, or the perpetual haibun. And maybe like Proust's two ways they might to our great surprise meet.

This chapter has been a kind of haibun, an itinerary prompted by several invitations, a mix of haikus or haiku-ish forms—mine and others'—amidst prose meditations. As for ongoing notations amidst ambient conditions:

Eclipse

I don't trust myself
not to look.[57]

CHAPTER THREE

notational/sufficiency...

notational
sufficiency: a wager

made some days
attention

seems wholly
enough

despite the danger
of a simplified

syntax, a mere
gleaning

from the surround—

so thought
hovered,

unstreaming,
punctual, rough[58]

* 4 *
Rhyme/Poetics

DIVAGATION I: WHAT ARE YOU DOING

I have a friend, an extremely accomplished, personally modest poet, who writes a beautifully etched, carefully considered poetry that often, subtly, rhymes. He is admired by many, from traditionalists to avant-gardists, who often seem to misrecognize him—not to say that he is not profoundly, traditionally, experimental. Some years ago he was invited to read at a gathering, and the audience—a sophisticated crew, deeply versed in postmodernism, post-post-structuralism, finance capitalism, etc.—grooved to his reading. At the Q&A, they asked him: J., what are you doing there with the *rhymes?!* And all J. could think to say was, Uh . . . I'm rhyming.

Rhyme is cheap.
So is pop.
Easy to be obese
in a land fat with rape.

"Another Day in This Here Cosmos"[1]

CHAPTER FOUR

But I do it and you do it
And we shoo-bee-doo-bee-doo it.

Rhyme is expensive
and thus I am pensive.

What are you doing with the rhymes?

There are many answers: historical, personal, physiological, musical, sonic, semantic, syntactic, expressionistic, cognitive, metaphysical, political, melodic, imitative, logical, alogical.

What are the rhymes doing with you?

You see it's leaders and it's followers
But I'd rather be a dick than a swallower.

YE, "New Slaves"[2]

OK!

There is of course no univocal unilateral "rhyme": there are many kinds of rhyme, rhyme schemes, rhyme occasions, rhyme traditions, emergent rhyming patterns, rhyme histories, and rhyme futurities. And it perhaps goes without saying that contemporary culture is awash in rhyme, most spectacularly in hip hop, which issues an ongoing challenge to (and inspiration for) contemporary poetry, as David Caplan argues in *Rhyme's Challenge: Hip Hop, Poetry, and Contemporary Rhyming Culture* (2014). Rhyming practices and taxonomies vary among languages and poetic traditions, the taxonomy for rhyme in poetries in English notably impoverished when compared to that of French.[3] And in terms of broader systematization, a number of modern European languages seem to have developed distinct "canons" and strictures when handling rhyme.⁴

What Susan Stewart says of meter might also apply to poetic rhyme:

> When we listen to a meter with a specific function and history we find that the choice of meter is not simply a matter of dipping into a repertoire of simultaneously available, and determined-by-occasion, metrical varieties. Meter has its own internal history, its own evolution, and along that temporal path it accrues a weight of allusion. The history of meter is tied to the specific development of national languages and at the same time to what might be called the creolization of forms as languages merge and are distinguished in political and historical contexts.⁵

Meter would seem to be more culturally bound and more historically conditioned than rhyme—which might, if some scholars are right, be a transpecific and not only a transcultural phenomenon. (Whales, it seems, are also rhymers.⁶) Rhyme per se, unlike meter, seems to bubble up in all human societies, as a crucial part of language learning. (Though can one talk of "rhyme per se"—given the etymological and philological entanglement of "rhyme" and "rhythm"? Certainly *rhythm* is immanent to the species, indeed to life: heartbeat, circadian rhythm, photosynthetic process, etc.⁷) Poetic rhyme likely has both internal and external histories, translinguistic histories and futurities. "Nevertheless," Stewart observes in "Rhyme and Freedom," "despite an apparently universal tendency for rhyming to be part of the process of language learning, most of the world's languages do not use poetic rhyme." She further notes that "the larger history of rhyme has yet to be written."[8] Perhaps her essay is a prologue to such a history, at least for poetic rhyme in English; she herself draws on the synoptic entry on "rhyme" in the 1993 edition of *The New Princeton Encyclopedia of Poetry and Poetics*.[9]

Behold rhyme reasoning and deranging along several axes: the axes of sound and sense; the "axis of combination" and the "axis of selection" (cf. Roman Jakobson[10]); the axes of verse and song; rhyme and reason/rhyme or reason/*Rhyme's Reason*—John Hollander's notable handbook.[11]

Jakobson launches his discussion of rhyme—within his larger inquiry into the relation of poetics to linguistics—with a meditation on Dwight Eisenhower's campaign slogan: "I like Ike." "Rhyme is only a particular, condensed case of a much more general, we may even say the fundamental, problem of poetry, namely *parallelism*."[12] It is clear, however, that the problem of parallelism will not restrict itself to poetry.

Parallelism: repetition with a difference? Or a spatialization of what's experienced in time? A rhyme felt as rhyme offers the possibility for a cognitive readjustment, a snap or a nod. The phonemes and morphemes and lexemes come trailing clouds of glory.

On rhyming and refrain: is refrain a subset of rhyme? repetition is not (only) parallelism.

With a hey and a ho.

Rhyme rhyme
with rhyme!
Rhyme rhymes

with rhyme.
Rhyme rhyme
with time.
Unrhyme
rhyme: one
less rhyme: un.

Roman Jakobson: "*The poetic function projects the principle of equivalence from the axis of selection into the axis of combination.*"[13]

The rhyming function projects the principle of sonic likeness ("the principle of equivalence") forward even as it retrojects itself backward as belatedly audible echo ("the axis of combination").

Rhyme measures time.
Rhyme carries time.
If, that is, rhyme's
perceived as rhyme.
"But a rhyme not felt
is not a rhyme."[14]

DIVAGATION 11: QUESTIONNAIRE: RHYME IS
SO NINETEENTH CENTURY: TRUE OR FALSE

Let us restrict ourselves to rhyme in poetry, poetic rhyme. To rhyme in Anglophone poetry.

Rhyme was left in a ditch when Ezra Pound and his modernist compadres gave the heave to the pentameter: true or false?[15]

CHAPTER FOUR

Virginia Woolf, "Mr. Bennett and Mrs. Brown":

> On or about December 1910, human character changed.
>   I am not saying that one went out, as one might into a garden, and there saw tha ft a rose had flowered, or that a hen had laid an egg. The change was not sudden and definite like that. But a change there was, nevertheless; and, since one must be arbitrary, let us date it about the year 1910.[16]

On or about 1910, rhyme in English changed: true or false?

> The apparition   of these faces   in the crowd   :
> Petals   on a wet, black   bough   .
>   EZRA POUND, "In a Station of the Metro" [1913][17]

> Whirl up, sea—
> whirl your pointed pines,
> splash your great pines
> on our rocks,
> hurl your green over us,
> cover us with your pools of fir.
>   H. D., "Oread" [1914][18]

Consider: Imagism—almost programmatically unrhyming—arose in part from Ezra Pound's, Amy Lowell's, and others' encounters with haiku, and flourished further as poets metabolized Ernest Fenollosa's arguable ideas about the Chinese ideogram. The doctrine of the image would seem to reign when composing haikus in English—whatever the actual protocols of Japanese poetries, contests, and erotics. But haikus in English float in a net whose filaments vibrate along other currents too—epigram, epitaph, couplet, aphorism: brief forms English has long known how to move through, move to. (As noted in the previous chapter, haikus flourish in English as an intermedial form: from the early twentieth century onward, a haiku-idiom and "haiku-technics" emerge, "poetry as audio-visual technique," with links to cinema and other new technologies.[19]) No surprise that haikus in English, unlike haikus in Japanese (and unlike paradigmatic "Imagist" poems), have sometimes rhymed[20]: it is as if the tendency toward rhyme in English verse began conditioning the haiku in English as soon as it made its translated debut.

Paul Muldoon's repeated adventures in and with the haiku form show just such an entanglement with rhyme and other medial forms: his poetic sequence "Hopewell Haiku" rhymes the first and third lines of each haiku tercet; "News Headlines from the Homer Noble Farm" rhymes haikus *across* the sequence, lines 1 and 3 of a tercet rhyming, and the second line's end word providing the opening rhyme of the next tercet, such that the series becomes a kind of compact terza rima—interrhyming triplets themselves flagrantly intermedial in conception (viz. "news headlines"); while his "90 Instant Messages to Tom Moore" offers yet another rhyming haiku sequence (though not with a terza rima effect), again explicitly presented as an intermedial form, in dialogue with that emergent short form, the instant message.[21]

But let us back up. Rhyming verse in English has, at least since the sixteenth century, danced around and with a persistent other, its definitional negation: "blank"—that is, unrhymed—verse. The *Oxford English Dictionary* registers this in its eighth definition for "blank, adj.":

> a. blank verse *n.* verse without rhyme; *esp.* the iambic pentameter or unrhymed heroic, the regular measure of English dramatic and epic poetry, first used by the Earl of Surrey.[22]

The essay "Rhyme" in the 2012 *Princeton Encyclopedia of Poetry and Poetics* draws on Robert Abernathy to make a similar point, that blank verse is not "rhymeless" but rather hypermarked—"antirhyme":

> Abernathy points out that it is not sufficient to characterize some types of verse as "unrhymed," for this fails to distinguish between "rhymeless" verse, wherein rhyme is neither required nor prohibited but merely unspecified, and "antirhymed" verse, such as blank verse, where rhyme is specifically proscribed.[23]

Since at least 1910 or so, the dominant "other" of rhyming metrical verse has been, of course, "free verse." (That "free verse" covers both nonmetrical and nonrhyming verse, which are not reducible to one another, is worth a whole other discussion.[24] Also: that Pound used the term "vers libre" points to the French and translational reverb of this early twentieth-century horizon. And further: one must agree with T. S. Eliot, and more recently with Marjorie Perloff, that "free" verse is never unmarked or unconditionally "free."[25]) Woven into this rhyming/unrhyming/anti-rhyming tapestry—far more intricately than any binary might suggest—are multiple threads, of many metrical forms and schemes, some rhymed, some not.

Free verse was itself, moreover, already fully capable of hackneyed automatism by 1918. As Pound mordantly observed in "A Retrospect":

> Indeed vers libre has become as prolix and as verbose as any of the flaccid varieties that preceded it. It has brought faults of its own. The actual language and phrasing is often as bad as that of our elders without even the excuse that the words are shoveled in to fill a metric pattern or to complete the noise of a rhyme-

sound. Whether or not the phrases followed by the followers are musical must be left to the reader's decision. At times I can find a marked metre in "vers libres," as stale and hackneyed as any pseudo-Swinburnian, at times the writers seem to follow no musical structure whatever.[26]

It's also true that modernist poets never simply abjured rhyme—as any turn to "Prufrock" or "Hugh Selwyn Mauberley" or countless other works attests. Also: Robert Frost. It is perhaps more useful to think of "a Modernist style of rhyming," as Daniel Albright suggested—complicatedly ironized, allusive, often dramatic, encoding its own critical relation to the history of rhyme in poetry.[27]

It's a long history. The horizon of rhyme's decay: historical, sonic. Rhyme > doggerel. The potential kitschiness of rhyme has been a feature of English poetry ripe for parody at least since Chaucer's self-satire as the poet in "The Tale of Sir Thopas" (in *The Canterbury Tales*), when the impatient Host interrupts the bumptious poet "Chaucer":

"Myne eres aken of thy drasty speche.
Now swich a rym the devel I biteche!
This may wel be rym doggerel," quod he.[28]

And when the pathetic poet begs sufferance, the Host continues:

　"By God," quod he, "for pleynly, at a word,
Thy drasty rymyng is nat worth a toord!
Thou doost noght elles but despendest tyme.
Sire, at o word, thou shalt no lenger ryme."[29]

The specter of rhyme as crap verse, word turds. As rhyme gone bad, "doggerel" appears early in the language not as a simple equivalent to or substitute for rhyme but more often as its degenerative modifier: as the *OED* notes, "in early use chiefly as postmodifier, esp. in rhyme doggerel."[30]

Of the poetry of Paul Muldoon and Frederick Seidel, a friend observed some years ago: *it is striking how often these poets have written so close to the edge of doggerel*. This is an edge Muldoon avowedly courts, or once allowed that he did. As he observed in an interview in 1994, speaking of his great complex poem *Madoc: A Mystery*:

> Often, these rhymes are completely crazy. I'm a great fan of Byron, and I really like these totally crazy rhymes. A lot of the time I just love to say, "Let's see what happens. Just how near the edge can you go without dissolving into outright doggerel?" That's something I'm very interested in. Again, it's a risky thing.[31]

Rhyme: a smuggling in of infantile pleasures amidst the grimmer workings of the ideating ego and superego? A networking of the fullest reaches of and beyond English, that voracious spangled language? That Muldoon hailed Byron points to the ways he continues that poet's crucial, complex double work of rhyming: honoring, as Anthony Madrid puts it, both the "desire for rhyme as an intoxicating agent, a figment of the rhythm completely operating below the reader's intellectual radar—and the sensibility of today's poet, who tends to subject each individual rhyme pair to judgments related to originality and wit."[32]

Miss Mary Mack Mack Mack All Dressed In Black Black Black will continue to take her whacks with Lizzie Borden and

Rhyme/Poetics

her axe. The plague will tell its story to the children through a posy through a ring-a-round-the-rosy.

Ashes, ashes.

All fall down.

What is your relation to surprise? To regularity? To an unrhymed singularity?

Scholars J. Paul Hunter and Anthony Madrid note that in the early twentieth century "rhyme more or less collapsed"—conventional poetic rhyming, that is. Yet (as already noted) rhyming did not quite disappear with modernism: Madrid has himself written an astute essay on Wallace Stevens as a rhymer.[33] More broadly, as David Caplan observes, "Canonical Anglo-American Modernism did not abandon rhyme; rather, it recrafted the technique."[34] Among these recrafters were Stevens and Gertrude Stein. And so, and lo:

DIVAGATION III: INSTRUCTIONS OF RHYME: WALLACE STEVENS'S RHYME EMERGENCIES

Wallace Stevens is in many ways a notably "'classic' rhymer" (in Madrid's terms), using rhymes wholly familiar to Alexander Pope: yet where Stevens differs from classically rhyming forebears is in his abandonment of through-rhyme, preferring instead an idiosyncratic "sneak-up" style of rhyming, intermittencies that refuse to resolve into a rhyme scheme or pattern.[35] One might consider Stevens's rhyming technique as part of a cognitive acoustic, arising from and soliciting and activating what Jeremy Prynne has called "mental ears."[36] As Prynne observes, "The rule-patterns of rhyme, for example, or of metrical regularity or strophic enclosure and repetition, are arbitrary in regard to grammatical structure, and much of their effect arises from cross-play between one system and another, maneuvered by composing habits of practice into productive contrasts and parallelisms" (131). In long poems, Stevens's play with, through, and against rhyme (cross-playing with stanza form, syntax, and so on) becomes part of his psychoacoustic technē, a distinct poetic materiality.

Consider the rhymes emerging and receding in this canto near the center of "The Man with the Blue Guitar" (1937), one of Stevens's more compulsively (albeit intermittently) rhymey poems:

XXV

He held the world upon his nose
And this-a-way he gave a fling.

His robes and symbols, ai-yi-yi—
And that-a-way he twirled the thing.

Sombre as fir-trees, liquid cats
Moved in the grass without a sound.

They did not know the grass went round.
The cats had cats and the grass turned gray

And the world had worlds, ai, this-a-way:
The grass turned green and the grass turned gray.

And the nose is eternal, that-a-way.
Things as they were, things as they are,

Things as they will be by and by . . .
A fat thumb beats out ai-yi-yi.[37]

In this passage, Stevens seems swiftly to establish a pattern of four-beat lines, printed as couplets, organizing themselves via rhyme into quatrains, *abcb*. Thus the opening two lines—a strongly accented iambic tetrameter—

He held the world upon his nose
And this-a-way he gave a fling.

soon become, as it were, as one hears, a component of a quatrain (*abcb*):

He held the world upon his nose
And this-a-way he gave a fling.

His robes and symbols, ai-yi-yi —
And that-a-way he twirled the thing.

Yet the implicit cognitive shaping here—the emergent quatrain structure—gets an immediate torque, as the next four lines emerge as another kind of quatrain, abbc:

Sombre as fir-trees, liquid cats
Moved in the grass without a sound.

They did not know the grass went round.
The cats had cats and the grass turned gray

Ah (so we might think,
as these phonemes morphing to morphemes to lexemes to syn-
    tagms punctuated by rhyme
fall upon our mind's ears),
Ah! we are in the realm of quatrains, variously rhyming!
    But Stevens then again throws a curve via rhyme. As if channeling somewhere an ostinato, the same string plucked in rhythmic figuration, the next three lines all rhyme:

And the world had worlds, ai, this-a-way:
The grass turned green and the grass turned gray.

And the nose is eternal, that-a-way.
Things as they were, things as they are,

Things as they will be by and by . . .
A fat thumb beats out ai-yi-yi.

As if to prove Susan Stewart's observation that strongly marked end rhymes work in part to hypermark those words that *don't* rhyme,[38] we are in this closing section suddenly back to the sonic and apodictic premising of "things as they are," the very phrase that is the humming rhythmic and rhyming core of this poem's guitar. Pivoting us out of the serial rhymes back into "things as they were, things as they are, / Things as they will be by and by . . . ," Stevens moves us into the final cadence, the fat thumb beating out "ai-yi-yi."

Here we encounter an apparent rhyme scheme that dissolves into other near-schemes (non-schemes?) even as rhyme persists, enlists, carries, and intermittently binds.

This swift scanning of emergent and fading and feinting rhyme here neglects several things—the many intricate patternings of repetition and variation throughout; the rhythmical skeleton and Stevens's metrical dance with and around it; the play of assonance and rhyme, all these threads co-woven with the more flagrant end rhymes. The rhymes here traverse as well as bind generations—of plants, of creatures, of worlds, and of course metapoetically the generation of lines themselves:

The cats had cats and the grass turned gray

And the world had worlds, ai, this-a-way:
The grass turned green and the grass turned gray.

The rhyme becomes the sonic pivot, the centering at the very proliferation of generational and worldly turnings (this-a-way, that-a-way), the returnings tuned in and by rhyme, the versing reversal continuing. Such phonemic, morphemic, lexical, and phrasal movements scale up to, or (we might say) rhyme with, the ideational movements of and in this poem. Co-ordination. Measure. Rhyme.

More locally, for me as a *reader* as well as a *sounder*, what was also emergent by this canto's end was a solution to a question I had had when encountering its third line—"His robes and symbols, ai-yi-yi": how to pronounce the vowel in those these last two syllables? Long "i" (/ay/) or long "e" (/ee/)? I had tended immediately toward the /ay/ but I wasn't sure if Stevens was here trying to channel (in line with his guitarist) a more "Spanish" orthographic and phonological system, thus giving us /ay yee yee/: this seemed to me a possibility even with the preceding syllable "ai," which seemed to admit one pronunciation only—a long diphthonged "/ay/."

A possible clue to, or further wrinkle in, pronunciation emerges in the ninth line of the passage, which also activates "ai": "And the world had worlds, ai, this-a-way." Is this "ai" a long "i," /ay/, as I was thinking, or might it rhyme with its neighbor "this-a-way"? My suspension of committed pronunciation, a question of audible mind, was released, however, in the final two lines of the passage. The rhyme itself taught me how to pronounce the earlier occurrence of "ai-yi-yi":

Things as they will be by and by . . .
A fat thumb beats out ai-yi-yi.

There was now no way not to hear the previous ai-yi-yi as a series of long "i's," /ay/. My question of sounding was by and by answered by the second ai-yi-yi.

I was, then, reading Stevens's rhymes as clues. As Stewart notes, "Rhymes fix sounds inflexibly at the ends of lines or freeze a local pronunciation like a fossil. Yet rhyme seems also to flourish in situations where dialects and languages meet and to form a record of how pronunciation is constantly changing by means of living language."[39] Such a passage enacts just such a flourishing—a guitar's sound and a Spanish cry haunting the American English of the ai-yi-yi-ing Stevens. And then too there is always haunting this phoneme for English speakers/hearers the cry of the I of subjectivity.

Now this may seem a lot of hullabaloo over a brief passage, but this experience of uncertain pronunciation reanimated for me the temporal forecasting that rhyme retroactively enables (as it were) and the astonishing cognitive as well as acoustic power of rhyme. Ringing his rhyming changes, Stevens manifests in sound how "things as they are / are changed upon the blue guitar" in time and over time, near and far. How does one ring changes on things as they are? By rhyming around, if not always on, that sonic /ar/.

A devolution, swerve, or dèrive into a call, a cry, a beating out, a measuring out of sound: "ai-yi-yi" is both a rhyme and a beat, "rhyme" and "rhythm" here restored to their etymological and conceptual entanglement.[40] Stevens's responsiveness to cries, ai-yi-yis, to calls, hoots, hoos, and hullaballos throughout his work is only one aspect of his extraordinary acoustic. "The Man with the Blue Guitar" is a poem conjuring a notional horizon of "gypsy" music, Picasso's painted Barcelonan guitarist ghosting the poem however much Stevens denied the connection.[41] One also hears in

CHAPTER FOUR

Stevens, I would suggest, not only the guitar but—via a network of thumb-beat and "this-a-way" and "that-a-way"—intimations of the children's song "Ha-Ha This a Way." I could not *not* hear in this passage this song, known to me in the first instance via another significant early twentieth-century artist, the American singer and guitarist Lead Belly (Huddie William Ledbetter): see, for example, his recording on *Lead Belly: The Smithsonian Folkways Collection* of "Ha-Ha This a Way," with its refrain:

Ha-ha this a way
Ha-ha that a way
Ha-ha this a way
Man oh man...[42]

Such a song, implicitly evoking dance movement, reminds us of the bodily and indeed planetary pulses coordinating at least some aspects of rhyme: rhyme as physical marker, as particularly notable in those poetries closest to song and dance. As Stewart notes, "When words are used at once linguistically and paralinguistically, separations between speech and sound do not hold and the performative power of words is strengthened."[43] Stevens is a master exploiter of both the semantic and sonic waves of/in rhyme, of the linguistic and paralinguistic dimensions of rhyme. The "performative power" of these words and phrases draws a complex charge from their intermedial reverb.

If the "mental ears" of Stevens's poems are vast, interlingual, and often intermedial, they are also, as is increasingly recognized, profoundly racialized.[44] For further evidence of Stevens's racialized sonic and rhythmic imaginary within "The Man with the Blue Guitar," consider the line from an earlier passage: "Tom-tom, c'est moi." We might take this code-switching as a bizarre encapsulation of Stevens's "négritude" (as it were)—a vexed position (to say the least), full of exoticized Africans and of notionally African instruments (though the tom-tom is in the first instance an East Indian drum, the term extended later, as the *OED* tells us, to the hand-beaten drums of Asia, Africa, and the Americas, and to drums included in drum kits in the early twentieth century).[45] "Tom-tom, c'est moi. The blue guitar / And I are one" (canto XII, *CPP*, 140). Most striking here: Stevens figures himself not as a Black or exotic drummer but as an exotic and potentially African *drum*—a figural claim asserted via the apocryphal, infamous, and refunctionable statement of French royalty, further torqued by Flaubert. (L'État, c'est moi > Madame Bovary, c'est moi > Tom-tom, c'est moi. Voilà!)

Even as Stevens is sounding out the thumb-beat ai-yi-yi, then, I would suggest he is also aspiring to channel Black sonics: not in any documentable way of influence but rather via resonance, approximation, appropriation. (Might "The Man with the Blue Guitar" channel, among other things, the man with the blues guitar?) Here we might invoke Toni Morrison, who in *Playing in the Dark: Whiteness and the Literary Imagination* tracks "the way black people ignite critical moments of discovery or change or emphasis in literature not written by them."[46] One hears in this passage, and elsewhere in Stevens's work, a presencing (simulating, appropriating) of a specular Black vernacular, of Black speech and song. (As I have argued elsewhere, this phenomenon is more broadly networked in Stevens's corpus via his performative forays into French, and into a French and more broadly a Latinate register in his "American" English, his idiolect.[47]) In Stevens's poems, ventures into (raids on) notionally "Black" sonics seem to function as a hypermarked "American" corrective to his explorations of French and Latin registers that some saw—and some still see—as dandyism. One might say that his is an "American" poetic Whiteness partially produced by performed access to "Blackness." To read Stevens's poems as if they manifested free and indifferent access to languages and linguistic registers is to miss precisely the differential and racialized dimensions of such work: the social basis and political economy of poetic soundings are exactly what has been usually underread in Stevens's oeuvre. Rhyme can offer one route into that inquiry, into Stevens's "mental ears" and our own.

"The Man with the Blue Guitar" is among many things a sustained inquiry into poetic instrumentality—*poiesis* figured as the playing of instruments, the poet as both player and instrument. Stevens accents the world-making as well as world-registering function of poetry: "I cannot bring a world quite round, / Although I patch it as I can" (canto II, *CPP*, 135). His idiosyncratic rhyming is a mode of such "patching": a world unable to be brought "quite round" via classic or conventional rhyme can still be brought toward us, before us, this-a-way, that-a-way. With its opening cantos establishing and then disestablishing rhyming horizons (against a steady background of fairly regular iambic tetrameter), Stevens thematizes refrain and "rounding" throughout, such that "things as they are on the blue guitar" are dispersed and sometimes ingathered, in changes wrung and rung through.

The man bent over his guitar,
A shearsman of sorts. The day was green.

They said, "You have a blue guitar,
You do not play things as they are."

Rhyme/Poetics

The man replied, "Things as they are
Are changed upon the blue guitar."

canto I, *CPP*, 135

The insistent rhymes of the first cantos wane as the poem unfolds, as if the rhythmic/rhyming entanglement of the blue guitar's music were meant to give way to reflections on that insistence. The foregrounding of the sonic-semiotic entanglement recedes, as a more semantic, even discursive, orientation moves to the fore. Yet as we have seen, Stevens can suddenly plug his guitar back into his rhyming amplifier, as in canto XXV, the "this-a-way" canto ("He held the world upon his nose"—the poet as comical performing seal, or clown, of world-making). And the poem closes—or is rather brought "round"—in a complex passage of Stevensian diminuendo:

Here is its actual stone. The bread
Will be our bread, the stone will be

Our bed and we shall sleep by night.
We shall forget by day, except

The moments when we choose to play
The imagined pine, the imagined jay.

canto XXXIII, *CPP*, 151

This rhyming emerges precisely and suddenly as a perceivable couplet, arising out of a complex preceding syntax, providing the "click" of poetic closure that Barbara Herrnstein Smith illuminated years ago.[48] These lines appear not as a couplet among couplets, not as a detachable unit or part of a through-composed rhyme scheme, but as the sole rhyming couplet in that final stanza: a decisive, resounding singular return to and in rhyme, to close out the poem, the *ta-da* of it sealed, the playing and jaying and surveying and strumming and excepting and acccepting. Stevens's rhyming is a vexed playing and a jaying in the dark.

DIVAGATION IV: STEINRHYME

Gertrude Stein is quite another champion of rhyme. Her work can further pluralize our sense of modernist horizons of rhyme. The oft-laid charge against her—that her work is indistinguishable from nonsense—may arise as much from her traffic in rhyme as from her giving the heave to normative syntax and to the referent. After all, Edward Lear, Lewis Carroll: nonsense poets, kings of rhyme. Gertrude Stein a king of rhyme. There is in English a long dance between rhyme and logic, or alogic: a structural link arising from rhyme's nature as an aspect of *measure*, of count, and thus of seriality, parallelism, and the various semantic/acoustic algorithms that are intermittently fixed in—or shaped through—such things as rhyme schemes. The rhyming mathematician, the chiming deranged logician: Lewis Carroll; the occasionally rhyming theoretician, the experimental scientist of rhyme, the cubist syntactical magician and technician: Stein.

At her most "accessible," in (for example) *The Autobiography of Alice B. Toklas*, Stein writes a prose that doesn't flagrantly foreground the poetic function, a prose that mutes her often hypermarked "figure of sound" (to invoke Gerard Manley Hopkins, invoked by Jakobson), that largely adheres to normative syntax and discursive flow.[49] Stein's more experimental works—her "abstract" writings, "Tender Buttons," say, or her "Portraits"—

infamously frustrate normative reading procedures and thus elicit all kinds of inventive and intermittently persuasive interpretive decodings. For purposes of this divagation I want to propose Stein as a theorist/performer of and in rhyme, especially in her work *Stanzas in Meditation*.[50] Stein is no mere stylist of rhyme: in *Stanzas in Meditation* she gives us a kind of anthology as well as handbook of and in rhyme.

Stein's tendency toward the gnomic and the aphoristic often manifests itself in rhyme—"pigeons on the grass alas," or "a rose is a rose is a rose," its apparently identitarian sequence self-disrupting precisely by continuing, that rose become another rose precisely through reiteration of the copula. If Stein's defamiliarizations don't necessarily make us feel the stoniness of the Stein or the rosiness of the rose, she certainly tests the limits of secure referentiality, as logical proposition and the law of identity ($A = A$) decay into a chain of reiteration—the syllable grown louder, as it were, than the semantic claim. What Stein brings to the fore is the proximity of babble to thought, and vice versa.

Reading Stein's *Stanzas in Meditation* as an excursus on rhyme, one might observe perhaps first that these are *stanzas*. Stein offers many examples of rhyme as a possible engine of stanza form. The question of the stanza itself increasingly emerges in the work as a subject of meditation, and as it does, rhyme does its queerly shaping work, becoming ever more prominent:

A stanza should be thought
And if which may they do
Very well for very well
And very well for you.

part IV, stanza XXIX, 111

Smuggled late into the *Stanzas* is a mini-rhyme-bomb she activates and defuses:

They did not know
That it would be so
That there would be a moon
And the moon would be so
Eclipsed

part V, stanza LXV, 136

This, the entirety of stanza LXV, offers a brilliant little meditation on what we think we know in advance, and after the fact, via rhyme. A logical and temporal order is conjured precisely to be thwarted—they did not know that it would be so: that there would be a moon, that a moon would likely rhyme soon, with June, say, or tune or croon, but Oh that line aborts or rather runs over enjambing and there we are, eclipsed. The wit of this stanza depends on our hearing the metrical patterning (and its frustration) *simultaneously* with the rhyming pattern, botched. And even as vehicular shapes of rhyme and meter appear here only to run off the rails, so too a virtual stanza flickers behind stanza LXV, a quatrain gone bust, not with a bang but a whimper. Such eclipsing of expectation, and the delight therein, is the cognitive and acoustic core of *Stanzas*.

Stanzas in Meditation is an extended meditation on the deictic echolocation of rhyme. What do I mean? That there is no where there but the there in the time of the where of the rhyme—back and forward.

. . . If a fisherman fishes
Or else a well

Rhyme/Poetics

Very well does an attack
Look back.

part III, stanza III, 40

An "attack" looks forward to, anticipates, "back," which retroactively seals the attack of "attack."

If the stanzas of *Stanzas in Meditation* disorient, this is a function of their intense engagement with orientation—temporal, spatial, erotic:

Full well I know that she is there
Much as she will she can be there
But which I know which I know when
Which is my way to be there then
Which she will know as I know here
That it is now that it is there
That rain is there and it is here
That it is here that they are there
But how foolish to ask them if they like it

part II, stanza I, 19

The compulsive iteration of such deictic markers at line ends—there / there / when / then / here / there / here / there—could be considered a species of near monorhyme, an emphatic epiphoric parallelism which stresses the matter of where "she is" and what "I know here." And one registers the microattentions to "*that* rain," the "now," and other deictic markers. The metrical regularity of these opening lines (a long stretch of which seems to be iambic tetrameter) emphasizes the line endings and the accented *then*, *here*, *there*, etc.: deictic echolocation incanted (though one might note the wonderful metapoetic disruption, tonal and metrical,

CHAPTER FOUR

of "But how foolish to ask them if they like it"). Here, one might argue, we have not so much rhyme per se but rather a more general case of parallelism and equivalence. But this parallelizing logic often centers itself throughout *Stanzas* via a more explicitly rhyming process, suggestively embedded in the ghosts of meters and other patterning counts.

Basil Bunting argued that "poetry and music are both patterns of sound drawn on a background of time."[51] But patterns of sound and thought are not drawn on a background of time: they are sounded through the medium of time. One falls into, moves through, time. Again, Stewart: "Lyric process is propelled by the sounded repetition of sameness and difference, of rhymes thrown forward as both moving line and anchor."[52] Line and anchor, fishing well in a well, an attack looks back, a hip-hop hook hooks.

What are you doing with the rhymes?

Consider how a number of stanzas begin with apparent couplets, which then mutate into other patterns, often unrhyming:

Just when they ask their questions they will always go away
Or by this time with carefulness they must be meant to stay

part I, stanza IV, 5

or

They may lightly send it away to say
That they will not change it if they may

part II, stanza III, 21

These rhyming gambits function as sonic teasers particularly when they seem to scan. (The first two couplets fall on my ear as fourteeners; the second two are harder to "lock in" to a meter but they seem to fall, provisionally, into four-beat lines.) These particular couplets soon dissolve or mutate into other discursive and stressed patterns, the ghost of sustainable rhyme and meter conjured here only to be abjured. Yet Stein intermittently gives us emergent stanzas in a more traditional key, little ditties that, however irregular, share a kinship with modes of light verse and popular song, as in:

Tell me darling tell me true
Am I all the world to you
And the world of what does it consist
May they be a chance to may they be desist
This came to a difference in confusion
Or do they measure this with resist with
Nor more which.
Than a conclusion
May they come with may then in with

part III, stanza X, 47

The swinging four-beat trochees of the first two lines locate us securely in a zone of light verse, in song lyric and song time, from which we immediately depart in line 3: "And the world of what does it consist," with its proliferation of syllables straining the apparent meter, and with its increasingly complicated syntax and technical language. We are further torqued in the syntactic stutters of line 4—"May they be a chance to may they be desist"—which one could read as enjambed self-interrupting fragments of thought, condensed in a line: May they be a chance to/may they be/desist.

We are now far from Tin Pan Alley, yet are we so far? "This came to a difference in confusion / Or do they measure this with resist with": these lines offer, perhaps, a gloss on the previous differentiations—the arrival at a metrical confusion, since while the rhyme persisted the syntax unmoored and so too the beat and notional meter. Do we measure this "with resist," as (or with) resistance? Is this confusion, or a strange kind of analytic clarity? Even as the initial metrical pattern devolves, even as the syntax increasingly deviates from the norm, the rhyme persists—in the end rhymes "consist"/"desist" and the internal (performative) "resist."

These kinds of extraordinary effects can't be accounted for, quite, by a *détournement* through defamiliarization, though surely they are a species of it. Such developments in these stanzas offer enactments in linguistic time of the multiple nonsynchronic streams that flow through and impede our reading ears' minds. A structure that might have kept time in one way—in a pop quatrain way, say—ends up keeping, moving, distending time in a way you, or at least I, could not anticipate. Meter right-foots you; Stein *wrong-foots* you. And if rhyme binds, it can also mark an unbinding in time, a resist amidst what briefly persists.

Among the several experiments in and on rhyme conducted here, perhaps the most profound is Stein's foregrounding of rhyme as measure, as count. Stewart notes: "The Old English word *rim* has a complex etymology indicating, among other meanings, counting or reckoning, as well as covering with 'rime' or hoarfrost.'"[53] And the *OED* offers this for "rhyme, n.": "1. a. Metre, measure (in verse). *Obs*."[54] I'd suggest that *Stanzas in Meditation* renders the *OED*'s judgment of rhyme as "metre, measure (in verse). *Obs*[olete]" obsolete. In *Stanzas*, Stein restores rhyme to its archaic measuring function precisely by refusing to deploy rhyme in standard meters. She also shows how rhyme moves along several axes—intersecting with poetic meters but also children's rhymes, counting games, advertisements. Stein's restriction of her vocabulary to a strongly monosyllabic, Germanic register of English has the effect of accenting *accent* itself; her lines are designed to enforce slow reading, a registration of microdifferences across a very limited set of data. The heavily stressed lines often resist phrasal groupings and the swift movements of accentual-syllabic verse: one has to discover and indeed to decide how to accent words in mind, how and what to emphasize, since there is a refusal of metrical subordination in such lines as

Nor not which one won for this is one.
I will not think one and one remember not.

part IV, stanza II, 64

Compare this to the previously quoted

Tell me darling tell me true
Am I all the world to you

with its clear accentual-syllabic patterning, its dip and swing. In *Stanzas*, as in so much Stein, what matters is the difference of the difference: "Now think of the difference of not yet" (part IV, stanza I, 62).

I said the difference is complicated
And she said yes is it it is
Or she said it is is it.
There seems so much to do
With one or two with six not seven
Either or.

part III, stanza III, 41

As the above extracts suggest, the *Stanzas* network lexis, grammar, syntax, meter, and *count*. Rhyme traverses these, binds and confounds these; rhyme also brings the sublexical (the phonemic, the morphemic) into play even as it scales up to complex cognitive operations. One must have a certain frame of mind, or a kind of patience, to immerse in the *Stanzas*, but they are the most delirious and delightfully instructive meditation on linguistics and poetics I have yet encountered, aside perhaps from her "Arthur a Grammar" (in *How To Write*, 1931).[55] And for my purposes here, what is most salient is the interface of rhyme and count as zones for, objects of, this meditation.

As in: "A stanza mine is a stanza nine. / My stanza is three of nine" (part V, stanza IX, 94). Or in the performative switchbacking here:

Stanza ten make a hen
Stanza third make a bird
Stanza white make a dog
Stanza first make it heard
That I will not not only go there
But here

part III, stanza XIII, 49–50

Children's counts and rhyming games, spells and incantations, deictic echolocation: such a stanza channels all this in a kind of idiot-savant half-rhyming wizardry. And the knotty syntax—the "not not only go"ing there—pressures us to think about where we're going, where the stanza's going, and where it's not not going: and all along the rhyming medium is not only the message but the vehicle for this going.

Rhyme/Poetics

Consider the following, a simultaneously compulsive yet free divagation on count, on "one" plus others, on declaring how "one" "won," homonymically, semantically:

I come back to think everything of one
One and one
Or not which they were won
I won.
They will be called I win I won
Nor which they call not which one or one
I won.
I will be winning I won.
Nor not which one won for this is one.
I will not think one and one remember not.
Not I won I won to win win I one won
And so they declare or they declare
To declare I declare I declare I win I won one
I win in which way they manage they manage to win I won
In I one won in which I in which won I won
And so they might come to a stanza three
One or two or one two or one or two or one
Or one two three all out but one two three
One of one two three or three of one two and one

part IV, stanza II, 64

What is it to think "everything" of one, of "one"? as sound, as sense, as number, as origin of a series, as impersonal pronoun? Let us permute; let us confute; let us count the ways. The permutational development of this stanza endlessly cleaves the denotative possibilities of "one" (and "won") both from each other and from the "acoustic image," despite the sonic identity of the "material envelope" (the homonym/won/)[56]; yet as Stein cleaves, she weaves. One notes too the hyperperformativity of this stanza ("I declare I declare"), and its brilliantly singing arithmetic. Stein's "or"s and "and"s become wholly operational conjunctions, plus signs, or symbols of distributive addition, logical operators: her "not"s similarly acquire a mathematical force, subtracting. Her "difference"(s) (a key Steinian word) become mathematical, algorithmic, an accounting gone viral: "The difference is spreading."[57]

Such performative thought is conducted precisely through rhyme, and acquires a metapoetic vibration in a later stanza, stanza IX—which conducts a kind of Skeltonic riff on the nineness of stanza nine, and on what's mine in nine.

How nine
Nine is not mine
Mine is not nine
Ten is not nine
Mine is not ten
Nor when
Nor which one then
May be not then
Not only mine for ten
But any ten for which one then
I am not nine
May be mine
Mine one at a time
Not one from nine
Nor eight at one time
For which they may be mine.

Mine is one time
As much as they know they like
I like it too to be one of one two
One two or one or two
One and one
One mine
Not one nine
And so they ask me what do I do
May they but if they too
One is mine too
Which is one for you
May be they like me
I like it for which they may
Not pay but say
She is not mine with not
But will they rather
Oh yes not rather not
In won in one in mine in three
In one two three
All out but me.
I find I like what I have
Very much.

part IV, stanza IX, 68–69

Certainly, as morphemes, "nine" is not "mine," nor "mine" "nine." And ten is not nine, neither as phoneme, morpheme, or lexis, nor as count. With her incremental shifts and permutations Stein activates and proliferates the axes of registration: sonic, semantic, numerical. Angle, referent; strangle referent; continuity, disruption; leap; dance; romance. Stanza IX in part IV offers the pure pleasure of soundplay but simultaneously rings its changes through brainteasers. This is only nonsense if you expect your sense to arrive on time. This is cognitive whiplash via chime. This is among other things an anatomy of rhyme.

In the final movement of this stanza, evoking a child's count, Stein conjures a move in a game, the pleasure of accounting and deranging the count:

In won in one in mine in three
In one two three
All out but me.
I find I like what I have
Very much.

I find I like mine, and nine. Says Stein.

This consummation in liking bespeaks a strong tendency in *Stanzas in Meditation*, especially toward its close, to assert the pleasures of liking itself, as if liking were itself a form of rhyme, even as rhyme encodes a complex mode of likening (recall Jakobson on "I Like Ike" as a paradigm for rhyme). Here the basic erotics of rhyme comes to the fore—a serious infantilism, I'd call it, rescued from mere infantilism (but what's wrong with that?) via its syntactic impediments, stumble as index of mind:

I like that I like.
Oh yes not if not I like
May they be a credit a credit to him
I like
If when if I like
Not if in choosing chosen.

part V, stanza LXXV, 141

Rhyme/Poetics

That is why a like in it with it
Which they gay which they gay
But not only just the same.

part III, stanza IX, 46

I wish once more to mention
That I like what I see

part V, stanza LXI, 133

Why spend so much time on Stein? Because she is so very fine. Her ways and means are near sublime though yes dementing at some times. Idiolectic and deictic, ludic not splenetic. And through her lines I came to see that rhyming need not mean poesy but need not not mean poesy too:[58] her prosing rhymes are dancing, true, but stanzas meditating true love rhymes are pleasing yes oh yes they are. And thus she takes us very far.

Or does she? Stein is, with rhyme as with much else, an outlier. This aspect of her work seems not much taken up by later writers. And again, in *Stanzas in Meditation*, Stein does not pursue an ironized or disjunctive "modernist style" of rhyming so much as a set of experiments in and through rhyme.

DIVAGATION V: PERSISTENCE / ENTANGLEMENT

Some twenty-five years ago, J. Paul Hunter noted the near-obsolescence of rhyme in "modern" (i.e., twentieth-century Anglophone) poetry:

> Rhyme, which was an indispensable feature of poetry in the age of the heroic couplet, has fallen badly out of favor in the modern era. Few poets now employ rhyme at all, and, conse-

quently, we are not used to regarding rhyme as an effective way of providing aural pleasure or as a structural device to convey meaning. We do have rhyme in our lives, but we reserve for it a quite specific and usually comic place.[59]

Perhaps Hunter spoke too soon. If rhyme is unlikely to regain its poetic hegemony, one does note its persistence and even a resurgence over the past twenty-five or so years. As Harryette Mullen said of her book *Muse and Drudge* (1995), "rhyme is too powerful a tool to be abandoned to advertising, greeting cards, or even platinum rap recordings. I hoped to reclaim it for my poem."[60] In David Caplan's view, "contemporary poets face a historical reversal; in Mullen's terms, they must 'reclaim' a technique once intimately associated with their art."[61] This reclaiming (various, heterogeneous, differently pointed) has proceeded apace.

In *Renegade Poetics: Black Aesthetics and Formal Innovation in African American Poetry* (2011), Evie Shockley documents a longer, rich history for such reclaiming in the tradition of experimental Black aesthetics. En route she foregrounds the innovative charge of Gwendolyn Brooks's and Sonia Sanchez's work with rhyme royal (in "The Anniad" [1949] and *Does Your House Have Lions?* [1997], respectively). For Shockley, Sanchez's blending of rhyme royal (a stanza form introduced to English by Chaucer) with contemporary rap exemplifies the technical virtuosity of Black aesthetics. And Shockley's own ventures in rhyme royal, ballads, blues, and refrains point to her ongoing contributions to "African American women's liberatory poetic projects," projects deeply invested in a reclaiming not only of rhyme but of stanzaic forms, genres, and poetic histories suffused by rhyme.[62] As Hannah Crawforth has written: "Rhyme is a particularly rich site for thinking about the process of negotiation that Shockley's own 'black aesthetics' might involve, bringing with it echoes of the past and existing always in relation to another moment."[63]

The reclaiming of rhyme is obviously no one thing (we might speak of "reclaimings") and should be assessed via the several nodes and traditions a poet's work engages. If some poets activate rhyme in dialogue with hip hop and/or as part of revived work in old genres, other poets (e.g., Urayoán Noel in *Transversal*, 2021) also exploit the possibilities of trans- and interlingual rhyme. (The Bronx-based Puerto Rican poet and scholar Noel moves across English, Spanish, and Spanglish, even as he pursues many modes of generic experiment and hybridization.) Some of the more ostentatious rhymers of recent decades take up rhyme as a power technology, a hypermarked reclaiming, a brandishing: one notes the pointed aggressivity of full-frontal rhyming in the work of Frederick Seidel (long a fan of the Arabic tradition of monorhyme), and in the first books of Michael Robbins—their polemical (white-)masculinist rhyming swagger, their rhyme-as-dagger.[64] We encounter something quite different in the work of, say, Kay Ryan, with her deft pivots and half rhymes embedded in brief lines; or in Devin Johnston, with his pacing care, his peerless ear; or in Cathy Park Hong, her "invented pidgin" and work in "bad English";[65] or in Christian Bök, his Oulipian recombinance in *Eunoia* (2001); or in Rowan Ricardo Phillips's neo-troubadour's air (in *The Ground*, 2012); or in Paul Muldoon, rhymer extraordinaire. Whether pyrotechnic or muted, these ongoing ventures in poetic rhyme only begin to suggest its ongoing fortunes.

These fortunes are of course entangled in broader horizons of *poiesis*, not least translational, transnational, post-/decolonial, and translinguistic. Pound claimed that every great age of literature is a great age of translation, and literary history and aesthetic judgment would seem to bear him out, at least in so-called English poetry: consider the efflorescence of poetries at the end of the fourteenth century (Chaucer, Gower, Langland); in Elizabethan and Jacobean England; in early twentieth-century Anglophone modernisms, Pound's own moment. Recent poetries in (and distressing and traversing) "English" suggest that we are in such another age—though very differently conditioned.[66] One finds in the past twenty-five or so years an upsurge of a cross-pollinating, awkwardly globalizing, at times neo-macaronic poetry, a sometimes brilliant mixing critically alive to the political as well as linguistic dimensions of mestijaze, creolization, "code-switching."[67]

Of "macaronic"—a term that comes to English from medieval French and then Italian, thereby indexing the phenomenon it specifies—the *OED* reports:

> 1. Of the nature of or designating a jumble or medley. *rare*.
>
> 2. Of or designating a burlesque form of verse in which vernacular words are introduced into the context of another language (originally and chiefly Latin), often with corresponding inflections and constructions; *gen*. of or designating any form of verse in which two or more languages are mingled together. Hence of language, style, etc.: resembling the mixed jargon of macaronic poetry.[68]

The potential political charge of a macaronic verse—and the aesthetic opportunities of it—are more apparent in an era of global capitalism, with its uneven and hierarchized financial, linguistic, phonotextual, and human flows. And here we can observe the relation of rhyme's charge to macaronic medleying and muddling. Stewart observes: "Moments of intense rhyming activity seem to coincide with the meeting of dialects and languages—the melting pot of troubadour culture, the macaronic verse of medieval scholasticism, Dante's turn between Latin and the Tuscan vernacular, Chaucer's encounter with Romance languages, Spenser's with Irish."[69] Such "intense rhyming activity" flourishes in the (sometimes antagonistic) encounter of standard contemporary "English" with a host of other languages and "dialects." "Macaronism" might be best understood as a heuristic, "macaronism" requiring intense historicization to sound out its reverberations, accommodations, and antagonisms.

As the above suggests, "macaronic" verse and doggerel share certain affinities: a relation to burlesque, to comedy, to satire; an embrace of the low, the mixed, the jumbled. With its worldly attunement and posture of a boulevardier's world-historical stroll, Frederick Seidel's poetry walks a fine line distinguishing poetry from doggerel: and macaronic means are sometimes key to his technique and effect. Jahan Ramazani considers "macaronic strategies" as part of a code-switching *poiesis*; he invokes poets like Derek Walcott, Bernardine Evaristo, and Cathy Park Hong to complicate any expectation that macaronism be held to mimesis.[70] These examples come from poets notably and differently alert to questions of migration, racialization, dispossession, and translanguaging. Seidel's work points to something else, a macaronism from above (we might say), a white haut-bourgeois dandyish macaronism.

In his poem "Do You Doha?," Seidel sustains insistent rhymes and plays with the pronunciation of "Qatar" as part of the network binding Sag Harbor, Texas, the Gulf oil states, contemporary economic and cultural regimes, jihadists, child suicide bombers, celebrities, cancer, weddings in America, certain death. (Rhymes include "Howard Street gutter"/"Doha, *Cutter*"/"utter"/"butter"; and later, "Pakistan"/"Afghanistan"/"marzipan"/"Taliban"/"God's plan."[71]) The poem concludes:

Do you Doha? Do you knowa how to Doha?
La Cina è vicina. It is time to say Aloha.⁷²

Seidel's poetic GPS breaks down into near-gibberish—"Do you knowa how to Doha?"—juxtaposed with world-historical bulletins in French ("China is near," etc.): a kind of parodic reversal of Eliot's *The Waste Land*, fragments not shored against but rather indexing ruins. The dizzying network here is both linguistic and political-economical, "Doha" ultimately rhyming with the Hawaiian "Aloha," signifying "an expression of welcome or farewell. Also: good wishes; love, affection" (*OED*), a word itself brought into English via settler colonialism.⁷³ Here the macaronic/doggereling tendencies of Seidel's verse fuel not so much burlesque or comedy as savage diagnosis.⁷⁴ Whether Seidel's jaunty macaronism is symptom or critique (or, unsteadily, both) of the racialized and racist global order he surfs makes for the cringe his work courts and sometimes induces.

One could cite numerous other poets who explore the complex contact zones among languages, peoples, nations; who insist on these zones as conflictual and not only contact zones; who channel complex histories in the sonic translinguistic textures, sonics, and antagonisms they generate. It is no accident that among the most brilliant rhyming poets today are those fully alive to several languages/"dialects" and their various historical claims, burdens, and weights. And then too there are those who are willing to play in this complex area, inventing and not only channeling collisions and contortions of/as/in rhyme. Among these poets is Cathy Park Hong. In her creolizing, minstreling, remixing verse, Hong might be seen as a neo-Elizabethan poet: her Desert City 2016 (in *Dance Dance Revolution*, 2006) and her boomtown China (see *Engine Empire*, 2012) are like Shakespeare's

Illyria, (partly) invented places where the most urgent human dramas are playing out: Hong's imagined places are structured by histories of war, colonialism, finance capital. Hong might be seen as a neo-Elizabethan in her profligate linguistic inventiveness and her wit: she ranges across languages and idiolects and repossesses (or invents) her materials—as in the supermiscegenating toast in *Dance Dance Revolution*:

Lo, brandied man en rabbinical cape
dab rosy musk en goy's gossamy nape,
y brassy Brahmin papoosed in sari's saffron sheet
swoon bine faire Waspian en 'im wingtip feet,
les' toast to bountiful gene pool,
to intramarry couple breedim beige population!
"Toasts in the Grove of Proposals"[75]

This is someone thinking about (and through) phonemes, morphemes, and ideologemes, about ads and clichés and commonplaces, about global flows, impasses, and globalized English.

And yet, and still?

DIVAGATION VI: PALINODE: RHYME REDUX[76]

I'd say it was high time
to retire rhyme
Hurry Up Please It's Time
(obviously not in hip hop
#can'tstopwon'tstop)
finally to give up and refuse rhyme
after centuries of jinglejanglery

this bathetic purported newfanglery
among the oldest things in soi-disant English verse
whether prolix or terse
which does nothing but betray the ears
into lockstep thoughts, mental arrears
—O really do you think so?
Where there is personal liking we go.[77]

Do the ladies these days not much rhyme?
Is it too obvious to chime
as if cooing one's gender
in so tender a sonic blender
were a thing to avoid:
one need not invoke Freud
to believe the fact of a feminine ending
is beyond all suspending
disbelief: What Does Woman Want?
Don't ask Immanuel Kant
whose purposive purposelessness
offers one gloss on *Troilus
and Criseyde* but, let's admit,
an inadequate
one: and since we're speaking of the ending
the fait accompli the telos the mending
wall good neighbors and good lovers both build
it would be remiss not to consider the *Bild-
ung* baked into blank verse
ever since Wordsworth got his unperverse
hands on it, wresting
it away from Milton's God to Man, cresting

as Man did around 1800 as Foucault
said, and he should know.

    Wordsworth
could hardly manage a curd's worth
of whey, didn't know a wren
from a lark, a hen
from a cock
except when his English cock-
ade tipped its hat to liberty in France
amidst its revolutionary dance
of death and love (O guillotine,
O libertin-
age ended!). His long epic poem *The Prelude*
famously eschewed
rhyme
and concealed as an episode a certain spot of time,
his dalliance,
his mésalliance
and illegitimate daughter
rewritten awkwardly as romance—
viz. the tale of Julia and Vaudracour—
take a glance
at Book IX when you get a chance
("Residence in France").
O liberté, égalité, fraternité
(O Dorothy O solidarité!)
He put a new blank
in blank verse, filled his tank
with Spenser, Milton, Shakespeare

and if elsewhere
he balladized and sonnetized we must concede
Wordsworth also an accomplished rhymer, indeed.
That's the point, or a point—
one can code-switch, refuse to disanoint
rhyme for some or all matters
no matter its tatters
and rags. It's a drag
always to be a man or a woman, to drag
your gender afore and behind,
to read *The Bonny Hynd*
and see how ballads sediment
the sexual politics of a long historical moment.
But back to rhyme, the ostensible
topic of this essay reprehensibl-
y deliquescing into errancy—
we can't deny its potency
even if we do not ourselves
indulge. One should leave rhyme on the table
if you're able.
I never ever rhyme
nor should you neither. For a time,
rhyme could align with the sublime,
as when in the eighteenth century
the couplet had a tendency
to swell into a verse paragraph
to register the play of thought better than an electrocardiograph
later measured the heart. Such couplet-work's now rarer than a giraffe
in Times Square—by which I don't mean to speak
of a supermodel during Fashion Week.
There's so much I'd wished to speak to you about,

the troubadours' ongoing clout
(see Devin Johnston's "Nothing Song"[78]
and another favorite, his "New Song"[79]);
about the slow then fast loosening
of eighteenth-century strictures via Pindaric, sprucing
up the English Ode—let's not repeat
tired clichés about the couplet's beat
as rhythm of reactionary thought—
maybe so, maybe not—[80]
Beyond the calumnies on Pope
who's still in the ring, rope-a-dope-dope,
the couplet had more poets ride him
than Pope and Swift, Waller and Dryden:
think Burns, with his insurgent rhymes—
his "Twa Dogs" gets me every time
though there his couplet's clear tetrameter
not heroic (*sic*) pentameter
more usually associated
with Augustan couplets, elevated.
This case of Burns is another one
to show complexities that come
with rhyme and meter, historically—
it's not an either/or you see—
Let's rather network
our way, work
it like Missy Elliott
flip it and reverse it
This A-Way
And That A-Way
so *Lifting Belly*
might salute Lead Belly.

CHAPTER FOUR

The sine waves of any synchronic slice
of rhymed display co-resonate nice-
ly and complexly or interfere
with the other waves you might hear
in any decade or on any day
— Funny the way
you have a period ear.[81]
usually without knowing it, too close to hear
the difference of the difference
of the relation of sound to sense
if we can even speak of such relation —
if it's not an abomination
to contrast them so —
by now you'll know
what I think of such things
as I sing
a song that can't but rhyme
(but as I told you I never rhyme).

And if I should say
on any given day
shiny china vagina
you would know very well
I was quoting Fred Seidel.[82]
And if I should pivot from Haggadah
to Haggaday
and later from fraochans
to paragon[83]
and elsewhere ride from syphilis
via Bucephalus[84]
you would know very soon

Rhyme/Poetics

I was invoking Paul Muldoon.
Sometimes rhyme's a signature
sometimes a hidden ligature
Kay Ryan with her half-buried
half-announced rhymes a figure
of wit but not only, the mind carried
over the ditch of a potential faltering, sure
for a moment of a landing
on safe ground, a standing
sure if skeptical,
unhysterical.

I want to disemplot
the plot
against rhyme, to save it
from neo-formalists who claim it
(though this is not a bawling
out of them: I like e.g. A. E. Stalling-
s's work a lot)
as if (e.g.)
John Ashbery, Ange Mlinko,
Rowan Ricardo
Phillips, Christian Bök
& Cathy Park Hong hadn't written books
time after time
crazed by rhyme.
The transcreative work of Urayoán Noel
is also notably swell—
cf. his *Transversal*—
and if you wonder what rhyme could do or did
see the work of Anthony Madrid

and for crossing Stein and Sappho with the blues
from Harryette Mullen take your cues.[85]
(Inger Christensen's another one
we must salute before we're done.
And her translator Susanna Nied
makes living poems that when cut bleed.)

O it's a cracked time—
good to have crackling rhyme
amidst the searing sun and hoarfrost,
the Robert-Frosty-lost-
in-the-woods
of it all, the Boyz-in-the-Hood-
of it all, please don't let me be misunderstood
of it all.

Let us recall.
To begin
again.
To end
what tends
to end.
To sound out the whole
—leaf blossom and bole—
and the broken.
Now then:

* 5 *
Choratopical/Poetics

"Poetry makes nothing happen," W. H. Auden infamously wrote—a line trotted out by various pundits whenever there's a need to opine on poetry and politics, or on whether poetry can "matter." But as anyone who thinks about it for two seconds realizes—and as Auden's poem "In Memory of W. B. Yeats" goes on to suggest—some poetries make some things happen (or offer "way[s] of happening"), especially if we scrutinize our sense of what "happening" might mean.[1]

One of my favorite chapbooks is Dorothea Lasky's *Poetry Is Not a Project* (2010), a witty meditation on the limitations of self-legislated administered poetic "projects," by which Lasky seems to mean mainly "works governed by procedures or rules or preset ideas or actions for generating 'poetry.'" A lot of writing has been and will be generated this way—good, bad, and mediocre. As Lasky herself notes, a number of her poetry "idols"—Bernadette Mayer, French surrealists—were project-meisters.[2] About the matter of poetic projects, I am, as about many things, agnostic.

CHAPTER FIVE

As someone partial some days to Keats's proclamation that "if Poetry comes not as naturally as the Leaves to a tree, it had better not come at all,"³ I find Lasky's hostility to projects salutary. The ghost of Taylorite factory production haunts some "projects," which can seem a lunging for a productive stimulus in default of any actual demand. (Let's leave aside, for the moment, inspiration or intuition or necessity: ah, those unobsolete eighteenth-century terms.) As Lasky observes, the concept or "project" behind project-generated poems often surpasses the poems in interest and vigor, so one might well wonder: why bother with the "poems," the outputs, the superfluous products of most "projects," at all?

There are, of course, as Lasky implicitly concedes, compelling works that might be categorized as "projects." (Hello *Aeneid*, hello *Divina Commedia*. Hello *Songs of Innocence and of Experience*, *Lyrical Ballads*, *The Prelude*. Hello *Leaves of Grass*, *Le Spleen de Paris*. Hello *My Life*. Hello *Revolutionary Letters*. The heterogeneity of this ad hoc list is diagnostic.) Confining ourselves (as Lasky does) to recent Anglophone poetries, we might think of the mordant *essais* and parables of Anne Boyer's *Garments against Women* (2015), the disjunctive resonant paragraphs of MC Hyland's *The End* (2019), the dystopian fable of Ilya Kaminsky's *Deaf Republic* (2019), the reverberant philosoundings of Fred Moten's *All That Beauty* (2019), the "scripts for situation videos" in Claudia Rankine's *Citizen: An American Lyric* (2014), the spare, devastating scenes in Prageeta Sharma's *Grief Sequence* (2019), the forensic-erotic inventories and ekphrases in Donna Stonecipher's *Transaction Histories* (2018) or her entries in *Model City* (2015), the incisive anatomies of feeling and encounter in Yanyi's *The Year of Blue Water* (2019). All these appear in what we might call "project books," but that won't get us very far in considering the specificities and complexities of their work.

Choratopical/Poetics

When I am not writing I am not writing a novel called *1994* about a young woman in an office park in a provincial town who has a job cutting and pasting time. I am not writing a novel called *Nero* about the world's richest art star in space. I am not writing a book called *Kansas City Spleen*. I am not writing a sequel to *Kansas City Spleen* called *Bitch's Maldoror*. I am not writing a book of political philosophy called *Questions for Poets*. I am not writing a scandalous memoir. I am not writing a pathetic memoir. I am not writing a memoir about poetry or love. I am not writing a memoir about poverty, debt collection, or bankruptcy. I am not writing about family court. I am not writing a memoir because memoirs are for property owners and not writing a memoir about prohibitions of memoirs.

ANNE BOYER, "Not Writing"[4]

To a person, everyone she aimed her camera at would demur, "Oh, I'm really not photogenic." Which, when she thought more about it, could only mean that everyone thought they were better-looking than they really were. The covert exhibitionists liked to hang out in banks, on subway platforms, and in front of embassies, sneaking glances at surveillance cameras with their sexy gray shoulders.

DONNA STONECIPHER, "Transaction History 3"[5]

She tells me she feels guilty for giving birth to me. What I am—I've gone further than gambling, drug addiction, death—I've killed the image of her daughter. I tell her she must feel so much pain, that I understand what she's going through. Then I hang up.

YANYI, "She tells me," *The Year of Blue Water*[6]

Such work suggests that not only are poetic "projects" highly variable in texture, procedure, and commitment: their multifariousness cuts across such descriptors as "prose poetry."

CHAPTER FIVE

Certainly one of the more successful and notorious wings of twenty-first-century poetic projects flew under the banner of Conceptual poetry. Various in project, procedure, and commitment, yet with a programmatic flair and incisive spokespeople, Conceptual poetry had charismatic, market-savvy practitioners, including Kenneth Goldsmith, with his neo-Warholian (indeed, neo-Duchampian) provocations, and a supportive critical cadre, not least the influential scholar and critic Marjorie Perloff. Continuing in a different key the hostility of the Language Poets to what Charles Bernstein called "official verse culture," Conceptual poets, ostentatiously indebted to Conceptual art, were great experimenters in poetry as appropriation, program, event, stunt, gimmick, plagiarism, critique, intermedial provocation, biotechnological collaboration. Mainstream (*sic*) poetry was—as Conceptual manifestos declared—so behind even visual art, so pathetic and moribund, that it could still be jump-started by what was then old news in the art world: conceptualism! Remediating weather reports, reframing rape victims' testimonies, collaborating with bioengineers, such work aimed to bring the frisson of the new to, while also dissolving normative parameters for, "poetry."[7] Many a forest has fallen, many an internet server gone down, in the surveying of such features of the poetic landscape; I wish not to add much more to that surveying but to register Conceptual poetry as a once-prominent but not exclusive zone of twenty-first-century poetic projects.

Turns out that many important lowercase-C conceptual poets—many of them poets of color—had been writing and publishing all along, unhitched to the capital-C Conceptual bandwagon (e.g., Bhanu Kapil, Harryette Mullen, Srikanth Reddy, Simone White). Among the most significant "conceptual" works of the past twenty years is surely M. NourbeSe Philip's *Zong!*

(2008), the devastating and influential book drawing its "word store" from the legal case *Gregson v. Gilbert*, 1783, concerning the murder-by-drowning of abducted Africans on the slave ship *Zong*.[8] And, to turn very much elsewhere: you might consider English poet Alice Oswald—often glossed as Ted Hughes's inheritor, certainly one of the prime examples of Anglophone "official verse culture"—to be a major conceptual poet, from *Dart* (2002), a work assembling voices along the River Dart in Devon, to *Memorial* (2012), the landmark work made from Iliadic death notices and similes. One might say—and scholars have—that there were conceptual poets long before, and there will be long after, the efflorescence of Conceptual poetry. And Conceptual poetry, with its avant-garde pronunciamentos and blinkered absolutisms, eventually generated a multipronged backlash, not least for its disdain for so-called identity politics and subjectivity, and for the "delusions of Whiteness in the avant-garde," as Cathy Park Hong's eponymous 2014 article had it.[9]

Again, returning to the multifariousness of poetic "projects," however announced, one might think of any number of works from the past two decades: Christian Bök's *Eunoia* (2001) manifests a neo-Oulipian dazzle in its lipogrammatic "chapters"; Susan Stewart's *Columbarium* (2003) enfolds within its "century form" (a seventeenth-century practice of making books of a hundred pages) an abecedarium of "shadow georgics"; Cathy Park Hong's *Dance Dance Revolution* (2006) and *Engine Empire* (2012) undertake (as previously noted) elaborate, linguistically profligate ventures in world-building, historical inquiry, and imaginative creolization; Srikanth Reddy's *Voyager* (2011) develops powerfully insinuating countertexts from Kurt Waldheim's memoir; Robin Coste Lewis's *Voyage of the Sable Venus* (2015) pointedly sounds out and reconfigures the poetics and politics of racist curatorial labels and inventories. One might note Aaron Kunin's procedurally exacting, cool work, in *Cold Genius* (2014) or the essays of *Love Three: A Study of a Poem by George Herbert* (2019). Or (to turn up the temperature, and toward narrative) Reddy's large-hearted time-traveling translational metempsychic catabasis (and portrait of a professorial "sad dad") in *Underworld Lit* (2020). Or consider Nathaniel Mackey's unfolding project, launched in the mid-1970s, *Song of the Andoumboulou*, which takes wing from the Dogon belief that humans are but "rough drafts," works in progress. Some of these works partake of the strikingly inventive documentary poetics arising in the past decade, a poetics committed not so much to a poetry of witness as to fiercely incisive critique — counterhistories, critical fabulations, speculative histories and futurities, polemical reportage and assemblage: as in (to cite very different works, beyond those invoked above) Don Mee Choi's *DMZ Colony* (2020); Layli Long Soldier's instantly canonical "38" in *Whereas* (2017); and Edgar Garcia's *Skins of Columbus: A Dream Ethnography* (2019), an experiment in which each night before sleep the poet reads Columbus's journal entries from his first voyage to the Americas, launching a counteroccupancy, a mythopoeic rewriting of colonial space-time.

Even if we restricted ourselves to the expansion of ecopoetics and pointed to work that is more than merely conservationist or genially inventorying, palliative "nature poetry," we would have many books to consider[10]: e.g., Brian Teare's propulsive "Toxics Release Inventory (Essay on Man)," in *Doomstead Days* (2019), which continues his project of geophysical positioning via lyric reckoning, charting the vulnerability and intimacy of bodies assembled in specifically distressed environs; or Juliana Spahr's work, which has long sounded out the politics, sonics, erotics, and violence of differential permeability — as in *This Connection of*

Everyone with Lungs (2005); or Ed Roberson's remarkable career and complex ecocritical vision, including *To See the Earth before the End of the World* (2010), *City Eclogue* (2006), and *Atmospheric Conditions* (1999); or Cecil S. Giscombe's sustained poetic mappings, his train routes, prairies, weather systems, regionalisms, and border towns (*Ohio Railroads*, 2014; *Prairie Style*, 2008); or Michael Dickman's deceptively dreamlike suburban dystopian incantation "Lakes Rivers Streams" in *Days and Days* (2019), which locates us "just upstream from a can of Red Bull & a pollen allergy," "just upstream from a can of Aqua Net & a Pepsi."[11]

I could go on; many have. The point here is: by their fruits ye shall know them, and the fruits of poetic projects are sometimes very fine. And also: enough surveying—let me turn to cases. Three recent books have made me consider further what poetic projects might offer—their horizons and possibilities. Poetry both is and is not a project, if we liberate "project" from its contemporary procedural (and sometimes careerist) associations and think of poetry as a projecting forth, something thrown forward into a given, multiple, and transformable world. In this sense, to write and to publish (and to read) poetry may be seen as an optimistic, generous wager, manifesting a faith in the ongoingness of a world of transmission, reception, creation, and possible transformation.

One feels the force of this generosity, and a semicovert optimism, even as—precisely as—these three books outline a terrain of precarity, anxiety, and trauma. These books take the measure of their differing occasions and attest to the complexity of their poetic condition/ing. Anne Boyer's *Garments against Women* (2015), already mentioned, gives us a portrait of an artist writing, not writing, thinking, sewing, stressing, as she navigates the mind-numbing corridors of officialdom, as she cooks, daydreams, and drives her daughter around the roads and parking lots of Kansas. Bhanu Kapil's *Ban en Banlieue* (2015) sustains a complex inquiry—autobiographical, historical, political-economical, material, postcolonial—into a figure, place, and body denominated "Ban," who is (among many other things) "a brown girl on the floor of the world," a girl lying down amidst a race riot in the suburbs of London.[12] Juliana Spahr's *That Winter the Wolf Came* (2015) locates itself amidst financial disaster, petroleum extraction, and Occupy Oakland, weaving together ecological meditation, political critique, and lyric inquiry.[13] *Each book activates a complex romantic/revolutionary inheritance, and each makes a claim for a poetry open to history as well as historicity.* Each book is a powerful, intricately made thing; each book indexes the often distressed conditions of its own making. Each book speaks, then, to the question of what *poiesis*—what making of any kind (of poems, books, lives, families, solidarity)—might require and might yet be. Arendt: to think what we are doing.

In thinking about poetry and possibility—on what the project of *poiesis* as *making or shaping* might be—I have in mind Anahid Nersessian's *Utopia, Limited: Romanticism and Adjustment* (2015). Drawing mainly on romantic-period writing (Shelley, Coleridge, Helen Maria Williams, Hazlitt, Kant), Nersessian's book is deeply informed by discussions of "the Anthropocene" (our own epoch, arguably inaugurated by the Industrial Revolution, marking the human impact on geology and ecosystems) and by contemporary reckonings with conditions and limits—the matter of living together in a constrained world of limited resources. Nersessian proposes "formal practices of limitation and adjustment," exploring *poiesis* as a complex co-forming in and of the world—a politically engaged and optimistic yet not necessarily radical-revolutionary aesthetic.[14]

Here I think (again) of Percy Bysshe Shelley, espouser indeed of radical-revolutionary aesthetics and politics—self-styled "Democrat, Philanthropist, and Atheist,"[15] hymnist of the French Revolution, passionately responding to hostile critics in his preface to *Prometheus Unbound* that he does indeed have "a passion for reforming the world":

> Let this opportunity be conceded to me of acknowledging that I have what a Scotch philosopher characteristically terms a "passion for reforming the world:" what passion incited him to write and publish his book he omits to explain.[16]

Modernity has offered us many things, not least a set of rationales for shaming poets who wanted (and who want) to reform the world, who thought (and think) that poetry might make things happen, who strove (and strive) to extend the domain of "what happens" to include such microscopic, barely perceptible events as a change of mood as well as such world-historical events as the French Revolution or mass extinction in the Anthropocene. The grotesque shifts in scale in that last sentence are precisely my point. We don't always know in advance what matters and to whom, and to recognize that—to rethink that—is an ongoing project. If modernity is, as Jürgen Habermas had it, an unfinished project, then negative capability (the Keatsian willingness not to know in advance, to be "capable of being in uncertainties") is an unfinishable project—or, rather, an important and renewable resource.

Boyer, Kapil, and Spahr manifest, to different degrees, a discomfort with and at times a violent refusal of "poetry"—certainly of "literature," and of any dream of a purportedly autonomous literary aesthetic. For "literature is against us," as Boyer writes—against women and against the poor (Boyer's primary "us");

against colonized peoples; against Black and brown and indigenous people; against immigrants; against trans and nonbinary writers; against anyone who isn't already imagined in, or willing to align with, the collectivities and subject positions to which official "literature" has traditionally addressed itself.[17] As Kapil writes in *Ban en Banlieue*, "I want a literature that is not made from literature" (32).

(Obviously I am suspending, as Boyer and Kapil certainly do, the question of whether their books are "poetry"—just as I earlier suspended the question of whether "poetry" is a "project." I mean to keep these questions suspended throughout this chapter, and indeed beyond, because the space for encountering, essaying, assaying, and shaping that these and kindred works open is the space of responsiveness I wish to dwell in and sponsor and test. It is also true that such institutions as publishers, libraries, and corporate booksellers must make their respective categorical calls.[18])

There is of course a long tradition of literature against literature, of poetry against poetry, of renunciation and critique: and Boyer, Kapil, and Spahr emerge from and contribute to that experimental tradition. One could see these books as experimental projects in life-writing, and also as examples of "autotheory" (as Maggie Nelson, following Paul Preciado, described her book *The Argonauts*, 2014).[19] We could see these writers as poet-venturers in a longer history of *poiesis*, writing not poetry "in a more restricted sense," as Shelley put it in his "Defence" (meaning metrical verse in recognizable forms), but rather poetry "in a general sense," complex acts of making which need not be in verse.[20] There is an argument to be made, in fact, that the proponents of the "New Sentence," a preoccupation of some Language Poets in the 1980s,[21] have found their best exponents a full generation or two later, in such writers as Boyer and Kapil, whose poetries are built primarily out of sentences. Kapil writes of *Ban*: "This is a bank for sentences" (61).

What does poetry sentence us to? What might it sentence forth, sentiently?

Boyer's book offers a savage, sometimes hilariously downbeat, peculiarly friendly poetics of precarity: emotional, financial, physical. She takes the risk of launching *Garments against Women* with a clinical, anesthetized discourse, "The Animal Model of Inescapable Shock," a series of paragraphs that lays out just that, in excruciatingly benumbed sentences. This studied neutrality, this polemically "objective" stance, could itself be understood as a stylistic mode proper to a shocked, traumatized female animal—the mice dragged across "electrified grids" in the lab pointing to Boyer herself, analyzed in "the infinite laboratory called 'conditions,'" the laboratory of "Capital" (1–2).

Boyer is a flaneur (flaneuse?) not of nineteenth-century Paris nor even of Kansas (where she lives) but of her own mind. The book registers many things, not least the specific material conditions conducive to, and inimical to, writing, sewing, and by extension any kind of making at all. It is difficult to convey the experience of reading Boyer without quoting vast swaths. There is great pressure and decision in her sentences and paragraphs, the force of a mind thinking and unspooling and backtracking. The power of the book seeps into you, as an ambient drip. The reiterative textures of much experimental writing are here mobilized toward powerfully and surprisingly emotional ends.

In its cumulatively mesmerizing weave, we come to realize that Boyer is writing toward a poetics of care, one that doesn't abjure the registering of envy, depression, embarrassment, abjection, failure. The most painfully tender passages in the book arise in exchanges with her young daughter, as in the mediated report of a dismal shoe-shopping expedition (there is not enough money for the desired shoes), which ends in tears, the daughter saying to her mother:

> "I am still a child and am learning to control my impulses and emotions. you have had many years of dreams and realities to learn from so there is no excuse for you to cry." she paused. "do you have enough dreams?" she finally asked. (38)

Wordsworth said poetry was "the *history or science of feeling.*"[22] *Garments against Women* is an absorbing book about what Sianne Ngai famously called "ugly feelings"—such "unprestigious" and "negative affects" as envy, anxiety, disgust, paranoia.[23] And Boyer is indeed envious, as well as embarrassed, embarrassing, culpably dreamy, cracked. "It is all this self-expression that makes me so ashamed," she writes. "I was too sad to slug in the face." "*I said that maybe everyone I knew was embarrassed by me. I went on being embarrassing*" (13, 63, 66).

It wouldn't be quite right to say that *Garments against Women* is leavened by its mordant humor (viz. such titles as "*Ma Vie en Bling*: A Memoir"). The book is made precisely out of this weave of pathos, resentment, tenderness, wit; out of a yes/no, neither this nor that, anti/pro toggling of a woman measuring out, sounding out, what she wants against the background noise of what she's supposed to want and what she doesn't have. Boyer writes in "A Woman Shopping" about the notional book she is supposedly *not* writing: "This book would be a book also about the history of literature and literature's uses against women, also against literature and for it, also against shopping and for it. . . . It will be a book about envy and a book about barely visible things" (47).

From one angle, this book is a sustained meditation on "making" itself: bad, failed, imperfect making, with occasional flashes of beauty, pleasure, good-enough use and reuse. Boyer tracks circuits and failed circuitry—of emotion, of efforts to make (books, clothes, dinner). Writing and sewing offer her imperfect and sometimes hostile garments, botched things in a botched world.

In her vexed romance with sewing, shopping, and thrifting, she occasionally and powerfully connects objects back to makers: in a wrap dress bought at the Salvation Army she detects "the odor of the extraordinary seamstress Louise Jones," whose name she discovers on the dress's label (28). Such thrilling moments are both documentary and theoretical, involving material attentiveness, sensual imagination, and a performative uncongealing of the "congealed labor time" that Marx said dwelled in, and was disguised by, every commodity.[24]

Boyer is writing a poetry "against information," which involves her in an analytic of information, of what informs us, forms in us, forms us, what is admissible and what is not: "Many kinds of inadmissible information are inadmissible because they provoke a feeling of pity, guilt, or contempt" (16, 9). Boyer offers a wizardly, bleakly funny anatomy of shame, contempt, resentment: the book refuses the partition of "thought" and "feeling" and contributes to the growing literature on the politics of feeling.

Boyer explores a poetics and politics of freedom, the linkages between "happiness" and "freedom" (two obsessively reiterated keywords here) and between their perversions: the obligation to be happy and to perform one's freedom. *Garments against Women* is a declaration of dependence, of interdependence, of hapless enmeshment: life, liberty, and the pursuit of happiness getting their thorough scouring and transvaluation.

> I am now constrained to abundance, "happiness" or its absence / infirmity. (12)

> To feel deeply, or to admit to feeling deeply, is also inadmissible, though not as inadmissible as to admit to having been un-free. (9)

> There are many things I do not like to read, mostly accounts of the lives of the free. (12)

Why is Boyer "un-free"? She has debts, she is invaded by bad feelings, toxins seep into her life, love goes awry, she watches the news. She expends herself on care, not least care for her young daughter, a care that falls outside the normative monetized and monetizable calculus of value. She is, in other words, a female human being in twenty-first-century America. She is also a writer, resisting mandates to be "productive" while also desiring to write, wanting recognition, fellowship, both as writer and as sentient creature: "Where is the true impermeable community?" (23).

In *Garments against Women*, "not writing" threatens to become, as it were, Boyer's métier—as it has for so many, the mute inglorious Miltons of the past and our present. In "What Is 'Not Writing'?" Boyer offers a bravura counter-reckoning, an arithmetic of negated productivity, productive negation:

> There are years, days, hours, minutes, weeks, moments, and other measures of time spent in the production of "not writing." Not writing is working, and when not working at paid work working at unpaid work like caring for others, and when not at unpaid work like caring, caring also for a human body [...] and when not reading and learning also making things (like garments, food, plants, artworks, decorative items) [...]
>
> . . .
>
> There is illness and injury which has produced a great deal of not writing. There is cynicism, disappointment, political out-

rage, heartbreak, resentment, and realistic thinking which has produced a great deal of not writing. There is reproduction which has been like illness and injury and taken up many hours with not writing.

. . .

There is shopping, which is a woman shopping. (44–45)

Among many things to register here, one might highlight the slyly pointed ferocity of the placement in the second passage above of the unmarked phrase "realistic thinking."

Boyer implicitly takes up Arendt's injunction "to think what we are doing" and torques it, tracking as well how we are feeling and regulating feeling. It is no accident that Boyer takes her epigraph from Mary Wollstonecraft, the great feminist thinker doubly smeared in life and after her death for daring to live a life of erotic as well as intellectual passion. Mary Wollstonecraft's own daughter, Mary Shelley, knew very well just how "literature" might be "against us": her greatest novel features a highly sensitive and literate creature who is nevertheless violently excluded from human fellowship.

From one monster to, perhaps, another; and from one project to another: "What is Ban?" asks the poet Bhanu Kapil in *Ban en Banlieue*. "Ban" is, Kapil writes, "the parts of something remixed as air: integral, rigid air, circa 1972–1979. She's a girl. A black girl in an era when, in solidarity, Caribbean and Asian Brits self-identified as black." She materializes in Kapil's work through a set of performances, notebooks, pilgrimages, embodiments: variously "a mixture of dog shit and bitumen (ash) scraped off the soles of running shoes," "a warp of smoke," "ivy-asphalt/glass-girl combinations," daffodils and mirrors arranged on a city street, the artist's body: "I want to lie down in the place I am from: on the street I am from" (30–32). "Ban" was also, it emerges, one of the poet's childhood nicknames.[25]

"Ban" is—becomes—many things. But she is above all else a girl lying on the street, an auto-sacrifice, a suicide, a self-protectively stilled and prone body, "a black (brown) girl," "lying on the floor of the world . . . lying on the floor of England" at the moment she hears glass shattering (42). That sound signals, it will unfold, a specific race riot of April 23, 1979, in Hayes, Middlesex, a suburb of London, "the outskirts of London: *les banlieues*" (33).

Ban speaks to Kapil's long-standing interest in the monster, the immigrant, materiality, (supposed) madness. The titles of her previous books evoke her theoretical dispositions: *Schizophrene* (2011), *Humanimal: A Project for Future Children* (2009), *Incubation: A Space for Monsters* (2006), *The Vertical Interrogation of Strangers* (2001). Through Ban, Kapil is writing not only about "social death"—the systematic denial of humanity to, for example, prisoners, slaves, or concentration camp inmates; the structuring of certain lives as disposable—but also about a never-having-been: a creature who never quite lived, perhaps an immigrant, perhaps a monster, ultimately neither. A charcoaled outline of a girl dying and already dead: "Some bodies don't somatize" (75).

Ban is situated between poetry and performance, between writing and ritual; the book emerges as well as a kind of durational default, the rejectimenta of an abandoned novel. The book appears as a series of notes and paratexts: endnotes and canceled epigraphs; autobiographical vignettes ("Five Fictions for Ban"); social reportage; lists of "installations and performances"; "Notes toward a Race Riot Scene"; further notes on rituals and performances undertaken in London, New York City, California, Colorado, and India (16, 33, 57). This material is all part of the "work," the project, of *Ban*. *Ban* is in part a record of the difficulty, the impossibility, of finding a form for Ban:

> Ban is a dessicating form on a sidewalk. . . . I should have written the alien body as a set of fragments, a ghazal with an omega mouth and a healing cry; instead I went with *historical fiction*, the narrative of a riot that had receded by 1983, to be overlain by other riots. The riot is a charnel ground in this sense. (21–22)

Kapil continues:

> The project fails at every instant and you can make a book out of that and I do, in the same time that it takes other people to write their second novel that is optioned by Knopf and which details the world they grew up in, just as I am—detailing—which is to say: scouring/burnishing—the world I grew up in too. (22)

Kapil puts one kind of project against another: excoriation—"scouring/burnishing"—is here her métier; her project is clearly not that of the ostentatiously successful realist immigrant novel. *Ban* itself announces its failure as a book, its failure as normative literature: it presents itself as the notes around a novel which this book first aspired to be, the novel which Kapil does not, cannot, give us—a realist novel about a brown girl in a race riot.

How to think about this "failure"? Is it apotropaic, designed to ward off a critical judgment of failure? A preemptive honesty? One sees this motif of failure in Boyer's work as well. It is powerful—both disarming and arming. (Note: Do men write about failure in this way?) Is this the writer's failure? A notational critique of the totalizing presumptions of genre? An unachieved or unachievable "work"? In the words of Ezra Pound—a perhaps obscene invocation—is it that Kapil "cannot make it cohere"?[26]

CHAPTER FIVE

Or that she won't? Or that coherence is itself obscene, offstage, beyond: *banlieue*?

One core, submerged, but centrally horrific element of this book is the way the ongoing project of *Ban* eerily predicts emerging Ban-figures—as if Ban were an image of violent abnegation vibrating across lands and times, for the brown girl lying on the floor of the world is not bound to one place or time. Kapil keeps her notebooks from 2009 to 2012—thinking and struggling with this work. In December 2012 a young woman in New Delhi is raped and left for dead, entrails streaming from her body on the street: "What was in the work—as an image—had appeared beyond it—as a scene."

> 11. . . . At that moment, I stopped writing Ban.
>
> 12. And there I lay down on the ground.
>
> 13. And this was the part of the project that could not be completed in the same place that the project was held . . . I knew that if I did this, if I continued to write—like this—then I myself—would not be able—to return. (25)

Poetry is not a project.
And yet poetry is not *not* a project.

Here the ethic of *Ban*'s form—its ethos and its morality—comes to the fore: the project of *Ban* must shift in the making, lest the writer of *Ban*, and the commitments animating *Ban*, be lost. For what, for whom, is this writing? *For Ban. Love Note for Ban. Anamorphia for Ban. Race Drops for Ban. Embryology for Ban.* Autobiography, theory, travel-journal, performance note, pilgrimage, remembrance, urban inquiry, photo-reliquary, elegy (for, among others, the Australian peace activist Blair Peach, killed in the riot of April 23, 1979): *Ban en Banlieue* encompasses yet is not reducible to these.²⁷

Ban resists normative, premature attempts at assessment: is it "good"? Kapil's book puts me in mind of Theodor Adorno's dictum from *Minima Moralia*, "Wrong life cannot be lived rightly" (*Es gibt kein richtiges Leben im falschen*).²⁸ Yet her book also puts pressure on that aphorism: for perhaps wrong life can be lived less wrongly if not rightly. (Such a proposal would likely earn Adorno's contempt, as a typically American weaseling, an effort to avoid and evade the totality of the situation of "the now" of "life." So be it. What is poetry to offer if not a specification and pluralization of the horizons of the now? *Poiesis*: form as adjustment. Not acceptance, not quiescence, but actual, transformable making toward the not-yet-known.) Kapil subjects herself to Ban, becomes Ban, enacts and refuses autobiography through Ban, "but Ban, in a sense, was waiting for me, in the darkness of the border, no longer proximal but centered, arms waving in a blur, waiting with everything that was wrong" (57).

Woven into this writing venture—the venture of life—is a sense of being in, writing toward, the wrong audience, the wrong space: "My mistake is that I perform works intended for a European audience—in California—and that I do not have the courage or means to go home" (24).²⁹ Elsewhere, Kapil makes perfectly clear that while "home" is England, she's not English: "What, for example, is born in England, but is never, not even on a cloudy day, English?" (30). Kapil writes in part out of, against, the resurgence of the British far right (both in the 1970s and 1980s and now); how might this resonate for US as well as other Anglophone audiences? Are our readerly intersectionalities, so to speak, sufficiently transnational (yet)? "What would I have written—

what would have become of these materials—had I stayed in the U.K.?" (22). Kapil thus sounds out the complexities and vulnerabilities of a postcolonial and immigrant literature testing its locations and destinations. (One of Kapil's recurring concerns is the traumatic impact of the 1947 Partition of India, a legacy—or, rather, a complex presence—haunting and maddening subsequent generations, diasporic and not.) This is one of many dimensions of Kapil's ongoing project—a postcolonial, migratory, deeply theorized poetics grounded in an analytic distinct from, yet related to, Boyer's orientation to economic and gender critique (recall, for example, Boyer's females/mice in the Lab of Capital with its "infinite 'conditions.'")

Kapil refuses the logic of mere persistence and moves toward "presence" (64). Thus curation and performance art, Ana Mendieta and Theresa Hak Kyung Cha, are her muses as much as other poets and novelists and Hindu epic. One infers from various acknowledgments that forms of healing bodywork also offer models and occasions for her art. The unfolding fragments making up *Ban*—slowly dilating into a more discursive prose before retracting into a more notational mode—suggest precisely the work of "form-as-adjustment" (see Nersessian): a form discovered, arrived at, adjusted to, out of very difficult conditions, a form adequate to those sensorimotor and political conditions.

Kapil has of course thought about all this—her book is as much autotheoretical as it is autosacrificial. For her, juxtaposition is precisely not about automatic resonance or reverberant collage: "One thing next to another doesn't mean they touch" (13). And further, "you can be a hybrid and not share a body with anything else. Thus, the different parts of 'Ban' do not touch." There is, she writes (quoting the writer Gail Scott), an "abyss between sentences" (58). Kapil will give us neither the rich integrative satisfactions of the realist novel nor the frissons of collage, and she more than tells us why.

In her end notes, Kapil writes, "I feel ashamed that I could not make *Ban* an amazing book" (100). The rawness of Kapil's profession of shame marks for me a vulnerability I would wish to turn away from: why would you write *that*, having written *Ban*? My reaction is a perfect symptom of the turning-away this book refuses, even as *Ban* marks and transforms the many moments in which Kapil had to stop, refuse, regroup, rethink "how to make (from this) (from these things): a form. A charnel: ground" (87). Kapil's is a *poiesis* of necessary extremity, of politicized vulnerability: "I'm writing about a person's attempt to maintain a level of psychic intensity at all costs" (68). This book does indeed "unfold the electrical mat of my nervous system" (108).

If Kapil's book is a network of notes around an ungrievable grievous place ("utopia" signaling here, etymologically, "no place"), Spahr's *That Winter the Wolf Came* traces a trajectory and sounds out a time, an epoch, not quite a "season in hell" (Rimbaud) but a season ("that winter") in exuberant, anxious protest, a season of uprisings collectively denominated "Occupy." The book follows an arc that might be called melancholy if that weren't already overpoeticized and typically depoliticized as a term. "That winter we just rhymed and rhymed on. Together" ("Went Looking and Found Coyotes," 60). Indeed, Spahr offers a politicized melancholy that asserts itself against defeatism. (Though perhaps one would want to keep a space open for clear-eyed defeatism.)

Spahr's book unspools around the songline:

> In this time song holds loss. And this is a time of loss. . . . Songs in their most popular versions tend to be epiphanic, gorgeous with swelling chord changes, full of lament too. And this song,

> like many, expresses the desire to be near someone who is now lost. It travels as something layered, infiltrated, unconfused with its refusals to make a simple sense. I want to give you this song sung in a bar in Oakland one night during the ongoing oil wars. ("Transitory, Momentary," 12)

The line itself, humming through sentences and permutations of sentences, is her unit, her subject, her object—as in this opening poem, which features a deft modulation from Brent geese flying to Brent crude oil: "The Brent geese fly in long low wavering lines on their migration"—an image of Spahr's own *poiesis*. Spahr is a deft weaver/waverer of lines, a permuter and transmuter, orchestrating into sinuous verse paragraphs the flow of the migratory lines of geese, the lines of her poetry, and how "the police move slowly, methodically in a line" ("Transitory, Momentary," 11).

That Winter the Wolf Came is a book about Occupy that largely eschews the term "Occupy": "I do not want to use the word occupy. I am trying to figure something out. Something I do not yet understand about my physical body, my real financial, medical, and social needs." Spahr presents herself, polemically, as unremarkable, one among others; in this she echoes Boyer's interest in being "ordinary."

> My body is unremarkable, not at all singular, as I walk up to join these other bodies, and it remains unremarkable, not at all singular, as it walks with others, takes off into the street when others do, usually after someone yells block up block up into a megaphone. ("Brent Crude," 21)

Spahr's is an art of entanglement and enmeshment, enacted via form: through lines, stanzas, verse paragraphs. Entanglement, enmeshment: these words could connote the cozy, the intimate, but should also connote a horizon of violence; you can't kettle a bunch of protesters without getting close. An oil spill kills the creatures it slicks. You can't but eat and breathe a complex, often poisonous biochemical life. As Spahr writes in a poem about mothering, about tending the not-me, the "not really me":

Later I pass the breast cup to not really me,
a breast cup filled with sound insulation panels and imitation wood
    with a little nectar and sweetness.
And not really me drinks it and then complains a little,
rebuking me, for my cakes of nuts and raisins
are cakes of extraction of crude petroleum and natural gas,
for my apples are filled with televisions and windshield wiper blades.
"Tradition," 54

The biblical Song of Songs—"Sustain me with cakes of raisins, refresh me with apples: for I am sick with love" (2:5)—is here infiltrated in its very substance, as are we, by contemporary commodities, petro-products.

    This is a book about vulnerable creaturely life and our petroscene, a book of poetry both rejecting and embracing poetry and "tradition"—or rather refunctioning tradition as "mothering," a mode of care:

I hold out my hand.
I hand over
and I pass on.
I hold out my hand.
I hold out my hand.
I hand over

and I pass on.
Some call this mothering.

"Tradition," 53

Spahr is a political formalist, or rather a politicized formalizer, one who *gives form* to the emerging, to emergency in its broadest sense. Here one can see how Spahr's project aligns with but also diverges from Boyer's and Kapil's: Spahr is more interested in old-school poetic tropes and techniques like apostrophe, refrain, and verse timing.[30] In "Brent Crude," the variations in oil pricing offer her a modulating, structuring principle—pricing over time a capitalist refrain and *punctum*:

> The Brent Crude Oil Spot price was 101.84, when the first of a series of meetings are held at a park. I stand at the back during these meetings and hold my son's hand as he jumps in mud puddles ... The Brent Crude Oil Spot price is 112.11 when the police come the first time. ("Brent Crude," 19)

A pointedly mobilized, glitchy iambic pentameter powers another powerful, disturbing poem, "Dynamic Positioning" (about the Deepwater Horizon explosion and resulting BP oil spill disaster of April 2010). Here and elsewhere Spahr makes a minimal yet powerful wager that form can adjust to—and do justice to—the currents of our moment: "Sometimes art can hold the oil wars and all that they mean and might yet mean within." This extraordinary wager is combined with polemically modest, minimal, and "minor" claims, even as her accumulations of apparently mere observations scale up into higher-order assertions of poetico-political entanglement.

> What I have to offer here is nothing revolutionary. They [the geese] learn the map from their parents, or through culture

rather than through genetics. It is just an observation, a small observation that sometimes art can hold the oil wars and all that they mean and might yet mean within. Just as sometimes there are seven stanzas in a song. And just as sometimes there is a refrain between each stanza. ("Transitory, Momentary," 11)

Toward the end of the book, she writes:

> This is where I am now, writing this story of the most minor of uprisings. A story about how when I entered into this one for a brief period of time I agreed to experience all the emotions and I realized there was a good chance that one of them would be sadness. Minor sadness, I had hoped. What I have now, even though minor, is a sadness that has made it hard for me to concentrate. ("It's All Good, It's All Fucked," 71)

Spahr's emphasis on the *minor*, on her "anxious body," her "nervous," unheroic self and engagements, is a big bold claim, and a sly "fuck you" to the heroic masculinist tradition of revolution.

In a book preoccupied (pre-Occupy'd) with questions of (not-quite) revolution, Spahr casts "Non-Revolution" as the provisional beloved, a sexy, earthy, tangy, promiscuous, intensely desired desire machine. Of "Non-Revolution's body," Spahr writes,

> Something about Non-Revolution's smell and body had gotten into me . . . it was like something so excellent I could not get enough of it.
>
>   . . . I wanted to be there all the time, to be inside every moment, to be always on the lips of Non-Revolution and whomever Non-Revolution was touching with their tongue, whatever parts of bodies of Mexico City, Santiago, El Alto, Madrid, Cairo, Suez, Istanbul, Yenagoa. ("It's All Good, It's All Fucked," 65–67)

Spahr has long written a poetry that confounded boundaries—between poetry and prose, erotics and politics, "private" and "public." The power of this book is undimmed and in fact propelled by its sadness, because hers is a deeply felt yet also limited sadness, a sadness alert to the "ever more about to be" (Wordsworth) that romantic writers also hoped for. Indeed Spahr takes her epigraph from Shelley's "Mask of Anarchy," a coruscating poem that has inspired left-wing radicals for two centuries:

When one fled past, a maniac maid,
And her name was Hope, she said:

What Spahr pointedly does not proceed to quote are Shelley's next lines:

But she looked more like Despair,
And she cried out in the air:[31]

A potentially crazy Hope sustained against the specter of Despair: this is Spahr's project, and it was—in another key—Shelley's. From Shelley—one of Marx's favorite poets—to our own moment: there is of course by now a long "revolutionary tradition" (Arendt again) that Spahr and her comrades at Commune Editions know very well—Joshua Clover's *Red Epic* (2015) is another such reckoning, as is Sean Bonney's *Our Death* (2019). Spahr's book is touching, endearing, winning, often thrilling—hardly the first adjectives one associates with revolutionary work: but perhaps they could be the qualities a revolutionized (non) revolution, a rethought utopia, could draw on and sponsor. Spahr makes one feel so.

∞

I have been discussing these books under the rubric of "the project" of poetry. I'd like to turn now, perhaps belatedly, to the governing term in this chapter's title—"choratopical." Sitting with these books and their complexities—of body, place, sound; *sôma, topos, phônê*—I began to consider this notion of a "choratope" as an analytic for poetic projects: and here I take wing from Mikhail Bakhtin's influential concept of "the chronotope," the space-time configuration of and in a literary work. One might think of "the chronotope" as the abstract a priori for any world-building—in a novel, a play, a movie, a video game. (Bakhtin wrote, for example, of "the castle" and "the road" as two important chronotopes; he also proposed such analytics as adventure-time, biographical-time, and so on, as differing historico-formal templates for fictional universes.[32])

In the term *choratope*, I am proposing something a bit different, a kind of echolocation, a sounding-out, that *poiesis* in particular is equipped to do. "Choratope," from the Greek *khôra*, denotes a location, place, or spot, and more specifically could specify that territory of the Greek *polis* outside the city proper; it conjures a clearing, receptacle, or site; it can also evoke one's country or nation. (Think of the extensive range of meanings of, say, "land" or "ground.") *Khôra* has a long and complicated philosophical career (from Plato through Heidegger to Derrida and Kristeva); it evokes as well the uterus, the feminine, a "matrix." Both related to and beyond the city, the "chora," for Julia Kristeva, is the underlining of symbolic order.[33] It specifies for her the domain of the semiotic, which pierces language in its bodily specificities: the cry, the laugh, the wail. The second component of "choratope"—

CHAPTER FIVE

topos—is Greek for "place," abbreviated from *tópos koinós*, "common place." The term is analogous to the Latin *locus* and conjures both a spatial location and a "commonplace" in rhetoric or literary art. *Chora/topos*: both components evoke, then, some dimension of "place," but with slightly different connotations—in what I hope might be a productive almost-redundancy: a *resonance*, a discrepant *reverberance*. Choratope: a sounding-out of place; poetry as sonar project, acoustic co-location, exploratory reverberance, whose resonances and dissonances and interferences are formed and reformed en route.

I came to the term "choratope" when thinking of the ritual (re)placing in Kapil, and of the potentially liberatory songs streaming through Boyer's and especially Spahr's work. Boyer writes some notably barbed lines about M.I.A. ("the anarchist pop star"), for example, and celebrates dance music: "My favorite arts are the ones that can move your body or make a new world" (18–19). For her part, Spahr captures a moment at a public assembly "as we all begin to call out I Love Michael Jackson one by one and then the sound guy puts on Smooth Criminal and everyone then rushes the stage, dancing hard" (67). Spahr's work is choratopic at the level of syntax as well as theme, "calling" and voicing the core tropes and iterative movements of her poetics.

For "chora" also connotes, in English, its close homonym "chorus." A strong preoccupation of all these books is the question of the collective, the group, the crowd—whether gathered in violence, in solidarity, in confusion, in labor, in dance, in consumption, in ebullience, in song, in Michael Jackson, in chants ("Hey hey ho ho"), in Occupy mic-checks, or in abstractions ("women," "Blacks," "citizens," "refugees"). Lyric is (in)famously the genre of solo, solitary voice. But a dialectical and historical conception of lyric (whether grounded in an awareness of ancient Greek choral lyric or in Adorno's and other Marxists' sense of modern lyric as social precisely in its apparent withdrawal from the social) impresses upon us the sociality of lyric: a sociality explored most impressively and recently by such poets and thinkers as Fred Moten and Claudia Rankine and Spahr herself.[34]

As in her previous *This Connection of Everyone with Lungs*, Spahr works in *That Winter* a subtle line between single and plural voicings, pivoting with ease between "I" and "we" as her subject. Important here: the medium of this collective movement, this oscillation between solo and collective voicing, is itself figured as poetry, a kind of collective rhyming, a choral speaking "together," a dispersed erotics "in which the we stood in for the beloved":

That winter we just rhymed and rhymed on. Together. Using words.
 Together. That winter everything suddenly written in our
 pentameters, our alexandrines, our heroic couplets, which was
 often an associational sentence-based quiet line, one indebted to
 lyric in which the we stood in for the beloved and yet there was
 almost never a description of this beloved, no listing of their red
 lips, their firm breasts, their smooth skin, leaving a sort of generic
 atmosphere.
I could tell you of the other things too.
A European influence.
A Middle Eastern influence.
              "Went Looking and Found Coyotes," 60

Spahr gives us a winter idyll, a provisional moment of communal *poiesis* itself aware of other transnational "influences."

CHAPTER FIVE

> The crowd in this moment. Complicated, but still joyous, transitory, momentary, experiencing this one moment of freedom before what we know is to come because we know history and we know the crowd will not win.
>
> ... We were with instead. But not just any old sort of with, but with each other in the hatred of capitalism. And if I was a poet of many centuries previous, I'd call that the sweetest wine of the beloved. ("It's All Good, It's All Fucked," 69)

Spahr can be bald—"hatred of capitalism" and so on. Then again, so could Blake and Shelley. She knows how hippy-dopey she can seem, and sound: "I was so classic, so clichéd those months" (67). Another word for cliché: commonplace (recall the *topos* in chora*tope*). This is a poetry dedicated to an emergent, precarious commons—of action, feeling, thought; of tradition as handing over, making it "together," hand in hand. As a poet Spahr is given to conceits so literal they threaten to collapse into bathos: lung-possessing creatures all breathing together, the ecstatic political moment as erotic, the poetic line become a line of protesters or geese or police, the expanding list as evocation of all creatures in the world. What is impressive is how often she brings this off, her incremental pulsing compositions emerging as patient end runs around cynicism, premature sophistication, been there done that. The combination of rigor and tenderness is notable, diagnostic.

Again, "choratope" specifies for me the sounding-out of place that these books undertake. And indeed, all these books—in good experimental fashion—offer a poetics as well as poems, a meditation on making as well as made things. Kapil orients us to the body in place, a body in one spot and then another spot, a body sometimes moving and sometimes still and stilled. This body, this imaged and created "Ban," is typically (Kapil tells us) an assemblage of disparate materials—not "matter out of place" (as anthropologist Mary Douglas famously defined "dirt") but "matter ritually placed," by Kapil, by her hands, her person, in her words.[35] Part of the force of *Ban* is its creation of a *Ban*-choratope: Hayes and Southhall, April 23, 1979; Uxbridge Road, London, 2012; Loveland, Colorado, 2012; South Delhi, India, 2014; "It is the last day. It is 1895. It is 1431. It is 1972. We have been married for five months." As Kapil writes, "A foreign body is a frequency" (62). Her work passionately receives and transmits and amplifies its frequencies into a reverberating space: *Ban*.

Spahr's work sounds out the question and location of voicing itself: solo/choral, local/global, national/transnational, human/nonhuman/transpecific. "It's All Good, It's All Fucked" stages the phrases of its title precisely as an inner refrain the poet chants to herself, uncertain and exhilarated, hopeful and despondent, as the charged season of "minor uprisings" gives way to disappointment. The poem tracks the transmutation of that titular refrain line into another possibility, that of "Non-Revolution"—which has "revolution as a possibility in their name but it is a modified and thus negated possibility so as to suggest they are possibly neither good nor fucked" (65).

The absolutism of the "It's All This or That" coexists with, and subtly turns toward, the horizon of what is merely, crucially, "possibly" just so. ("Verse" is, etymologically, a "turning.") Spahr thus floats her refrains on a vast ocean of revolutionary theory and specific historical experience, condensing complex ideological positions into song lines. For a while Spahr becomes one who "now goes around muttering fuck y'all," a refrain for this later moment of disappointment, resentment, blockage—which, movingly, a younger activist friend talks her through: *con-verse* (74). Again, what Spahr is doing here, it seems to me, is conducting a choratopic sounding-out of an experiential trajectory—how excitement modulates into sadness, hope toward despair, yet not quite: "I begin walking, determined, head down" (77).

Spahr's book begins with a meditation on song ("in this time song holds loss") and ends with a similar, pointed turn, as we modulate toward a layered, experienced sadness.

> I put on my earphones and click on the app that imitates the radio. A country song about abandonment is playing, about laying down on the bathroom floor, about wasting all those tears. The song is simple in its structure. Three chords, of course. Two four line stanzas and one half stanza . . . The song begins and ends with the singer crying on the bathroom floor but the song resolves it too. I'm through with all the crying the song states, even though the song gets all its power from being about the soft crying after being left standing on the street corner. I begin walking, determined, head down. ("It's All Good, It's All Fucked," 77)

To hear the clichéd crying, the patterns we all know, and to feel their power; to hear one kind of song and make another; to register how "the song resolves it" and to hold that yet move toward other resolutions; to transmute supposedly familiar songs into lyrical-critical materials; to feel out the difference between feelings and given forms; to abjure outworn songs for new patternings of solo and collective; to take song as prompt for thought and not only refrain; to be "through with crying" and embrace "determination" without abandoning the cry: here is a manifesto of and in form, not only in propositional content. Here the project of Spahr's book suspends itself. And in the pun in "determined," we get a rebooted Marxian horizon for *poiesis*, with the poet living in a social order perhaps "determined in the last instance" by the economic, or (more persuasively) co- or overdetermined in multiple ways, yet a poet also determined to move complicatedly into a co-made emerging present we call the future.

And what of this future, for poetries and projects? Let us return to the work with which I began, Dorothea Lasky's *Poetry Is Not a Project*. Lasky ends her chapbook thus: "There's a lot we have to do in this new century to make our world better and to make our world better for poets. Let's start first by valuing poems over projects." I can neither agree nor disagree with this—not least because Boyer, Kapil, and Spahr remind me of the force of Lasky's final claim: "Because poems, the way they are created and the way they exist, can, in a small way, remind the world of what's still possible."[36] As Spahr writes: "Sometimes it feels like it is over and it's not" (81). In negation, possibility. If Winter comes, can Spring be far behind? So Shelley asked, and the question remains open. What is required to sound out our shifting season, our moment? What forms, what materials, what choratopic sensors, antennae? How even to define "our moment"? The Anthropocene? Late capitalism? The drone era? Middle age? A gust of wind? A passing cloud? A slap, a kiss, shattering glass? Where are the songs of spring, of springs transforming? As Wallace Stevens might have said, these are the poems of our changing climate.

CHAPTER FIVE

Moonrise

The moon rose in the sky
as the moon rose in the poem
the new held in the lap of the old
and we talked about the weather
and imminent disaster forestalled
since we were together.

Comrades, I am with you
under this very full moon!
and we shall not yet set forth
but will talk about the shape
of things and thereby shape
this hour this day if not
this life –

                Are you depressed?
Does the reflection of bright objects
themselves reflecting brighter
objects' pulsing energies make you cry
your face toward the darkening sky?
Are you too always mooding
the air, sulfurous or snowcleaned,
windwashed, particulated
with microplastics?
I cannot see what I breathe
except when I freeze.
There's a streak on the lake
of a yellowy white you could drown
in for real. Please don't.

All you believers in total immersion
all you who hope yet to surface
I salute you, I on a far shore
but thinking of you as no wind
tears the bare branches away –

There's a stillness and another
        stillness.
There's a whiteness whitening
        the gray.
There's a fullness plain
        as day
in the dawning night,
        an impersonal rock
drawing the waves far away
        to their ebb.
You wanted real things
        food and trucks
and diapers and OK a moon a baby
        says goodnight to.
Good morrow! I haven't given up
        yet! we haven't!
The connectivity is good!
        Today every conversation
found an open channel.[37]

Acknowledgments

—*Was it for this . . . ?* (Wordsworth.)

A conditional poetics can't but be shaped by ambient conditions: so too *My Poetics*. This is in part a pandemic book, alas, though its origins long precede the advent of COVID, and I hope the book is not excessively deformed by the claustrophobia, constriction, and duress of recent years. Then again, perhaps it's not for me to gainsay deformation. *O the wind and rain.*

What mitigated the various forms of duress brought to you (or at least to me) by the twenty-first century was the ongoing good fortune of friendship and solidarity, with the living as well as the dead. And so, as to the where and with whom and for whom of reading, thinking, writing:

Colleagues and students at New York University, as well as lecture and seminar audiences at Heinrich-Heine-Universität Düsseldorf, Nottingham Trent University, Princeton University, Sorbonne

ACKNOWLEDGMENTS

Université, Stony Brook University, the Tin House Summer Workshop, the University of Cambridge, the University of Chicago, and the University of Edinburgh, engaged with this work as it developed; their responses and questions pointed me in new directions, sharpened my thinking, and sustained me en route.

At the University of Chicago Press, Alan Thomas expressed interest in this project when it was still inchoate. His support and trenchant comments helped to shape this book. So too the two anonymous readers for the Press offered acute, searching, and transformative readings: they know very well how indebted this book is to them, though they should be blamed for nothing, certainly not for my inability to metabolize all of their brilliant suggestions. Randy Petilos and the staff at the University of Chicago Press have guided me through the final stages of book production; Tamara Ghattas brought her acute eye to every page.

I am grateful to the editors of *Critical Inquiry*, the *Keats-Shelley Journal*, the *Los Angeles Review of Books*, and *Representations* for allowing me to adapt or reuse material that first appeared in their pages: a brief passage in chapter 1, revised, first appeared in "Meanwhile Romanticism / Romanticism Meanwhile," in the *Keats-Shelley Journal* 68 (2019): 142–46. An earlier version of chapter 2 appeared as "Compositionism: Plants, Poetics, Possibilities—or, Two Cheers for Fallacies, Especially Pathetic Ones!" in *Representations* 140, no. 1 (Fall 2017): 101–20. Chapter 3 first appeared in *Critical Inquiry* 50, no. 2 (Winter 2024), © The University of Chicago, all rights reserved. An early version of chapter four appeared as "Divagations on Rhyme: For Rhyme, Or Rhyme," in *On Rhyme*, ed. David Caplan (Presses Universi-

ACKNOWLEDGMENTS

taires de Liège, 2017), 46–78, and a few passages in that chapter also draw on "Hoobla-hoo and Hullabaloo: Divagations with Wallace Stevens," in *Wallace Stevens, Poetry, and France: Au pays de la métaphore*, ed. Juliette Utard, Bart Eeckout, and Lisa Goldfarb (Presses Universitaires d'Ecole Normale Supérieure [Éditions rue d'Ulm], 2018). And, finally, an earlier version of chapter 5 appeared as "Projects, Poetries, Choratopes: On Anne Boyer, Bhanu Kapil, and Juliana Spahr," in *Los Angeles Review of Books* (June 5, 2016). My thanks to these editors for their invitations and the opportunity to rehearse these ideas first in their publications.

Farrar, Straus and Giroux has long supported my work as a poet; I am grateful especially to Jonathan Galassi, who first saw *My Poets* for what it was and thereby helped to lay the groundwork for *My Poetics*.

Core peeps Hillary Chute, Lennie Hanson, Celeste Langan, Wendy Anne Lee, Anahid Nersessian, Crystal Parikh, Jini Kim Watson, and Clair Wills read and/or heard early versions of a number of these chapters: their comments, responses, and critical solidarity have been an ongoing beacon, refuge, and spur. My life is better for their friendship, and this book is too. Langdon Hammer and Erica McAlpine were crucial readers of this book and invaluable interlocutors; both pushed me to be clearer and yet welcomed the flying of freakish flags. Having offered extensive commentary, they tolerated late-breaking questions and were unfailingly generous and acute in their responses. They know how much I owe them: more anon. And a salute too to David Caplan, who generously read the entire manuscript and offered helpful comments, and especially to Catherine Barnett, another magnanimous and astute reader, whose responses allowed me to see this book afresh.

Other crucial interlocutors: Jeff Dolven and Brooke Holmes, who invited me to think about the secret life of plants; Penny Fielding, who invited me to Edinburgh and whose work and long-standing friendship is a gift; Anne-Lise François, ditto (except the part about Edinburgh); Lisa Goldfarb, who invited me years ago to think more about Wallace Stevens; Anna Henchman, who invited me back in the day to think about poetry and breakthroughs (and, always, cats); Elizabeth Metzger, who welcomed new writing on several contemporary poets; Rowan Ricardo Phillips, who asked me to think about contemporary poetry in a new key; Elisa Tamarkin, who invited me to think about the pathetic fallacy. Luminaries all. Deborah Nelson invited me to give the 2021 Frederick Ives Carpenter Lectures at the University of Chicago; I am grateful to her and to the English department for their lively hospitality and intellectual verve, and to Bill Brown, Suzanne Buffam, James Chandler, Frances Ferguson, and Srikanth Reddy.

Karen Russell and Tony Perez and Oscar and nearly-born Ada welcomed me to Portland, OR, and to the Tin House universe: karaoke forever! Claire Connolly welcomed me to University College Cork; Bart Eeckhout welcomed me to Bogliasco; Celeste Langan welcomed me to Berkeley and to NASSR; Peter Manning welcomed me to Stony Brook; Anahid Nersessian to LA and to the ACLA; Clair Wills to Princeton; Ross Wilson to the University of Cambridge on Zoom; Juliette Utard to the Sorbonne; and Nancy Yousef to the MLA on Zoom. Mary Favret and Deidre Lynch offered sage counsel at a crucial juncture.

ACKNOWLEDGMENTS

Stephanie Kelley came on as my research assistant just as this book was beginning to take shape: I am grateful for her help, acuity, and mojo. She knows where the bodies, or at least the footnotes, are buried.

Thinking and writing require time and material support. Fellowships at the Max-Planck-Institut für Wissenschaftsgeschichte (Berlin), the New York University Global Research Initiative, T. S. Eliot House and Foundation, and Yaddo supported the writing of this book. I am grateful to these institutions and the provisional communities and enduring friendships they sponsored. All thanks to Lorraine Daston for the invitation to Berlin, to Catherine Robson and Clair Wills for camaraderie in London, and to Claire Reihill for the invitations to T. S. Eliot House, including a miraculous response to a last-minute SOS.

I would never have persisted without the support and camaraderie of my colleagues at New York University, especially the chair of the English department, Elizabeth McHenry, and Dean Una Chaudhuri. Staff members Alyssa Leal and Jaysen Henderson-Greenbey offered invaluable logistical support throughout the writing of this book.

Over the past decade, students in my "Lyric Discontents," "Reading as a Writer," "Romanticisms/Modernisms/Now," and "Some Contemporary Poetries" seminars have been fellow voyagers and key companions on poetic seas: my poetics is indebted to theirs—especially to MC Hyland's, and to conversations with Alliya Dagman, Andrew Gorin, Luke McMullan, Bérengère Riou, Isaac Robertson, and Colin Vanderburg.

ACKNOWLEDGMENTS

And to others who asked or answered, my thanks: Matthew Bevis, Celia Brickman, Matthew Campbell, Michelle Chihara, Valerie Cotter, Gregory Cowles, Robyn Creswell, Ian Duncan, Angela Esterhammer, Neil Fraistat, Saskia Hamilton, Walt Hunter, Bruce King, Yoon Sun Lee, Marjorie Levinson, Anthony Madrid, Peter Manning, Paul Muldoon, Jonathan Mulrooney, Christopher Nealon, Joanne O'Leary, Ruth Perry, Katie Peterson, Rebecca Ariel Porte, Sonya Posmentier, Alice Quinn, Emily Rohrbach, Linda Diamond Shapiro, Mark Shapiro, Alice Spawls, Elizabeth Taylor, Lindsay Turner, and Gillian White.

My cat Biscuit kept me company throughout these years. *O the wind and rain.*

Also in memory: William Corbett, Saskia Hamilton, Susan Manning.

For Laura, who definitely "suffered what I wrote, or viler pain!" (Shelley), who yet helped me enjoy all there is to enjoy, Laura who keeps the questions open and for just long enough, Laura whose poetics are my poetics.

ACKNOWLEDGMENTS

envoi

the vanish
of the shore-

drift the last
rift unsutured

assured the cloud

knowing goes in
song in stars inscaped

        clouds gathering
           do I go
        with the gathering
          clouds or the sun
             seen an hour
                  ago

Notes

CHAPTER ONE

1. Hannah Arendt, *The Human Condition*, 2nd ed. (Chicago: University of Chicago Press, 2018), 5.
2. William Godwin, *Enquiry Concerning Political Justice and its Influence on Modern Morals and Happiness*, ed. Isaac Kramnick (New York: Penguin, 1985), 783.
3. Liane Carlson, "What Is Called Thinking in the Anthropocene?" *The Revealer*, August 9, 2019, https://therevealer.org/what-is-called-thinking-in-the-anthropocene/.
4. Margaret Ronda, "Mourning and Melancholia in the Anthropocene," *Post45*, June 10, 2013, https://post45.org/2013/06/mourning-and-melancholia-in-the-anthropocene/; also as chapter 4, "Mourning and Melancholia at the End of Nature," in *Remainders: American Poetry at Nature's End* (Stanford, CA: Stanford University Press, 2018), 91–112.
5. Dipesh Chakrabarty, "The Climate of History: Four Theses," *Critical Inquiry* 35, no. 2 (Winter 2009): 197.
6. Thomas Robert Malthus, *An Essay on the Principle of Population*, ed. Joyce E. Chaplin (New York: Norton, 2018), 151.
7. Shelley, "The Triumph of Life," line 545, in *The Complete Poetry of Percy Bysshe Shelley*, vol. 7, ed. Nora Crook (Baltimore: Johns Hopkins Press, 2021), 30.
8. See also the unpublished and uncollected work collected in Arendt, *Thinking without a Banister: Essays in Understanding, 1953–1975*, ed. Jerome Kohn (New York: Schocken, 2021).
9. See Fred Moten, "Refuge, Refuse, Refrain," in *The Universal Machine: Consent Not to Be a Single Being* (Durham, NC: Duke University Press, 2018), 92. Note too his critique of the "constant assertion of a supreme, and even supremacist, intelligence," the assertion thereof enmeshed in anti-Blackness. Of the

"belief in the supremacy of a certain mode of intelligence and the supremacy of anyone who could be said to carry it. Fuck that intelligence" (66). For a countermodel of thinking and care, powerfully sustained in and against the ongoing afterlife of slavery (one of the many senses of "the wake"), see Christina Sharpe: "I want to think 'the wake' as a problem of and for thought. I want to think 'care' as a problem for thought. I want to think care in the wake as a problem for thinking and of and for Black non/being in the world... thinking and care need to stay in the wake" (*In the Wake: On Blackness and Being* [Durham, NC: Duke University Press, 2016], 5).

10. Samuel Taylor Coleridge, "Dejection: An Ode," section VI, line 87, in *The Collected Works of Samuel Taylor Coleridge: Poetical Works I; Poems (Reading Text): Part 2*, ed. J. C. C. Mays (Princeton, NJ: Princeton University Press, 2001), 700.

11. Wordsworth, "Ode: Intimations of Immortality from Recollections of Early Childhood," lines 1–9, in *Poems, in Two Volumes, and Other Poems*, ed. Jared Curtis (Ithaca, NY: Cornell University Press, 1983), 271.

12. "The Marriage of Heaven and Hell," line 70, in *The Poems of William Blake*, ed. David V. Erdman, 3rd ed. (London: Longman, 2007), 111.

13. Lucy Ives, *The Hermit* (n.p.: Song Cave, 2016), no. 21.

14. See Reinhart Koselleck, *Futures Past: On the Semantics of Historical Time*, trans. Keith Tribe (New York: Columbia University Press, 2004); also *Radical Future Pasts: Untimely Political Theory*, ed. Romand Coles, Mark Reinhardt, and George Shulman (Lexington: University Press of Kentucky, 2014).

15. Jerome McGann, "Shelley's Poetry: The Judgment of the Future," in *The Romantic Ideology: A Critical Investigation* (Chicago: University of Chicago Press, 1983), 118–122.

16. Louis Althusser, *L'avenir dure longtemps; suivi de Les Faits*, ed. Olivier Corpet and Yann Moulier Boutang (Paris: Stock/IMC, 1992); published in English as *The Future Lasts Forever: A Memoir*, trans. Richard Veasey (New York: New Press, 1992).

17. *Archean to Anthropocene: The Past is the Key to the Future*, proceedings of the Geological Society of America Annual Meeting and Exposition, October 9–12, 2011, Minneapolis (Boulder, CO: Geological Society of America, 2011).

18. Arendt, *On Revolution* (New York: Viking, 1963).

19. Shelley, canto 9, stanza XXVII, lines 239–41, *Laon and Cyntha*, ed. Anahid Nersessian (Peterborough, ON: Broadview Editions, 2016), 186. Further quotations will be cited in text from this edition, by canto and stanza number.

20. Francis Fukuyama, "The End of History?" *National Interest* 16 (Summer 1989): 3–18.

21. "A Defence of Poetry," in *Shelley's Poetry and Prose: Authoritative Texts, Criticism*, 2nd ed., ed. Donald H. Reiman and Neil Fraistat (New York: Norton, 2002), 508.

22. Bruno Latour, "An Attempt at a 'Compositionist Manifesto,'" *New Literary History* 41, no. 3 (Summer 2010): 486. As Latour observes, "we are progressively discovering that, just at the time when people are despairing at realizing that they might, in the end, have 'no future,' we suddenly have many prospects."
23. Peter Frase, *Four Futures: Life after Capitalism* (London: Verso, 2016).
24. Lee Edelman, *No Future: Queer Theory and the Death Drive* (Durham, NC: Duke University Press, 2004).
25. For Jarcho's fuller engagement with Muñoz's "then and there" of queer futurity, see Julia Jarcho, *Writing and the Modern Stage*, "Introduction: Negative Theatrics," in *Writing and the Modern Stage: Theater beyond Drama* (Cambridge: Cambridge University Press, 2017), 3–22. Jarcho invoked Muñoz at a presentation at New York University in spring 2017, alluding to this passage: "The present is not enough. It is impoverished and toxic for queers and other people who do not feel the privilege of majoritarian belonging, normative tastes, and 'rational' expectations." José Esteban Muñoz, *Cruising Utopia: The Then and There of Queer Futurity*, 10th anniversary ed. (New York: New York University Press, 2019), 27.
26. Latour, "Compositionist Manifesto," 487.
27. Gertrude Stein, "Van or Twenty Years After: A Second Portrait of Carl Van Vechten," in *Gertrude Stein: Writings 1903–1932*, ed. Catharine R. Stimpson and Harriet Chessman (New York: Library of America, 1998), 504.
28. Weisman, *The World Without Us* (New York: St. Martin's, 2007); McKibben, *The End of Nature* (New York: Random House, 1989), 54.
29. Lisa Robertson, *The Weather* (Vancouver: New Star Books, 2001), 59.
30. This distinction borders on many contentious theoretical zones—from logic to theology to Marxist analytics to medical hermeneutics. "Determination" is itself a famously vexed category: see Raymond Williams's mordant anatomy of the term and its conceptual leverages in Williams, "Determine," in *Keywords: A Vocabulary of Culture and Society* (London: Routledge, 1976), 87–91. For a reanimation of "determination" via eighteenth-century medical hermeneutics, see Kevis Goodman, *Pathologies of Motion: Historical Thinking in Medicine, Aesthetics, and Poetics* (New Haven, CT: Yale University Press, 2022).
31. For weather as the register of prevailing conditions, see "Weather and Atmosphere," Fondriest Environmental Learning Center, April 14, 2014, https://www.fondriest.com/environmental-measurements/parameters/weather/: "Weather is made up of multiple parameters, including air temperature, atmospheric (barometric) pressure, humidity, precipitation, solar radiation and wind. Each of these factors can be measured to define typical weather patterns and to determine the quality of local atmospheric conditions." See too the *OED* on "weather" as atmospheric condition: "The condition of the atmosphere (at a given place and time) with respect to heat or cold, quantity of sunshine, presence or absence of rain, hail, snow, thunder, fog, etc., violence

or gentleness of the winds. Also, the condition of the atmosphere regarded as subject to vicissitudes" (*OED Online*, s.v. "weather (*n.*)," sense 1a, last modified September 2022, https://www.oed.com/).

32. John Durham Peters pointedly reminds us that "weather" is also an abstraction in modernity: see *The Marvelous Clouds: Toward a Philosophy of Elemental Media* (Chicago: University of Chicago Press, 2015), 252. Even more pointed is Christina Sharpe's gloss on weather and climate in *In the Wake*: "In my text, the weather is the totality of our environments; the weather is the total climate; and that climate is antiblack" (104). There is no way in which weather and climate are not deeply embedded in political economy as well as in abstracting rhetorics—as my later, albeit brief, discussion of wind, breathing, and precarity suggests.

33. "NASA—What's the Difference between Weather and Climate?," rev. August 7, 2017, https://www.nasa.gov/mission_pages/noaa-n/climate/climate_weather.html.

34. *OED Online*, s.v. "instrument (*n.*)," senses 1a–c, last modified December 2022, https://www.oed.com/.

35. Dipesh Chakrabarty, *The Climate of History in a Planetary Age* (Chicago: University of Chicago Press, 2021), 21.

36. Arendt offers this caution: "The conditions of human existence—life itself, natality and mortality, worldliness, plurality, and the earth—can never 'explain' what we are or answer the question of who we are for the simple reason that they never condition us absolutely." See too her rejection of the notion of a human "nature" or "essence": "Nothing entitles us to assume that man has a nature or essence in the same sense as other things." Arendt, *Human Condition*, 10–11.

37. John Durham Peters, *Marvelous Clouds*, 51.

38. In *Pathologies of Motion*, Kevis Goodman invokes biologists Richard Levin's and Richard Lewontin's notion of "codetermination" to bring home the complexities of eighteenth-century medical hermeneutics: see Levin and Lewontin, *The Dialectical Biologist* (Cambridge, MA: Harvard University Press, 1985).

39. Karl Marx, "The 18th Brumaire of Louis Bonaparte (1852)," chap. 1, para 2, http://www.marxists.org/archive/marx/works/1852/18th-brumaire/ch01.htm.

40. Arendt, *Human Condition*, 169.

41. Arendt, *Human Condition*, 170.

42. "Hymn to Intellectual Beauty" (*Examiner* Version—1817), stanza 1, lines 1–12, in *The Complete Poetry of Percy Bysshe Shelley*, vol. 3, ed. Neil Fraistat and Nora Crook (Baltimore: Johns Hopkins University Press, 2012), 3:73. Further quotations from this poem will be cited in text by stanza and line.

43. I nod here to Geoffrey Hartman's powerful and influential readings, particularly in *Wordsworth's Poetry: 1787–1814* (New Haven, CT: Yale University Press, 1964) and in his 1968 essay on Marvell, "'The Nymph Complaining for

the Death of Her Faun': A Brief Allegory," *Essays in Criticism* 18, no. 2 (April 1968): 113–35. See too Anne-Lise François's revisiting of Hartman's reading under the sign of climate change, in "'A Little While' More: Further Thoughts on Hartman's Nature as Paraclete," *Essays in Romanticism* 22, no. 2 (2015): 133–149.

44. Susan Stewart offers a characteristically magisterial reading of this poem in chap. 4 of *The Poet's Freedom: A Notebook on Making* (Chicago: University of Chicago Press, 2011), 85–110. Stewart notes that while "Shelley used the term 'Intellectual Beauty' in his own translation of Plato's *Symposium*, here his use of the phrase evidently came from the influence of Plotinus's *Enneads* upon his summer 1816 reading" (100).

45. Here and in the next paragraph I allude to Eve Kosofsky Sedgwick's celebrated essay "Paranoid Reading and Reparative Reading, or, You're So Paranoid You Probably Think This Essay Is about You," in *Touching Feeling: Affect, Pedagogy, Performativity* (Durham, NC: Duke University Press, 2003), 123–51.

46. Celeste Langan acutely suggests that such *copia* may be aligned with an overproduction endemic to capital (private communication). Yohei Igarashi has recently argued that such Shelleyan profusions are critical of, and not merely complicit with, such overproduction. See Igarashi, "The Calculating Principle: Indexing Shelley," presented over Zoom at *1820: Aesthetics, Politics, and the Legacies of Romanticism: A K-SAA Curran Symposium*, Harvard University, October 29, 2021. For a dazzling anatomy of "accumulation" as a logic of dispossession, and of romantic-era figuration as a core archive for thinking this through, see Lenora Hanson, *The Romantic Rhetoric of Accumulation* (Stanford, CA: Stanford University Press, 2022).

47. Regarding "music by the night wind sent / Thro' strings of some still instrument": this Aeolian relay would seem susceptible to an Aristotelian analytic in its coordination of efficient, material, final, and formal causes. It is *music*, the final cause, the apparent telos of this embedded simile, that is sent *by* the night wind (efficient cause) *through* strings (material cause) *of* some still instrument (formal cause: instrument as blueprint, design). Yet the recursivity of this action, as well as of Shelley's broader tropologics, defies any neat Aristotelian partitioning of causes and stable telos.

48. This passage resonates with the famous questions and impasse in Wordsworth's "Immortality" ode (in many ways the template for Shelley's hymn): "Whither is fled the visionary gleam? / Where is it now, the glory and the dream?" Wordsworth, "Ode: Intimations of Immortality," lines 56–57, in *Poems, in Two Volumes*, 272.

49. Shelley, "The Triumph of Life," line 544, in *The Complete Poetry of Percy Bysshe Shelley*, vol. 7, ed. Nora Crook (Baltimore: Johns Hopkins University Press, 2021), 30.

50. In the *Scrope Davies Notebook*, the names that sages and poets give to their longed-for addressees include "God & Ghosts & Heaven." See Shelley, *The*

Scrope Davies Notebook, summer 1816, British Library, Loan MS. 70 8, fol. 2v, digitized at the Shelley-Godwin Archive, http://shelleygodwinarchive.org/sc/bl/loan_ms_70_08/#/p4. Shelley altered this triad in the published version, the addressees there specified as "Demon, Ghost, and Heaven." For "obstinate questionings," see Wordsworth's "Ode: Intimations of Immortality," line 144, in *Poems, in Two Volumes*, 275.

51. See Fredric Jameson on "the great Althusserian (and Lacanian) redefinition of ideology as 'the representation of the subject's *Imaginary* relationship to his or her *Real* conditions of existence.'" *Postmodernism: Or, The Cultural Logic of Late Capitalism* (Durham, NC: Duke University Press, 1991), 51. See too Althusser's central chapter "Ideology and Ideological State Apparatuses," from the section "Ideology is a 'Representation' of the Imaginary Relationship of Individuals to Their Real Conditions of Existence," in *Lenin and Philosophy* (New York: Monthly Review Press, 1971), 109–15.
52. See the *Post45* series edited by Margaret Ronda and Lindsay Turney, "Poetry's Social Forms," April 22–26, 2019, https://post45.org/sections/contemporaries-essays/poetry-social-forms/. Samuel Delany terms this quality of speculative writing "subjunctivity," as it explores what has "not happened yet," what "might happen," and other permutations of potentiality and counterfactual conjecture. Delany, "About 5,750 Words," originally presented at the December 1968 meeting of the MLA Seminar in New York City, first published in *Extrapolation* 10 (May 1970), 52–66; reprinted in *The Jewel-Hinged Jaw: Notes on the Language of Science Fiction* (Middletown, CT: Wesleyan University Press, 2009), 11–13.
53. For an incisive consideration of the philosophical implications of this mode, see Nelson Goodman, "The Problem of Counterfactual Conditionals," *Journal of Philosophy* 44, no. 5 (February 1947): 113–28.
54. Shelley, "Ode to the West Wind," lines 69–70, in *Shelley's Poetry and Prose*, 301.
55. Anne Boyer, *Garments against Women* (Boise: Ahsahta, 2015), 20.
56. Jacques Rancière, "Ten Theses on Politics," in *Dissensus: On Politics and Aesthetics*, ed. and trans. Steven Corcoran (New York: Continuum, 2010), 37. Italics in original.
57. See Shelley, *The Scrope Davies Notebook*, http://shelleygodwinarchive.org/sc/bl/loan_ms_70_08/#/p3, and compare to Shelley's phrasing in *Prometheus Unbound* in the infernal pedagogy and catechism of Demogorgon and Asia, II.4. In Asia's hymn (act II, scene v), she envisions a paradise "peopled by shapes too bright to see"; in act IV, Panthea unfurls a vision of multiple involved spheres and orbs, "peopled with unimaginable shapes." Unimaginable: precisely!
58. *Shelley's "Prometheus Unbound": A Variorum Edition*, ed. Lawrence John Zillman (Seattle: University of Washington Press, 1959), 272.
59. For more on Percy Shelley's critique of Malthusian discourses on population,

and on Mary Shelley, *Frankenstein*, Malthus, and "peopling," see Maureen N. McLane, *Romanticism and the Human Sciences: Poetry, Population, and the Discourse of the Species* (Cambridge: Cambridge University Press, 2000), particularly chaps. 1 and 5.

60. Here I should note that Moten's "sociality" is not at all equivalent to Arendt's "plurality" and indeed rejects its assumptions—plurality presupposing "the individual" and a logic of possessive individuality. Moten argues in *The Universal Machine* "for the necessity of a social (meta)physics that violates individuation" (xii). More broadly, Moten is highly critical of Arendt's conception of the political (imagined against, and cordoned off from, the social): his "ante- and antipolitical" sociality—which is decidedly not "prepolitical" (79)—rejects both her terms and her partitions, including of "private" from "public" (100). See Moten, "Refuge, Refuse, Refrain," in *Universal Machine*.

61. For an intriguing reading of "the multiverse" as itself an expression of population anxiety—the "anxiety of [and about] the explosion of subjects under decolonisation and globalization"—see Fredric Jameson, "In Hyperspace," *London Review of Books* 37, no. 17 (September 2015), https://www.lrb.co.uk/the-paper/v37/n17/fredric-jameson/in-hyperspace.

62. Ariana Reines, "The World Is Not Enough," lines 1–2, *Artforum International*, January 10, 2020, https://www.artforum.com/slant/ariana-reines-s-full-moon-report-81838.

63. Reines, "The World Is Not Enough," lines 7–17.

64. Shelley, "Ode to the West Wind," lines 61–62, in *Shelley's Poetry and Prose*, 300.

65. Stevens, "A Clear Day and No Memories," lines 7–9, in *Collected Poetry & Prose*, ed. Frank Kermode and Joan Richardson (New York: Library of America, 1997), 475.

66. "Your head so much concerned with outer, / Mine with inner, weather." Robert Frost, "Tree at My Window," lines 15–16, in *Collected Poems, Prose, & Plays*, ed. Richard Poirier and Mark Richardson (New York: Library of America, 1995), 231. Amidst a vast bibliography, see M. H. Abrams's landmark essay "The Correspondent Breeze: A Romantic Metaphor," in *English Romantic Poets: Modern Essays in Criticism* (New York: Oxford University Press, 1960), 37–54, in which the complex of breath, air, and wind becomes a historically specific matrix for romantic *poiesis*. For this legacy in twentieth-century poetry, see Michael O'Neill's rich study *The All-Sustaining Air: Romantic Legacies and Renewals in British, American, and Irish Poetry Since 1900* (Oxford: Oxford University Press, 2007). This romantic-period naturalization of divine inspiration has a long prehistory and wide extension, as Abrams observed; and it has more recent critical and poetic vitalities—whether we look to the program of the line-as-breath in Charles Olson's "Projective Verse" or to Allen Ginsberg's poetics or to Allen Grossman's theory of poetry as composed on the "dead breath" or to Juliana Spahr's ecopoetics in *This Connection of Everyone with*

Lungs (Berkeley: University of California Press, 2006). For Grossman's theory of the second, poetically central "Lesser, or Dead, or Speech Breath" of exhalation (vs. inhalation), see Allen Grossman, Commonplace 29, "Scholium on line and breath," "Summa Lyrica: A Primer of the Commonplaces of Speculative Poetics," in *The Sighted Singer: Two Works on Poetry for Readers and Writers*, with Mark Halliday (Baltimore: Johns Hopkins University Press, 1991), 279.

67. See, for example (to invoke very divergent projects), John Durham Peters, *Marvelous Clouds*, and Julius S. Scott, *The Common Wind: Afro-American Currents in the Age of the Haitian Revolution* (London: Verso, 2018).

68. Regarding the biopolitics of breath: among the most significant recent reflections on "breathing while Black" is Christina Sharpe's in *In the Wake*. As she notes, "there is, too, a connection between the lungs and the weather: the supposedly transformative properties of breathing free air—that which throws off the mantle of slavery—and the transformative properties of being 'free' to breathe fresh air. These discourses run through freedom narratives habitually. But who has access to freedom? Who can breathe free?" (112). For further trenchant analyses related to poetics, see, e.g., Nathaniel Mackey on a "radical pneumatics of black poetics," and Jennifer Scappettone's essay "Precarity Shared: Breathing as Tactic in Air's Uneven Commons," in *Poetics and Precarity: The University at Buffalo Robert Creeley Lectures in Poetry and Poetics*, ed. Myuang Mi Kim and Cristanne Miller (Albany: State University of New York Press, 2018), 1–30, 41–58. See too Lindsay Turner's review of this volume in *ASAP Journal*, February 14, 2019, http://asapjournal.com/poetics-and-precarity-lindsay-turner/.

69. "The Twa Sisters," often known since Child's work as "Child No.10," appeared in numerous antiquarian ballad collections, from the eighteenth century onward, including Walter Scott's *Minstrelsy of the Scottish Border* and Francis James Child's later monumental compendium *The English and Scottish Popular Ballads*, 5 vols. (Boston: Houghton, Mifflin, 1882–98). "The Cruel Sister," in Walter Scott, *Minstrelsy of the Scottish Border*, 2 vols (London: James Ballantyne, 1802), 2:143–150; "The Twa Sisters," in *The English and Scottish Popular Ballads*, pt. 1, ed. Francis James Child (Boston: Houghton, Mifflin, 1882), 1:118–141.

70. See David Atkinson, "Magical Corpses: Ballads, Intertextuality, and the Discovery of Murder," *Journal of Folklore Research* 36, no. 1 (January 1999): 5.

71. See *The English and Scottish Popular Ballads*, pt. 1, 1:127. See also Lesley Nelson, "Variants for Child Ballad #10, The Twa Sisters: Version B," *The Contemplator*, n.d., http://www.contemplator.com/child/variant10.html#B.

72. See Bertrand Harris Bronson, "The Two Sisters (Child No. 10)," in *The Traditional Tunes of the Child Ballads*, vol. 1 (Princeton, NJ: Princeton University Press, 2015), 143–84. Bronson documents ninety-seven tune variants of this ballad.

73. Child, *The English and Scottish Popular Ballads*, 1:128.

74. See too "Child Version J," "from the north of Ireland," with its similarly self-playing harp: "He set it down upon a stone, / And it began to play its lone." If "program music" is, as Wikipedia says, "a type of instrumental art music that attempts to render an extra-musical narrative musically," we have here a kind of recursive ballad logic for program[med] music, whereby what first seems "extra-musical narrative" repeatedly becomes determinatively, musically rendered. Program music is typically understood to be instrumental, not vocal, music. See *Wikipedia*, s.v. "program music," https://en.wikipedia.org/w/index.php?title=Program_music&oldid=1090635164. See too *Encyclopedia Britannica* on program music as "instrumental music that carries some extramusical meaning, some 'program' of literary idea, legend, scenic description, or personal drama"; program music is typically defined against so-called "absolute music." *Encyclopedia Britannica*, s.v. "program music," last modified January 31, 2014, https://www.britannica.com/art/program-music.

75. Among those who have performed or recorded this version are Jerry Garcia, Peggy Seeger, Gillian Welch, and the Irish band Altan: Jerry Garcia, vocalist, "Oh, the Wind and Rain," recorded live April 26, 1988, track 8 on Jerry Garcia Acoustic Band, *Almost Acoustic,* released December 6, 1988, Grateful Dead Records; Peggy Seeger, vocalist, "O the Wind and Rain," track 11 on *Bring Me Home*, released January 22, 2008, Appleseed; Altan, "The Wind and Rain," track 11 on *Local Ground*, released January 1, 2005, Compass Records.

76. See Celeste Langan, "Repetition Run Riot: Refrains, Slogans, and Graffiti," *Wordsworth Circle* 52, no. 2 (Spring 2021): 287–307, 288. Invoking Marx, Langan "links an examination of phrasal repetition to historical repetition" (288). As she observes, "the refrain opens the question of what is not repetition" (289). For John Hollander's classic essay, see "Breaking into Song: Some Notes on Refrain," in *Lyric Poetry: Beyond New Criticism*, ed. Chaviva Hošek and Patricia Parker (Ithaca, NY: Cornell University Press, 1985), 73–89.

77. See Peters, *Marvelous Clouds*, 167: "Sea and sky, 'the extraterrestrial commons,' are the twin sublimities that ring the human estate."

78. See Thomas Percy's version, "Sir Patrick Spence: A Scottish Ballad," in his *Reliques of Ancient English Poetry* (London: J. Dodsley, 1765), 71–73; or a slightly different and longer version, "Sir Patrick Spens," Scottish Poetry Library, https://www.scottishpoetrylibrary.org.uk/poem/sir-patrick-spens/.

79. Consider Jerry Garcia's refrain, "Oh the wind and rain"; vs. "oh, the wind and rain" registered by the Traditional Music Library, http://www.traditionalmusic.co.uk/folk-song-lyrics/Oh_the_Wind_and_Rain(The_Two_Sisters).htm; vs. Peggy Seeger's "O, the wind and rain," on her album *Bring Me Home* (the title intriguingly appears there both with and without the comma).

80. Wordsworth, "Song," lines 11–12, in *Lyrical Ballads, and Other Poems, 1797–1800*, ed. James Butler and Karen Green (Ithaca, NY: Cornell University Press, 1992), 163.

81. As set out in Hollander, "Breaking into Song," 34, and more recently in Langan, "Repetition Run Riot," 290.
82. Coleridge, "Dejection: An Ode," section I, line 14, in *Poetical Works*, 1:698.
83. I owe this formulation to Celeste Langan.
84. *OED Online*, s.v. "instrument (*n*.)," senses 1a–c, last modified December 2022, https://www.oed.com/.
85. Louis Althusser, "The Underground Current of the Materialism of the Encounter," in *Philosophy of the Encounter: Later Writings, 1978–1987*, ed. François Matheron and Oliver Corpet, trans. G. M. Goshgarian (London: Verso, 2006), 197.
86. Althusser, "Underground Current," in *Philosophy of the Encounter*, 170–171.
87. Langan, "Repetition Run Riot," 301.
88. Althusser, "Underground Current," in *Philosophy of the Encounter*, 174.
89. Althusser, 176.
90. Reines, "The World Is Not Enough," lines 56–67.
91. Reines's apparently imperative mode—"you have to be the sound of the world"—partakes of the *modus irrealis* we have seen before: and perhaps we might see this turn not as a simple imperative but as shading toward other irrealis moods: the hortatory (*you have to be* exhorted, implored, insisted, encouraged), or the jussive (*you have to be* pleaded, implored, or asked), or even toward the irrealis mood shared by Armenian and Turkish, the *necessitative* (*you have to be* is necessary, or it is both desired and encouraged: a combination of the hortative and jussive).
92. Wordsworth, *The Thirteen-Book Prelude*, vo. 1, ed. Mark L. Reed (Ithaca, NY: Cornell University Press, 1991), 287.
93. Christopher Nealon, "Last Glimpse," in *The Shore* (Seattle: Wave Books, 2020), 75.
94. Nealon, *The Shore*, 75.
95. Maureen N. McLane, from "Saratoga August," in *World Enough* (New York: Farrar, Straus & Giroux, 2011), 46–47.
96. McLane, "Preferences," in *What You Want* (New York: Farrar, Straus & Giroux, 2023), 15–16.
97. McLane, "They Were Always Thinking," in *World Enough*, 4.

CHAPTER TWO

1. Latour, "An Attempt at a 'Compositionist Manifesto,'" *New Literary History* 41, no. 3 (Summer 2010), 474, 487. Latour here proposes "compositionism" as an "alternative to critique": see his previous "Why Has Critique Run Out of Steam? From Matters of Fact to Matters of Concern," *Critical Inquiry* 30, no. 2 (2004): 225–48. I remain agnostic as to whether critique has "run out of steam."
2. Latour, "Compositionist Manifesto," 489n25.

3. Marjorie Levinson, *Thinking through Poetry: Field Reports on Romantic Lyric* (Oxford: Oxford University Press, 2018), 171.
4. Susan Manning, *The Poetics of Character: Transatlantic Encounters, 1700–1900* (Cambridge: Cambridge University Press, 2013), 96.
5. Latour, "Compositionist Manifesto," 476.
6. See Timothy Morton, *The Ecological Thought* (Cambridge, MA: Harvard University Press, 2010); Jane Bennett, *Vibrant Matter: A Political Ecology of Things* (Durham, NC: Duke University Press, 2010); Margaret Ronda, *Remainders: American Poetry at Nature's End* (Stanford, CA: Stanford University Press, 2018); Anahid Nersessian, *The Calamity Form: On Poetry and Social Life* (Chicago: University of Chicago Press, 2020); Ada Smailbegović, *The Poetics of Liveliness: Molecules, Fibers, Tissues, Clouds* (New York: Columbia University Press, 2021); Levinson, *Thinking through Poetry*. This is a heterogeneous and incomplete listing which risks obscuring quite different commitments. It is worth noting, for example, that while Ronda draws on Latour, Nersessian invokes him primarily to set him aside, not least for his hostility to Marx.
7. Percy Bysshe Shelley, "The Triumph of Life," lines 182 and 204, in *Shelley's Poetry and Prose*, ed. Donald H. Reiman and Neil Fraistat, 2nd ed. (New York: Norton, 2002), 489; John Ruskin, "Of the Pathetic Fallacy," in *Modern Painters*, 3rd ed. (London: Smith, Elder and Co, 1872), 157–58.
8. Eleanor Ainge Roy, "New Zealand River Granted Same Legal Rights as Human Being," *The Guardian*, March 16, 2017, https://www.theguardian.com/world/2017/mar/16/new-zealand-river-granted-same-legal-rights-as-human-being. See also Te Awa Tupua (Whanganui River Claims Settlement) Act (2017 no. 7), https://www.legislation.govt.nz/act/public/2017/0007/latest/DLM6830851.html.
9. Michael Marder, *Plant-Thinking: A Philosophy of Vegetal Life* (New York: Columbia University Press, 2013), 10.
10. On the burgeoning (scholarly and popular) literature—dare one say a cornucopia—on whether plants think (which unsurprisingly requires an inquiry into "thinking") and how they communicate, see, e.g., Michael Pollan, "The Intelligent Plant," *New Yorker* 89, no. 42 (December 23/30, 2013): 92–117; Richard Mabey, *The Cabaret of Plants: Forty Thousand Years of Plant Life and the Human Imagination* (New York: Norton, 2016), which argues for "a new language" with which to accommodate the "selfhood" of plants; Peter Wohlleben, *The Hidden Life of Trees: What They Feel, How They Communicate—Discoveries from a Secret World* (Vancouver: Greystone, 2016); David Chamovitz, *What a Plant Knows: A Field Guide to the Senses* (New York: Scientific American/Farrar, Straus & Giroux, 2012); Michael Marder, *Plant-Thinking: A Philosophy of Vegetal Life* (New York: Columbia University Press, 2013); Ferris Jabr, "The Social Life of Forests," *New York Times Magazine*, December 20, 2020, https://www.nytimes.com/interactive/2020/12

/02/magazine/tree-communication-mycorrhiza.html, which highlights the work of Canadian ecologist Suzanne Simard; and Suzanne Simard's own *Finding the Mother Tree: Discovering the Wisdom of the Forest* (New York: Knopf, 2021).

11. Gilles Deleuze and Félix Guattari, "Introduction: Rhizome," in *A Thousand Plateaus: Capitalism and Schizophrenia*, trans. Brian Massumi (Minneapolis: University of Minnesota Press, 1987), 11.

12. For another route into "roots," see Tristram Wolff's ramifying inquiry into etymological thought, method, and poetics: Wolff, *Against the Uprooted Word: Giving Language Time in Transatlantic Romanticism* (Stanford, CA: Stanford University Press, 2022).

13. Louise Glück, "The Red Poppy," lines 12–20, in *The Wild Iris* (Hopewell, NJ: Ecco, 1993), 29.

14. Paul de Man, "Anthropomorphism and Trope in Lyric," in *The Rhetoric of Romanticism* (New York: Columbia University Press, 1986), 255.

15. Maureen N. McLane, "OK Fern," in *This Blue* (New York: Farrar, Straus & Giroux, 2014), 8.

16. See Sidney Burris, "Pathetic Fallacy," in *The Princeton Encyclopedia of Poetry and Poetics*, 4th ed., ed. Roland Greene, Stephen Cushman, Clare Cavanagh, Jahan Ramazani, and Paul Rouzer (Princeton, NJ: Princeton University Press, 2012), 1009–10.

17. "What are the implications for the charge of anthropocentrism leveled at thinkers grappling with the diverse forms of agency that make up nature or for poets who attribute thought and feeling to aspects of the physical world? If we are willing to grant that the human side of things is just as constitutionally heterogeneous as most of us are now willing to allow nature (as in, always already culture), then labeling the agential view of nature as subjectivist makes no sense." Levinson, "Of Being Numerous," in *Thinking through Poetry*, 190.

18. Latour, "Compositionist Manifesto," 483.

19. See especially Virginia Jackson's work on "lyric" as an effect of reading (to wit: "lyricization"), and on the historical construction of "lyric" (and the critical suppression or elision of other historical-poetic modes, practices, and horizons), in, e.g., *Dickinson's Misery: A Theory of Lyric Reading* (Princeton, NJ: Princeton University Press, 2005); and see also Jackson and Yopie Prins, eds., *The Lyric Theory Reader: A Critical Anthology* (Baltimore: Johns Hopkins University Press, 2014).

20. For a fuller meditation on ballad *poiesis* as simultaneously a historical, transhistorical, and transmedial phenomenon, see my *Balladeering, Minstrelsy, and the Making of British Romantic Poetry* (Cambridge: Cambridge University Press, 2008). In late eighteenth-century balladeering and in romantic-era *poiesis*, we find poets and poetries increasingly alert to, as well as conditioned by, their complex historicity and mediality.

21. Thomas Ravenscroft, *Melismata: Musicall Phansies. Fitting the Court, Citie,*

and *Countrey Humours. To 3, 4, and 5. Voyces* (London: Printed by William Stansby for Thomas Adams, 1611), 20–21.

22. See Francis James Child, ed., "26. The Three Ravens," in *The English and Scottish Popular Ballads*, 5 vols (Boston: Houghton, Mifflin, 1884), 1:253–254.
23. For these several versions and sources, see Maureen N. McLane, "Child No. 26 and *Poiesis* Unbound," in *Child's Children: Ballad Study and Its Legacies*, ed. Joseph C. Harris and Barbara Hillers (Trier: Wissenschaftlicher Verlag Trier, 2012), 140–54.
24. Child, *English and Scottish Ballads*, 1:254.
25. William Wordsworth, "Ode: Intimations of Immortality from Recollections of Early Childhood," lines 51–57, in *Poems, in Two Volumes, and Other Poems*, ed. Jared Curtis (Ithaca, NY: Cornell University Press, 1983), 272.
26. See, e.g., Marjorie Levinson's landmark reading of the ode in her *Wordsworth's Great Period Poems: Four Essays* (Cambridge: Cambridge University Press, 1986), 80–100.
27. I am indebted to Anahid Nersessian for this formulation.
28. Child, *English and Scottish Ballads*, 1:254; emphasis added.
29. Child, *English and Scottish Ballads*, 1:254.
30. *OED Online*, "down (*adv.*)," last modified December 2022, https://www.oed.com/.
31. Wallace Stevens, "Sunday Morning," in *Collected Poetry & Prose*, ed. Frank Kermode and Joan Richardson (New York: Library of America, 1997), 56.
32. "It is, however, in English only that the word has given rise to an adverb and a preposition." *OED2*, s.v. "down (n^1)," published 1989, https://www.oed.com/oed2/00069237/. Note the mordant sense 26 of "down (*adv.*)": "Used in ballad refrains, without appreciable meaning." *OED2*, "down (*adv.*)," published 1989, https://www.oed.com/oed2/00069241.
33. *OED Online*, "down (n^3)," last modified December 2018, https://www.oed.com/.
34. Latour, "Compositionist Manifesto," 476.
35. Samuel Pepys, January 2, 1666, in *The Diary of Samuel Pepys*, vol. 7, *1666*, ed. Robert Latham and William Matthews (Berkeley: University of California Press, 1972), 1. See Child (inter alia) for Pepys's diary entry: "84. Bonny Barbara Allan," in *English and Scottish Ballads*, ed. Child, 2:276–78. Further quotations from this ballad will be cited from myself (in good native-informant balladeering fashion), drawing on Child; North American versions recorded by (among others) Bob Dylan and Joan Baez; and Charles Seeger, ed., "Versions and Variants of the Tunes of 'Barbara Allen,'" *Selected Reports of the Institute of Ethnomusicology* 1, no. 1 (1966): 120–167.
36. See Walter Scott, *The Poetical Works of Walter Scott, Bart.*, 12 vols (Edinburgh: Robert Cadell, 1830–1833). On North American versions invoking the young man as "Sweet William," see Ed Cray, "Comment on the Words," quoted in Seeger, "Versions and Variants," 164.

37. For "Martinmas" vs. springtime / May versions (the former considered older), see Seeger, "Versions and Variants"; see too the variants in Child. And see both as well for the various localizations in "Reading Town," "London Town," and "Scarlet Town"; and see Cray (cited in Seeger) for the "corrective" of print on oral tradition. Seeger, "Versions and Variants," 164.
38. See Gerry Webster and Brian Goodwin, *Form and Transformation: Generative and Relational Principles in Biology* (Cambridge: Cambridge University Press, 1996) — whose work I first encountered in Levinson, "Of Being Numerous," in *Thinking through Poetry*, 187n85, 189.
39. For other poeticritical compostings, see Jed Rasula, *This Compost: Ecological Imperatives in American Poetry* (Athens: University of Georgia Press, 2002): a book titled after a poem by Whitman — further evidence that compositionism / composting has long been "in the air" of poetics.
40. Barbara Johnson, "Anthropomorphism in Lyric and Law," in *Persons and Things* (Cambridge, MA: Harvard University Press, 2008), 206.
41. Alain Badiou, *Being and Event*, trans. Oliver Feltham (London: Continuum, 2006), 59.
42. Levinson, "Notes and Queries on Names and Numbers," *Thinking through Poetry*, 205.
43. Deleuze and Guattari, *A Thousand Plateaus*, 11.
44. Deleuze and Guattari, 25.
45. Latour, "Compositionist Manifesto," 489n25.
46. Ruskin, *Modern Painters*, 165–66.
47. For the fullest elaboration of his argument, see Jonathan Culler, *Theory of the Lyric* (Cambridge, MA: Harvard University Press, 2015).
48. Burris, "Pathetic Fallacy," in *Princeton Encyclopedia of Poetry and Poetics*, ed. Greene et al., 1010.
49. Johnson, *Persons and Things*, 206–7.
50. See Barbara Johnson, chap. 1, "Toys R Us: Legal Persons, Personal Pronouns, Definitions," in *Persons and Things*, 3–23: "Personification and anthropomorphism have an important thing in common: they are figures of being, not address. What matters in them is their predicates, not their voices. Instead of the phenomenalization of human speech, they endow the world with meaning centered around the representation of human being" (18).
51. de Man, *The Rhetoric of Romanticism*, 241.
52. Latour, "Compositionist Manifesto," 487.
53. Gertrude Stein, "In the Grass (On Spain)" (1913), in *Gertrude Stein: Writings 1903–32* (New York: Library of America, 1998), 381.
54. *OED Online*, "nigh (*v.*)" and "nigh (*adv., prep., adj., n.*)," last modified December 2022, https://www.oed.com/.
55. Adapted from Child, *English and Scottish Ballads*, 1:254, to reflect the weave in performance of verse and refrain.
56. Gertrude Stein, *Writings 1903–32*, 374.

57. Latour, "Compositionist Manifesto," 476.
58. Child, *Popular English and Scottish Ballads*, 1:253.
59. Maureen N. McLane, "Haunt," in *World Enough* (New York: Farrar, Straus & Giroux, 2011), 33–34.
60. McLane, "Crows," in *What You Want* (New York: Farrar, Straus & Giroux, 2023), 68–69.
61. McLane, "Weeds," in *What You Want*, 81–82.
62. McLane, "Trees," in *What You Want*, 61–62.
63. McLane, "Taking a Walk in the Woods after Having Taken a Walk in the Woods with You," in *Some Say* (New York: Farrar, Straus & Giroux, 2016), 16.

CHAPTER THREE

1. Lauren Berlant, "Starved," *South Atlantic Quarterly* 103, no. 3 (2007): 433; see too Berlant's subsequent gloss on the phrase, recurring in (e.g.) *Cruel Optimism*: "The phrase 'political depression' emerges from discussions in a working group on Public Feelings." Berlant, *Cruel Optimism* (Durham, NC: Duke University Press, 2011), 272n11.
2. Fred Wah, *Rooftops* (1998), in *Scree: The Collected Earlier Poems, 1962–1991* (Vancouver: Talonbooks, 2015), 355.
3. Wah's poem implicitly announces itself as a transmedial, transnational venture, with artistic practices crossing and co-resonating, as *ut pictura poiesis* meets ikebana : : poem. Wah's *Rooftops* (1988) is a volume invested in exploring Japanese forms, temples, and the specific vibrations of the time he and his family spent in Japan. On Wah's notable trajectory and singular contributions to Asian Canadian literature, experimental poetics, "racial hybridity" (as he has termed it), and a localized poetics of place also alert to transnational and global pulses, see Jeff Derksen, "Reader's Manual: An Introduction to the Poetics and Contexts of Fred Wah's Early Poetry," in *Scree: The Collected Earlier Poems, 1962–1991*, 1–16.
4. Wallace Stevens, "Anecdote of the Jar," lines 9, 3, 6, in *Collected Poetry & Prose*, ed. Frank Kermode and Joan Richardson (New York: Library of America, 1997), 60.
5. The variable practices, aims, technologies, and entanglements of note taking—across periods, disciplines, professions, cultures—exceed the remit of this chapter, but one might point to the efflorescence of work on early modern note taking, its relation to common-placing and composition, its entanglement with discourses of knowledge, its transformation under the pressures of Baconian science. Ann Blair's work has been central: see "Note Taking as an Art of Transmission," *Critical Inquiry* 31, no. 1 (2004): 85–107; "The Rise of Note-Taking in Early Modern Europe," *Intellectual History Review* 20, no. 3 (2010): 303–16; and *Too Much to Know: Managing Scholarly Information before the Modern Age* (New Haven, CT: Yale University Press, 2010), in particular chap. 2, "Note-Taking as Information Management," 62–116. See too Richard

Yeo, *Notebooks, English Virtuosi, and Early Modern Science* (Chicago: University of Chicago Press, 2014).

6. As Ueda observes, "haiku—the free-standing seventeen-syllable verse form—develops historically from "*hokku*, the opening verse of *renku*, which was required to present a season word" ("*kigo*"). See Makoto Ueda, "True before It Is Made Truth," interview with Eve Luckring, *Roadrunner* 12–13, nos. 3/1 (December 2012–May 2013): 27–39, 19–31.

 See too the discussion of "hokku" under "Haikai" and the entry on "Haiku, Western" in Roland Greene, Stephen Cushman, Clare Cavanagh, Jahan Ramazani, and Paul Rouzer, eds., *The Princeton Encyclopedia of Poetry and Poetics*, 4th ed. (Princeton, NJ: Princeton University Press, 2012), 592–95. It is striking that this fourth edition refines the previous discussion of this terrain in the 1993 edition of the *Princeton Encyclopedia*, in which "H" launched with "Haiku (also called *haikai* or *hokku*)"—a parenthetical that risked dehistoricizing and amalgamating differences, poetic processes, and compositional situations that are worth articulating, modern "haiku" having been developed in particular by Masaoka Shiki in the late nineteenth century. See Alex Preminger, Frank J. Warnke, and O. B. Hardison, eds., *The New Princeton Encyclopedia of Poetry and Poetics* (Princeton, NJ: Princeton University Press, 1993), 334–35. For my own work on antiquarians' headnotes, see Maureen N. McLane, *Balladeering, Minstrelsy, and the Making of British Romantic Poetry* (Cambridge: Cambridge University Press, 2008), particularly chaps. 1 and 2; and also McLane, "Mediating Antiquarians in Britain, 1760–1830: The Invention of Oral Tradition, or, Close-Reading before Coleridge," in *This Is Enlightenment*, ed. Clifford Siskin and William Warner (Chicago: University of Chicago Press, 2010), 247–64.

7. See Rosalind Krauss on "approaching the works of Jasper Johns . . . through the grid of Roland Barthes, on whom I am now working," Krauss, "Liar's Paradox," *Artforum* 60, no. 22 (January 2022), para 2, https://www.artforum.com /print/202201/rosalind-e-krauss-on-jasper-johns-87451.

8. Roland Barthes, *The Preparation of the Novel: Lecture Courses and Seminars at the Collège de France (1978–1979 and 1979–1980)*, ed. Nathalie Léger, trans. Kate Briggs (New York: Columbia University Press, 2011), 127. Further citations from this translation of Barthes will be cited in text by page.

9. See Claude Coste: "Barthes was always equipped with a notebook in which to record his reactions. Using these notebooks he would then write up more extensive files, passing from the *notula* (sometimes just a single word) to the *nota* (as long as a sentence)." "Roland Barthes's Visits to Greece," trans. Sam Ferguson, *Barthes Studies* 5 (2019): 19n5. Coste's account of Barthes's notational practices in Greece in 1978 aligns with what Barthes set forth in his lectures of that same year. Regarding Barthes's use of filing cards in his final two years, Coste observes, "Between the initial *notula* and the rewritten *nota*, the filing cards bear witness to this difficult process of materialisation that

allows each subject, each consciousness to take the first step towards transforming an individual experience into a text for other readers" (17). See also Coste, "From *Fichier* to *Œuvre*: Barthes and the 'Our Literature' Project," in *Interdisciplinary Barthes*, ed. Diana Knight (Oxford: Oxford University Press, 2020), 252–75.
10. Roland Barthes, "An Introduction to the Structural Analysis of Narrative," trans. Lionel Duisit, *New Literary History* 6, no. 2 (Winter 1975): 237–72.
11. See Jean-Paul Sartre, *"What Is Literature?" and Other Essays* (Cambridge, MA: Harvard University Press, 1988), 48–69.
12. See, e.g., Barthes, "Rhetoric of the Image," in *Image-Music-Text*, trans. Stephen Heath (New York: Hill and Wang, 1977), 32–51.
13. For a fuller unfolding, see Charlton T. Lewis and Charles Short, *A Latin Dictionary: Founded on Andrews' edition of Freund's Latin dictionary. revised, enlarged, and in great part rewritten with many instances of use adduced from Cicero* (Oxford: Clarendon Press, 1879), archived at http://www.perseus.tufts.edu/hopper/text?doc=Perseus:text:1999.04.0059.
14. *OED Online*, s.v. "notation (*n.*)," senses 1–7, last modified December 2022, https://www.oed.com/.
15. Maureen N. McLane, "Note to Self (Strandhill)," in *Some Say* (Farrar, Straus & Giroux, 2016), 57.
16. Harryette Mullen, *Urban Tumbleweed: Notes from a Tanka Diary* (Minneapolis: Graywolf, 2013), ix. On tanka, another notably brief Japanese form long adapted into other languages and poetic traditions, see the subsection "Tanka" in the entry "Japan, Modern Poetry Of," in Greene et al., eds., *Princeton Encyclopedia of Poetry and Poetics*, 750–66.
17. Mullen, *Urban Tumbleweed*, 8.
18. Fanny Howe, "2000," in *Love and I* (Minneapolis: Graywolf, 2019), 45.
19. See the project, and ensuing volume, Sam Buchan-Watts and Lavinia Singer, eds., *Try to Be Better*, (London: Prototype, 2019).
20. Graham was referring here to reviews of "difficult poetry like Pound's Cantos." W. S. Graham, "From a 1949 Notebook: Given to the Late Elizabeth Smart in the 1950s," *Edinburgh Review* 75 (1987): 25.
21. Graham, "From a 1949 Notebook," 24, 25, 33, 35. Buchan-Watts and Singer collected and collated these prompts from across the notebook pages; see Buchan-Watts and Singer, eds., *Try to Be Better*.
22. Maureen N. McLane, "Take Down Actual Speech," in Buchan-Watts and Singer, eds., *Try to Be Better*, 24–25, and in McLane, *What You Want* (New York: Farrar, Straus & Giroux, 2023), 53–55.
23. Tonya Foster, *A Swarm of Bees in High Court* (New York: Belladonna, 2015), 122. Further quotations from this work will be cited in text by poem title and page.
24. See Makoto Ueda on twentieth-century postwar developments in Japanese haiku, including "social," "avant-garde," and "surrealist" haiku. Ueda, "True

before It Is Made Truth," interview by Eve Luckring, *Roadrunner* 13, no. 1 (May 2013): 19–31.

25. See, for example, Christopher Bush's incisive and mordant observations on Barthes and a wider horizon of modernist Orientalism: "The distance between Asia and its modernist refunctionalizations testified to a deliberate program of cross-cultural *non*-interpretation of which such later East Asian-inspired *écritures* as Tel Quel Maoism and Roland Barthes's *Empire of Signs* might be seen as the theoretically self-conscious descendants." And further, "much of what we might today call modernist Orientalism either explicitly disavowed any relationship to a contemporaneous, or even a real East, or did such a poor job of understanding it that it might as well have." Bush, "Modernism, Orientalism, and East Asia," in *A Handbook of Modernism Studies*, ed. Jean-Michel Rabaté (Malden, MA: Wiley, 2013), 193–94.

26. The programmaticism of "uncreative writing" and its affines (Conceptual poetry, inter alia) renders it quite another project than Barthesian haiku, and indeed than the notational, though certainly some twentieth- and twenty-first-century experimental poetries — even some Conceptual poets! — have been central to "the minimal" (cf. Barthes on "the minimal act of writing that is notation"). See Paul Stephens, *absence of clutter: minimal writing as art and literature* (Boston: MIT Press, 2020). See also Craig Dworkin and Evan Goldsmith, eds., *Against Expression: An Anthology of Conceptual Writing* (Evanston, IL: Northwestern University Press, 2011); Kenneth Goldsmith, *Uncreative Writing: Managing Language in the Digital Age* (New York: Columbia University Press, 2011); and Marjorie Perloff, *Unoriginal Genius: Poetry by Other Means in the New Century* (Chicago: University of Chicago Press, 2010).

27. Consider, as Paul Stephens and others have invited us to, such examples of and inquiries into "minimal/ist" writing as Jack Spicer: "A really perfect poem has an infinitely small vocabulary"; or Raymond Queneau and François Le Lionnais, "how few words can make a poem?"; or Aram Saroyan's famous "lighght" (1965). Jack Spicer, *After Lorca* (New York: NYRB/ Poets, 2021), 24; Queneau and Lionnais, *Oulipo Compendium*, ed. Alistair Brotchie and Harry Matthews (London: Atlas, 1998), 178; Saroyan, "lighght" (printed by Brice Marden, 1966), quoted in Stephens, *absence of clutter*, 93, 100.

28. As Antoine Compagnon pointedly remarks, Barthes's "bibliography is always restricted and almost entirely made of secondary sources, without his taking the trouble to return to the primary texts. Thus almost all the examples of French poetry that he compares to haiku come from a strange *Anthology of Single Stanzas* by Georges Schéhadé." Compagnon, "Roland Barthes's Novel," trans. Rosalind Krauss, *October* 112 (Spring 2005): 26.

29. The original French subtitle as published in *Cahiers du Cinéma* 222 is "Notes de recherche sur quelques photogrammes de S. M. Eisenstein"; the essay appeared in English as Roland Barthes, "The Third Meaning: Notes on Some of Eisenstein's Stills," trans. Richard Howard, *Artforum* 11, no. 5 (January

1973): 46–50. In his later and now more broadly disseminated translation, Stephen Heath restores the "recherche." See Barthes, *Image-Music-Text*, 52–68.

30. Hillary Chute advised me at a crucial moment to return again to Barthes on Eisenstein: I am indebted to her reflections on Barthes's essay, and to her transmedial and formal acuities regarding the film still and the grammar, syntax, and medium-specificity of comics (not least the gutter and the frame as "box-of-time"). See, for example, Chute, *Graphic Women: Life Narrative and Contemporary Comics* (New York: Columbia University Press, 2010), particularly the section of the introduction titled "An Elliptical Form," 7–15, and the chapter "Animating an Archive; see also *Disaster Drawn: Visual Witness, Comics, and Documentary Form* (Cambridge, MA: Harvard University Press, 2016), particularly the introduction, "Seeing New," 2–24, on Barthes and Eisenstein.

31. Barthes, "The Third Meaning: Research Notes on Some Eisenstein Stills," in *Image-Music-Text*, 62–63.

32. For another suggestive, indeed explicit, turn to haiku, see Barthes on the puppets of Bunraku theater in his "Lesson in Writing," which footnotes a quotation of Bashō: "Haiku by Bashō: 'A white onion / freshly washed. / Feeling of cold.'" Barthes, "Lesson in Writing," in *Image-Music-Text*, 170n.

33. Barthes, "The Third Meaning," in *Image-Music-Text*, 61.

34. McLane, from "Notationals/ Songs of a Season III," in *Some Say*, 25, 27.

35. McLane, "Update," in *Some Say*, 85.

36. Makoto Ueda, *Matsuo Bashō* (Tokyo: Kodansha International, 1970), 53; Robert Hass, trans. and ed., *The Essential Haiku: Versions of Basho, Buson, & Issa* (New York: Ecco, 1994), 18. The last version here is by me.

37. Lorine Niedecker, "Five Poems," *Poetry* 106, no. 5 (August 1965): 341–44.

38. Sasha Weiss, "Taylor Mac Wants Theater to Make You Uncomfortable," *New York Times Magazine*, April 2, 2019, https://www.nytimes.com/2019/04/02/magazine/taylor-mac-gary-broadway.html/.

39. Shelley, "On Life," in *Shelley's Poetry and Prose*, 2nd ed., ed. Donald H. Reiman and Neil Fraistat (New York: Norton, 2003), 505–8; "The Triumph of Life," line 544, in *The Complete Poetry of Percy Bysshe Shelley*, vol. 7, ed. Nora Crook (Baltimore: Johns Hopkins University Press, 2021), 30.

40. "Es gibt kein richtiges Leben im falschen" ("*Wrong life* cannot be lived rightly," in Jephcott's translation). Theodor W. Adorno, *Minima Moralia. Reflexionen aus dem beschädigten Leben*, ed. Rolf Tiedemann (Frankfurt am Main: Suhrkamp, 1980), 43; *Minima Moralia: Reflections from a Damaged Life*, trans. E. F. N. Jephcott (London: Verso, 2005), 39. As Judith Butler observed in their 2012 Adorno Prize Lecture: "We are left with the question, how does one lead a good life in a bad life?" Thinking of Arendt, Butler meditates further: "It may be that the question of how to live a good life depends upon having the power to lead a life as well as the sense of having a life, living a life or, indeed, the sense of being alive." Butler, *Notes toward a Performative Theory of Assembly* (Cambridge, MA: Harvard University Press, 2015), 193, 212.

41. See Achille Mbembe, "Necropolitics," trans. Libby Meintjes, *Public Culture* 15, no. 1 (2003): 11–40, and his book of the same name (Durham, NC: Duke University Press, 2019). Mbembe posits the necropolitical as not just "the right to kill" but the right to "expose" other people (including a country's own citizens) "to death." Mbembe, "Necropolitics," 12.
42. Claudia Rankine, *Citizen* (Minneapolis: Graywolf, 2014), 135.
43. Wilson's testimony was widely reported in the national (US) news. For Rankine's reflections, see her remarks in an interview: "When [Darren Wilson] said that thing—that seeing Michael Brown was like seeing Hulk Hogan, that he was a demon—I don't disbelieve him. I think that for him the black body is this thing that is larger than life.... The ways in which the racial imagination has been created for whiteness and blackness in this country, it has at its root this kind of... this sense of fear and loathing, basically, of the other." Rankine, "The Poetry of Race," interview by Charles Monroe-Kane, *To the Best of Our Knowledge* (podcast), February 1, 2015, https://www.ttbook.org/interview/poetry-race.
44. See Jacques Rancière, "Ten Theses on Politics," trans. Davide Panagia and Rachel Bowlby, *Theory & Event* 5, no. 3 (2001): 1–16. While this essay also appears in Jacques Rancière, *Dissensus: On Politics and Aesthetics*, ed. and trans. Steven Corcoran (New York: Continuum, 2010), 27–44, I prefer Panagia's and Bowlby's translation here.
45. Rancière, "Ten Theses," 3.
46. Rancière, "Ten Theses," 8, 14. Rancière further observes that the dissensus that constitutes the political is not assimilable to or resolvable through other modes of action, i.e. *poiesis* (giving form to matter) and *praxis* (the capacity to initiate).
47. On this, there is an extended bibliography: see n6, above.
48. A haibun is "a literary form developed in Japan that employs a combination of prose and haiku. A haibun may be as brief as a single terse paragraph followed by a single haiku or an extended work involving an alternation of prose and verse." Wenthe, "haibun," in Greene et al., eds., *Princeton Encyclopedia of Poetry and Poetics*, 592.
49. See Christopher Bush, who resists "the ideologically opposed but often mutually reinforcing critical tendencies of traditionalism and Orientalism critique"; he insists on an "inherently global" modernity, in which "Orientalist modernism should be understood not primarily as a more or less flawed representation of 'the Orient' but as a geopolitically specific iteration of aesthetic *modernism*'s problematic relationship to the history of *modernity*." Bush, "Modernism, Orientalism, and East Asia," 195–96. As Ueda observes, haiku was also crucial for *Japanese* modernism. See also Tollof Nelson, "Theoretical Apparitions of Haiku: An Intermedial Interrogation of Modernity," *Cinemas: Journal of Film Studies* 10, nos. 2–3 (2000): 185–203.
50. Anthony (Vahni) Capildeo, "Interview with Vahni Capildeo by Zannab

Sheikh," *I Don't Call Myself a Poet: Interviews with Contemporary Poets Living & Working in Britain* (blog), August 15, 2012, https://idontcallmyselfapoet.wordpress.com/category/poets-a-e/capildeo-vahni/.

51. Nelson, "Theoretical Apparitions of Haiku," 185.
52. See Barthes, *Image-Music-Text*, 67.
53. Eve Kosofsky Sedgwick, "A Dialogue on Love," first published in *Critical Inquiry* 24, no. 2 (Winter 1998): 611–31, and later expanded into a book of the same title (Boston: Beacon, 2003); Brian Teare, "Toxics Release Inventory (Essay on Man)," in *Doomstead Days* (New York: Nightboat Books, 2019), 42–91.
54. Ezra Pound, "How I Began," *T.P.'s Weekly* (June 6, 1913): 707 (reprinted in *The Literary Essays of Ezra Pound*, ed. T. S. Eliot [New York: New Directions, 1976], 15–40); also in "Vorticism," *Fortnightly Review* 96 (September 1, 1914): 461–71. With Barthes in mind, one might register the notable deixis of "*these* faces."
55. John Ashbery, "The New Spirit," in *Collected Poems 1956–1987*, ed. Mark Ford (New York: Library of America, 2008), 247.
56. Jeremy Noel-Tod, "The Quizzical Priest: Inside John Ashbery's Everyday Magical Thinking," review of Karin Rofmann, *The Songs We Know Best: John Ashbery's Early Life*, *Prospect Magazine*, March 19, 2018, https://www.prospectmagazine.co.uk/magazine/the-quizzical-priest-inside-john-ashberys-everyday-magical-thinking.
57. McLane, "Envoi: Eclipse," in *Some Say*, 129.
58. Maureen N. McLane, "notational/sufficiency," in *Same Life* (New York: Farrar, Straus & Giroux, 2008), 98.

CHAPTER FOUR

1. Maureen N. McLane, "Another Day in This Here Cosmos," in *This Blue* (New York: Farrar, Straus & Giroux, 2014), 13.
2. Ye (formerly Kanye West), vocalist, "New Slaves," track 4 on *Yeezus*, Def Jam, 2013, http://genius.com/Kanye-west-new-slaves-lyrics.
3. See T. V. F. Brogan, Stephen Cushman, K. S. Chang, R.M.A. Allen, W. L. Hanaway, and C. Scott, "Rhyme," in *The Princeton Encyclopedia of Poetry and Poetics*, 4th ed., ed. Roland Greene, Stephen Cushman, Clare Cavanagh, Jahan Ramazani, and Paul Rouzer (Princeton, NJ: Princeton University Press, 2012), 1182–92.
4. J. H. Prynne (among others) has invoked Viktor Zhirmunsky regarding the automatisms of rhyme and its challenges in Russian poetics. On various comparative "canons" of rhyme, see Zhirmunsky's "Introduction to Rhyme: Its History and Theory" (1923), trans. John Hoffman, *Chicago Review* 57, nos. 3–4 (Winter 2013): 119–27. On English vs. French taxonomies of rhyme, see Brogan et al., "Rhyme," in *Princeton Encyclopedia*, 1190–91.
5. Susan Stewart, *Poetry and the Fate of the Senses* (Chicago: University of Chicago Press, 2003), 119.

6. "The inevitability of rhyme suggested by this study becomes harder to deny in light of evidence that rhyme-like structures apparently exist even in non-human langs., such as that of whales (Guinee and Payne), challenging those who think of rhyme as more artificial than natural to reconsider." Brogan et al., Section D, "Analogues," in "Rhyme," in *Princeton Encyclopedia*, 1191.
7. See Susan Stewart, "Rhyme and Freedom," in *The Sound of Poetry/The Poetry of Sound*, ed. Marjorie Perloff and Craig Dworkin (Chicago: University of Chicago Press, 2009), 31–32; this essay also appeared with slight modifications as chap. 6, "Rhyming," in *The Poet's Freedom: A Notebook on Making* (University of Chicago Press, 2011), 142–60. See also Brogan et al., "Rhyme," in *Princeton Encyclopedia*, 1190–91; and the *Oxford English Dictionary* for the etymological, linguistic, and historical entanglements of "rhyme" and "rhythm."
8. Stewart, "Rhyme and Freedom," 33, 44.
9. See Stewart, "Rhyme and Freedom," 294n7, for her salute to T. V. F. Brogan's essay "Rhyme" in an earlier 1993 edition of *The Princeton Encyclopedia of Poetry and Poetics*. Other scholars notable for their contributions to work on rhyme, including rhyming forms and stanzas, include David Caplan; J. Paul Hunter (particularly with regard to eighteenth-century verse and the heroic couplet); and Anthony Madrid, who makes a trenchant, dazzling argument about "classic" rhyme, the "decommissioning" of certain rhymes, and broader historical shifts in rhyming technique from the Restoration period onward: see his "Seventeen Quotations with Commentary," in *On Rhyme*, ed. David Caplan (Liège: Presses Universitaires de Liège, 2017), 123–39. Also crucial: Evie Shockley, who vivifies Black poets' complex rhyming ventures as part of her inquiry into formal innovation in *Renegade Poetics: Black Aesthetics and Formal Innovation in African American Poetry* (Iowa City: University of Iowa Press, 2011).
10. See Roman Jakobson, "Closing Statement: Linguistics and Poetics," in *Style in Language*, ed. Thomas A. Sebeok (Cambridge, MA: MIT Press, 1960), 358: "The poetic function projects the principle of equivalence from the axis of selection into the axis of combination."
11. John Hollander, *Rhyme's Reason: A Guide to English Verse*, 3rd ed. (New Haven, CT: Yale University Press, 2001). For one classic statement, see W. K. Wimsatt, "One Relation of Rhyme to Reason," in *The Verbal Icon: Studies in the Meaning of Poetry* (New York: Noonday Press, 1958), 152–66.
12. Jakobson, "Closing Statement," 357, 368.
13. Jakobson, 358. Italics in text.
14. Brogan et al., "Rhyme," in *Princeton Encyclopedia*, 1189.
15. "(to break the pentameter, that was the first heave)": Pound, canto LXXXI, *The Pisan Cantos*, in *The Cantos of Ezra Pound* (New York: New Directions, 1934), 96.
16. Virginia Woolf, "Character in Fiction" [repr. "Mr Bennett and Mrs Brown"], in *The Essays of Virginia Woolf*, vol. 3, *1919–1924*, ed. Andrew McNeillie (London: Hogarth, 1986), 421–22.

NOTES TO PAGES 000–000

17. Ezra Pound, "In a Station of the Metro," *Poetry* 2, no. 1 (April 1913): 12.
18. H. D., "Oread," in *Collected Poems 1912–1944*, ed. Louis L. Martz (New York: New Directions, 1983), 55. Note that when the poem was first quoted by Ezra Pound in *Blast*, it was untitled.
19. See Tollof Nelson, "Theoretical Apparitions of Haiku: An Intermedial Interrogation of Modernity," *Cinémas: Revue d'études cinématographiques*, 10, nos. 2–3 (2000): 190.
20. It is striking that in his influential book, scholar and translator Kenneth Yasuda argued that in English the first and third lines of haiku should in fact rhyme. See Yasuda, *The Japanese Haiku: Its Essential Nature, History, and Possibilities in English, with Selected Examples* (Boston: Tuttle, 2001), 71.
21. Paul Muldoon, "Hopewell Haiku," in *Hay* (London: Faber and Faber, 1998), 56–73; "News Headlines from the Homer Noble Farm," in *Moy Sand and Gravel* (London: Faber and Faber, 2002), 50–54; "90 Instant Messages to Tom Moore," in *Horse Latitudes* (London: Faber and Faber, 2006), 53–75. That Muldoon (born and educated in Northern Ireland, long resident in the US) is a poet (and translator) conversant in several linguistic, poetic, and rhyming traditions inflects his pronounced rhyming bravura (as well as, more obviously, his multilingual rhymes). Then too, his work as a songwriter and lyricist suggests other dimensions of a commitment to rhyme.
22. *OED Online*, s.v. "blank (*adj.*)," sense 8, last modified December 2022, https://www.oed.com/.
23. Brogan et al., "Rhyme," in *Princeton Encyclopedia*, 1189. The entry's authors footnote Robert Abernathy's "Rhymes, Non-Rhymes and Antirhyme," *To Honor Roman Jakobson* 1 (1967): 1–14.
24. As the editors of *The Princeton Encyclopedia of Poetry and Poetics* have it (drawing on Cornulier), "rhyme does not exactly reside at line end: its positioning shapes the entire structure of the line, so that we should more accurately say that the rhyme resides in the entire line. Removing rhymes from lines does not merely render them rhymeless; it alters their lexical-semantic structure altogether." Brogan et al., "Rhyme," in *Princeton Encyclopedia*, 1185.
25. T. S. Eliot: "No verse is free for the man who wants to do a good job." Eliot, *On Poetry and Poets* (New York: Farrar, Straus & Cudahy, 1957), 31. We might recast this is the terms of structural linguistics: no verse ("free" or otherwise) is "unmarked." In his 1917 "Reflections on Vers Libre," Eliot writes, "there is only good verse, bad verse, and chaos." Eliot, *To Criticize the Critic* (New York: Farrar, Straus & Cudahy, 1965), 189. On the historicity of "free verse," see Marjorie Perloff's classic essay, "After Free Verse: The New Non-Linear Poetries," in *Poetry On and Off the Page* (Evanston, IL: Northwestern University Press, 1998), 141–67.
26. Ezra Pound, "A Retrospect: A Few Don'ts," in *Pavannes and Divagations* (New York: Knopf, 1918), 95–96.
27. Daniel Albright, "Modernist Poetic Form," in *The Cambridge Companion to*

Twentieth-Century English Poetry, ed. Neil Corcoran (Cambridge: Cambridge University Press, 2007), 26.
28. Geoffrey Chaucer, "The Tale of Sir Thopas," fragment VII, lines 923–25, in *The Riverside Chaucer*, ed. Larry D. Benson (Oxford: Oxford University Press, 1998), 216.
29. Chaucer, "Tale of Sir Thopas," lines 929–32.
30. *OED Online*, s.v. "doggerel (*adj.* and *n.*)," sense 1a, last modified March 2022, https://www.oed.com/.
31. Paul Muldoon, "An Interview with Paul Muldoon," interview by Lynn Keller, *Contemporary Literature* 35, no. 1 (Spring 1994): 18.
32. Anthony Madrid, "Wallace Stevens's Place in the History of English Rhyming: A Talk Given at the 43rd Annual Louisville Conference on Literature and Culture Since 1900," transcript, February 27, 2015, *Prelude* 2, https://preludemag.com/issues/2/wallace-stevenss-place-in-the-history-of-english-rhyming. Madrid argues that, before Byron, "the issue of wit and originality and portability of a given rhyme pair did not exist. With Byron, it suddenly exists."
33. See Madrid, "Wallace Stevens's Place." See also J. Paul Hunter's seminal work on rhyme, particularly in its eighteenth-century modalities, e.g., "The Heroic Couplet: Its Rhyme and Reason," *Ideas from the National Humanities Center* 4, no. 1(1996): 22–29.
34. See David Caplan, *Rhyme's Challenge: Hip Hop, Poetry, and Contemporary Rhyming Culture* (Oxford: Oxford University Press, 2014), 5–6.
35. See Madrid, "Wallace Stevens's Place": "Stevens pretty clearly preferred to deploy rhyme effects in a 'sneak up' style" (para 31). While Madrid does not address "The Man with the Blue Guitar," and while I drafted this chapter at first unaware of Madrid's essay, our accounts of his rhyming technique align. Madrid's excellent essay offers a synoptic description of Stevens's rhyming art across the corpus and situates his work within broader historical transformations.
36. J. H. Prynne, "Mental Ears and Poetic Work," *Chicago Review* 55, no. 1 (Winter 2010): 126–57.
37. Wallace Stevens, "The Man with the Blue Guitar," canto XXV, lines 1–14, in *Wallace Stevens: Collected Poetry and Prose*, ed. Frank Kermode and Joan Richardson (New York: The Library of America, 1997), 146. Hereafter abbreviated *CPP* and cited in text by canto and page number.
38. Stewart, "Rhyme and Freedom," 46.
39. Stewart, "Rhyme and Freedom," 44.
40. See again the *OED* and the *Princeton Encyclopedia*: "*Rhythm* and *rhyme* are, thus, intimately related not only etymologically but conceptually"; Brogan et al., "Rhyme," in *Princeton Encyclopedia*, 1185.
41. "I had no particular painting of Picasso's in mind and even though it might help to sell the book to have one of his paintings on the cover, I don't think we

ought to reproduce anything of Picasso's." Stevens to Renato Poggioli, July 1, 1953, in *The Letters of Wallace Stevens*, ed. Holly Stevens (Berkeley: University of California Press, 1966), 786.

42. Lead Belly, performer, "Ha-Ha This a Way," track 13 on *Lead Belly: The Smithsonian Folkways Collection*, Smithsonian Folkway Recordings, 2015.
43. Stewart, "Rhyme and Freedom," 45.
44. See, for example, Mark Mayer, "Using the Rotted Names: Wallace Stevens's Racial Ontology as Poetic Key," *Twentieth-Century Literature* 65, no. 3 (September 2019): 217–36. Mayer notes that "the predominating critical approach to Stevens's racial imagination is neglect." This is perhaps less true in recent years, with critics and poets increasingly alert to Stevens's racial imagination. For further reflections, see two essays in *Poetry and Poetics after Wallace Stevens*, ed. Bart Eeckhout and Lisa Goldfarb (London: Bloomsbury, 2016): Lisa M. Steinman, "Unanticipated Readers," 288–302, which explores the engagement of several poets of color, including Terrance Hayes, with Stevens; and Rachel Galvin, "'This Song Is for My Foe': Olive Senior and Terrance Hayes Rewrite Stevens," 303–322, which discusses Hayes (including his racialized reception by critics) alongside the Jamaican Canadian Senior. For other reckonings, see Major Jackson, "Wallace Stevens after 'Lunch,'" *Harriet* (blog), Poetry Foundation, February 4, 2008, https://www.poetryfoundation.org/harriet-books/2008/02/wallace-stevens-after-lunch; Saeed Jones, "Self Portrait of the Artist as Ungrateful Black Writer," *BuzzFeed*, April 3, 2015, https://www.buzzfeed.com/saeedjones/self-portrait-of-the-artist-as-ungrateful-black-writer; Rickey Laurentiis, "Of the Leaves That Have Fallen," first published in *Boston Review* in March 2014, https://bostonreview.net/poetry/rickey-laurentiis-timothy-donnelly-leaves-have-fallen, and later collected in Laurentiis's volume *Boy with Thorn* (Pittsburgh: University of Pittsburgh Press, 2015); and Terrance Hayes, "Snow for Wallace Stevens," in *Lighthead* (New York; Penguin, 2010), 57.
45. *OED Online*, s.v. "tom-tom (n. and int.)," senses 1a and 1c, last modified March 2023, https://www.oed.com/.
46. Toni Morrison, *Playing in the Dark: Whiteness and the Literary Imagination* (Cambridge, MA: Harvard University Press, 1993), viii.
47. See Maureen N. McLane, "Hoobla-hoo and Hullabaloo: Divagations with Stevens," in *Wallace Stevens, Poetry, and France: "Au pays de la métaphore,"* ed. Juliette Utard, Bart Eeckhout, and Lisa Goldfarb (Paris: Éditions Rue d'Ulm, 2018), 81–96.
48. Barbara Herrnstein Smith, *Poetic Closure: A Study of How Poems End* (Chicago: University of Chicago Press, 1968), 237.
49. "Gerard Manley Hopkins, an outstanding searcher in the science of poetic language, defined verse as 'speech wholly or partially repeating the same figure of sound.'" Jakobson, "Closing Statement," 358–59.
50. All passages quoted from *Stanzas in Meditation* (1932) will be cited in text

by part, stanza, and page: see Gertrude Stein, *Writings 1932–1946*, ed. Catharine Stimpson and Harriet Chessman (New York: Library of America, 1998), 1–146. These passages have all been checked against the definitive *Stanzas in Meditation: The Corrected Edition*, ed. Susannah Hollister and Emily Setina, (New Haven, CT: Yale University Press, 2012). For further cases of Stein-Rhyme, one might look to her portrait of Picasso, "If I Told Him: A Completed 'Portrait' of Picasso," in *Writings: 1903–1932*, ed. Catharine R. Stimpson and Harriet Chessman (New York: Library of America, 1998), 282–84, a festival of parallelism and rhyme and count; or to her short poems.

51. Basil Bunting, "The Codex," in *Basil Bunting on Poetry*, ed. Peter Makin (Baltimore: Johns Hopkins University Press, 1999), 4.
52. Stewart, "Rhyme and Freedom," 30.
53. Stewart, "Rhyme and Freedom," 32.
54. *OED Online*, s.v. "rhyme (*n*.)," sense 1a, last modified December 2022, https://www.oed.com/.
55. Gertrude Stein, "Arthur A Grammar," in *How to Write* (Craftsbury Common, VT: Sherry Urie, 1977), 37–101.
56. Here I draw on Saussure—who distinguishes between the "material envelope" (the sound of a word, its pronunciation) and the "image acoustique," the latter a mental imprint or auditory generalization provoked by a sound/word: the competing vibrations of which Stein relentlessly exploits. Ferdinand Saussure, *Course in General Linguistics*, ed. and trans. Roy Harris (London: Bloomsbury Academic, 2013), 168. On the difficulty of translating Saussure's concepts, see Harris's introduction to the volume, xxi.
57. Gertrude Stein, *Tender Buttons*, in *Writings 1903–1932*, 313.
58. See, e.g., the rhyming textures throughout Stein's *Everybody's Autobiography* (1937), a work I believe we can say is "in prose."
59. Hunter, "The Heroic Couplet," 25. Hunter's remarks on rhyme are a subset of his trenchant meditation on the couplet, hegemonic vector of rhyme for 150 years in Anglophone verse: "With a few exceptions in the nineteenth century and with even fewer in the twentieth, the couplet has disappeared, along with most other traditional forms of rhymed verse" (24).
60. Harryette Mullen, interview by Daniel Kane, in *What Is Poetry: Conversations with the American Avant-Garde*, ed. Daniel Kane (New York: Teachers and Writers, 2003), 129.
61. Caplan, *Rhyme's Challenge*, 131.
62. Drawing on Gwendolyn Brooks's and Sonia Sanchez's work, Shockley makes clear how "rhyme royal (and other received stanzaic forms) might lend themselves to African American women's liberatory poetic projects" (*Renegade Poetics*, 17). For Shockley's own poetry, see (for example) in *semiautomatic* (Middletown, CT: Wesleyan University Press, 2017) the rhyme royal of "the way we live now ::" (6) and the section called "refrain" (43–78), within it the poem "a-lyrical ballad (or, how america reminds us of the value of family)"

(43–45)—a devastating update of the murder ballad as a catalogue and grieving of anti-Black violence.
63. See Hannah Crawforth, "Queer Echoes: Reading 'The Faerie Queene' with Evie Shockley," *Spenser Review* 51, nos. 2–3 (Spring–Summer 2021), para 8, http://www.english.cam.ac.uk/spenseronline/review/item/51.2.3.
64. See Frederick Seidel, *Poems 1959–2009* (New York: Farrar, Straus & Giroux, 2010); Michael Robbins, *Alien vs. Predator* (New York: Penguin, 2012) and *The Second Sex* (New York: Penguin, 2014). Robbins has since moved to a more meditative post–New York school idiom, less surcharged with flashing rhyme.
65. For Cathy Park Hong on what she calls her "invented pidgin," see her interview with Ken Chen in *Bomb*, January 8, 2020, https://bombmagazine.org/articles/cathy-park-hong/. For her anti-assimilationist commitment to "bad English" as a wellspring for poetry, see chapter 4 of *Minor Feelings: An Asian American Reckoning* (New York: One World, 2020), 92–109.
66. Of global/ized/izing poetry, some significant considerations include Walt Hunter, *Forms of a World: Contemporary Poetry and the Making of Globalization* (New York: Fordham University Press, 2019); Christopher Nealon, *The Matter of Capital: Poetry and Crisis in the American Century* (Cambridge, MA: Harvard University Press, 2011); and Jahan Ramazani, *Poetry in a Global Age* (Chicago: University of Chicago Press, 2020). In invoking "distressing," I allude to Susan Stewart's seminal work "Notes on Distressed Genres," in *Crimes of Writing: Problems in the Containment of Representation* (Oxford: Oxford University Press, 1991), 66–101.
67. See Jahan Ramazani, chap. 9, "Code Switching, Code Stitching: A Macaronic Poetics?" in *Poetry in a Global Age*, 193–212, for more extended meditations on the macaronic. Ramazani argues for a "polytemporal, polyspatial poetics" underwriting twentieth- and twenty-first-century poetries: "A macaronic poetics foregrounds the always-already dialogic nature of even the supposedly unitary poetic voice" (40). Ramazani notes Helen Vendler's reservations about what she termed Derek Walcott's "macaronic" aesthetics, but—with younger poets and extensive work in postcolonial and world literature/s in mind—he offers a more sanguine view. It's worth noting that many poets and critics would not accept a "two languages" notion of the macaronic, nor the ratios, terms, hierarchies, and distributions assumed therein. And as Ramazani himself notes, any notion of a "macaronic poetics" has to reckon with the historically situated stakes of multilingual (or plurilingual) poetics.
68. *OED Online*, s.v. "macaronic (*adj.* and *n.*)," senses 1–2, last modified September 2022, https://www.oed.com/.
69. Stewart, "Rhyme and Freedom," 44.
70. Ramazani, "Code-Switching," 195–208.
71. Seidel, "Do You Doha?," in *Poems 1959–2009*, 36–37.
72. Seidel, "Do You Doha?," 38.

73. *OED Online*, s.v. "aloha (*n.* and *int.*)," etymology, last modified March 2023, https://www.oed.com/.
74. It is perhaps more precise to read Seidel as tending toward monorhyme rather than macaronism: his insistent expressionist end rhymes tend to pile up extravagantly. Seidel has expressed his admiration for the great Arab poets of the classical period and their monorhyming poetry. See, for example, his "'Stars and Stripes Forever' cross-species salute" to Imru al-Qays's poem "Mu'allaqa," and the accompanying author's note praising its "utter foreignness, the monorhymes which I have been trying and failing to translate for twenty years, the magnificence," in *Poetry* 192, no. 2 (April 2008): 21–25.
75. Cathy Park Hong, *Dance Dance Revolution* (New York: Norton, 2006), 92. Hong's political-aesthetic inquiries took up new forms, not least the ballad, in her *Engine Empire* (New York: Norton, 2012), employing Oulipian constraints as part of its poetic world-building (including sections evoking a nineteenth-century US western frontier town, a contemporary Chinese boomtown, and a futuristic cybernetic city).
76. Erica McAlpine has observed that this divagation borders on doggerel. Well, yes.
77. Marianne Moore, "The Hero," line 1, in *New Collected Poems*, ed. Heather Cass White (New York: Farrar, Straus & Giroux, 2017), 97.
78. Devin Johnston, "Nothing Song," in *Traveler* (New York: Farrar, Straus & Giroux, 2011), 5–6.
79. Devin Johnston, "New Song," in *Far-Fetched* (New York: Farrar, Straus & Giroux, 2015), 24–25.
80. See J. P. Hunter's magisterial "Form as Meaning: Pope and the Ideology of the Couplet," *Eighteenth Century* 37, no. 3 (Fall 1996): 257–70.
81. For the concept of "the period eye," see Michael Baxandall, "The Period Eye," chap. 2 of *Painting and Experience in Fifteenth-Century Italy: A Primer in the Social History of Pictorial Styles* (New York: Oxford University Press, 1988), 29–70. One might think as well of a "period ear," though it is even more difficult to reconstruct. Rhyme is however one possible route. On the question of the historicity of couplets and of socialized hearing itself, consider J. Paul Hunter: "Can the fading of couplet verse be explained as an instance of the 'exhaustion' of the form? Were poetic imaginers no longer up to the task, as traditional literary history has implied? Or, over time, did the ears of listeners change, or did structures of thought and expression change so that 'hearing' was no longer the same?" Hunter, "The Heroic Couplet," 24.
82. Seidel, "That Fall," in *Poems 1959–2009*, 363.
83. "(for she is of blueberry-browsers the paragon)": Paul Muldoon, "The Mudroom," in *Hay* (London: Faber and Faber, 1998), 3–4.
84. "he's so shot-through, so spangled / with the cankers and carbuncles / of syphilis. / Three nights ago, Southey lay down with Bucephalus": Paul Muldoon, *Madoc: A Mystery* (London and Boston: Faber and Faber, 1990), 181.

85. See Urayoán Noel, *Transversal* (Tuscon: University of Arizona Press, 2021); Anthony Madrid's critical work on rhyme, already invoked, and his books of poems *I Am Your Slave, Now Do What I Say* (2012) and *Try Never* (2017), both published by Canarium Books (Ann Arbor, MI); Harryette Mullen, *Muse & Drudge* (San Diego: Singing Horse Press, 1995); later collected in *Recyclopedia: Trimmings, S*PeRM**K*T, and Muse & Drudge* (Minneapolis: Graywolf, 2006).

CHAPTER FIVE

1. W. H. Auden, "In Memory of W. B. Yeats," line 36, line 41, in *Collected Poems*, ed. Edward Mendelson (New York: Vintage, 1991), 248. For a profound meditation on Auden's ramifying engagement with history, as well as his reverberance in (and appropriation by) contemporary culture, see Susannah Young-ah Gottlieb, *Auden and the Muse of History* (Stanford, CA: Stanford University Press, 2022).
2. Dorothea Lasky, *Poetry Is Not a Project* (Brooklyn: Ugly Duckling Presse, 2010), 7–8, 15–16.
3. John Keats to John Taylor, February 27, 1818, in *The Letters of John Keats*, vol. 1, *1814–1818*, ed. Hyder Edward Rollins (Cambridge: Cambridge University Press, 2011), 238–39.
4. Anne Boyer, *Garments against Women* (Boise: Ahsahta 2015), 41. Further quotations from this book will be cited in text by page.
5. Donna Stonecipher, "Transaction History 3," in *Transaction Histories* (Iowa City: University of Iowa Press, 2018), 25.
6. Yanyi, *The Year of Blue Water* (New Haven, CT: Yale University Press, 2019), 40.
7. I here allude to the following works: Kenneth Goldsmith, *The Weather* (Los Angeles: Make Now, 2005); Vanessa Place, *Statement of Facts* (Los Angeles: Blanc Press, 2010); Christian Bök's ongoing "Xenotext" experiment.
8. M. NourbeSe Philip, "Notanda," in *Zong!* (Middletown, CT: Wesleyan University Press, 2008), 191. There is a burgeoning scholarship on Philip's *Zong!*; for one meditation on this work and more broadly the wake of the slave ship *Zong*, see Christina Sharpe's discussions in chap. 2, "The Ship," and chap. 3, "The Hold," in *In the Wake: On Blackness and Being* (Durham, NC: Duke University Press, 2016).
9. See Cathy Park Hong's "Delusions of Whiteness in the Avant-Garde" (2014), first published in *Lana Turner* 7 (2014), https://arcade.stanford.edu/content/delusions-whiteness-avant-garde. Here I wish not to go too far down a specialist wormhole which has a burgeoning bibliography, but for work on the crises in Conceptual poetry, and its racist/racialized logics, see Michael Leong, "Conceptualisms in Crisis: The Fate of Late Conceptual Poetry," *Journal of Modern Literature* 41, no. 3 (2018): 109–31; Jahan Ramazani's introduction to the "Poetry and Race" issue of *New Literary History*, 2019; Cathy Park

Hong's article "There's a New Movement in American Poetry," *New Republic*, October 1, 2015, https://newrepublic.com/article/122985/new-movement-american-poetry-not-kenneth-goldsmith; John Keene's "On Vanessa Place, Gone With the Wind, and the Limit Point of Certain Conceptual Aesthetics," *Atticus Review*, May 27, 2015, https://atticusreview.org/on-vanessa-place-gone-with-the-wind-and-the-limit-point-of-certain-conceptual-aesthetics-2/; Ken Chen's "Authenticity Obsession, or Conceptualism as Minstrel Show," in *The Margins* (New York: Asian American Writers' Workshop, 2015), https://aaww.org/authenticity-obsession/. For groundbreaking considerations of race/racialization and experimental poetries, see Dorothy Wang's *Thinking Its Presence: Form, Race, and Subjectivity in Asian American Poetry* (Stanford, CA: Stanford University Press, 2013); Evie Shockley, *Renegade Poetics: Black Aesthetics and Formal Innovation in African American Poetry* (Iowa City: University of Iowa Press, 2011); and Anthony Reed, *Freedom Time: The Poetics and Politics of Black Experimental Writing* (Baltimore: Johns Hopkins University Press, 2014).

10. The domain of ecopoetics is of course vast: significant books include Camille Dungy, ed., *Black Nature: Four Centuries of African American Nature Poetry* (Athens: University of Georgia Press, 2009); Joyelle McSweeney, *The Necropastoral: Poetry, Media, Occults* (Ann Arbor: University of Michigan Press, 2014); Margaret Ronda, *Remainders: American Poetry at Nature's End* (Stanford, CA: Stanford University Press, 2018); Angela Hume and Gillian Osborne, eds., *Ecopoetics: Essays in the Field* (Iowa City: University of Iowa Press, 2018); and Jed Rasula, *This Compost: Ecological Imperatives in American Poetry* (Athens: University of Georgia Press, 2002). (It's worth noting too that ecologically minded poetries are not necessarily ecocritical.) For ecological preoccupations in twentieth-century Black poetics, see, e.g., Sonya Posmentier, *Cultivation and Catastrophe: The Lyric Ecology of Modern Black Literature*. (Baltimore: Johns Hopkins University Press, 2017). Ronda dates the term "ecopoetics" to 2001, to the founding of the eponymous journal at Buffalo, though certainly (as Dungy's anthology suggests, and as the scholarly turn in the 1990s to "green romanticism" suggested), "ecopoetics" might be seen to have been launched long in advance of the term. But Ronda orients us specifically to "poetry as an essential site for postwar reflections on ecological calamity" (129), and in that sense, and in terms of a consciousness of anthropogenic climate change, "ecopoetics" is historically specific, emergent in the late twentieth century.

11. Michael Dickman, "Lakes Rivers Streams," in *Days & Days* (New York: Knopf, 2019), 45, 50.

12. Bhanu Kapil, *Ban en Banlieue* (New York: Nightboat, 2015), 48. Further quotations from this book will be cited in text by page.

13. Juliana Spahr, *That Winter the Wolf Came* (Oakland, CA: Commune Editions, 2015). Quotations from this book will be cited in text by page.

14. Anahid Nersessian, *Utopia, Limited: Romanticism and Adjustment* (Cambridge, MA: Harvard University Press, 2015), 220n74.
15. See Gavin de Beer, "An 'Atheist' in the Alps," *Keats–Shelley Memorial Bulletin* 9 (1958): 1–15.
16. Shelley, preface to *Prometheus Unbound*, in *Shelley's Poetry and Prose*, ed. Donald H. Reiman and Neil Fraistat, 2nd ed. (New York: Norton, 2002), 208–9.
17. Boyer, "'Literature Is against Us': In Conversation with Anne Boyer," interview by Amy King, Poetry Foundation, August 30, 2015, https://www.poetryfoundation.org/harriet-books/2015/08/literature-is-against-us-in-conversation-with-anne-boyer.
18. Boyer's book is categorized by its distributor (Small Press Distribution) as "Poetry. Literary Nonfiction. Women's Studies," a categorization followed by vendors from Amazon to independent bookstores. Comparatively, the New York University library catalog puts *Ban* under the subject headings "Performance Poetry," "Nationalism—Poetry," "Race Riots—Poetry," and "Laments—Poetry," and glosses Spahr's book as "Experimental fiction, American." Yet all have been primarily reviewed—as far as I can discover—as "poetry." Product page for Anne Boyer's *Garments against Women*, Small Press Distribution, https://web.archive.org/web/20170715052948/http://www.spdbooks.org/Products/Default.aspx?bookid=9781934103593.
19. Maggie Nelson, *The Argonauts* (Minneapolis: Graywolf, 2015).
20. Shelley, "A Defence of Poetry," in *Shelley's Poetry and Prose*, 513, 511.
21. See Ronald Silliman, *The New Sentence* (New York: Roof, 1989); and Kaplan Harris, "Causes, Movements, Theory: Between Language Poetry and New Narrative," in *A Companion to American Poetry*, ed. Mary McAleer Balkun, Jeffrey Gray, and Paul Jaussen (Hoboken, NJ: Wiley Blackwell, 2022), 151–52.
22. Wordsworth, note to "The Thorn," in *Lyrical Ballads, and Other Poems, 1797–1800*, ed. James Butler and Karen Green (Ithaca, NY: Cornell University Press, 1992), 351.
23. Sianne Ngai, *Ugly Feelings* (Cambridge, MA: Harvard University Press, 2005), 6, 3.
24. Karl Marx, *Capital*, vol. 1, trans. Ben Fowkes (London: Penguin, 1990), 130.
25. See Kapil, *Ban*, 94.
26. Pound, canto CXVI, in *The Cantos of Ezra Pound* (New York: New Directions, 1971), 796.
27. For these sections, see Kapil, *Ban*, 63, 66, 69, 74, 98.
28. Adorno, "Es gibt kein richtiges Leben im falschen" ("*Wrong life* cannot be lived rightly," in Jephcott's translation). Theodor W. Adorno, *Minima Moralia. Reflexionen aus dem beschädigten Leben*, ed. Rolf Tiedemann (Frankfurt am Main: Suhrkamp, 1980), 43; *Minima Moralia: Reflections from a Damaged Life*, trans. E. F. N. Jephcott (London: Verso, 2005), 39.
29. In the years since publishing *Ban en Banlieue*, Kapil has returned to the UK, in part to secure better care for her mother. Her widely reviewed and prize-

winning *How to Wash a Heart* analyzes and dramatizes "host-guest chemistry" and takes clear and sardonic aim at liberal pieties about im/migration, and does so in a lyric, verse-lineated, through-composed mode. Kapil, *How to Wash a Heart* (Liverpool: Liverpool University Press, 2020), 40.

30. On Spahr's use of refrain, and on refrain's long romantic-revolutionary history and linkage to riotous upsurge, see Celeste Langan, "Repetition Run Riot: Refrains, Slogans, and Graffiti," *Wordsworth Circle* 52, no. 2 (Spring 2021): 287–307.

31. Percy Bysshe Shelley, "The Mask of Anarchy," lines 86–89, in *Shelley's Poetry and Prose*, 319.

32. Mikhail Bakhtin, "Forms of Time and of the Chronotope in the Novel," in *The Dialogic Imagination: Four Essays*, ed. Michael Holquist, trans. Caryl Emerson and Michael Holquist (Austin: University of Texas Press, 1981), 84–258. For the "chronotope of the road," see 98; for "the castle" and "the historicity of castle time," see 245–47. Note that this chapter is subtitled "Notes toward a Historical Poetics."

33. See, e.g., Julia Kristeva, *Desire in Language: A Semiotic Approach to Literature and Art* (New York: Columbia University Press, 1980) and *Revolution in Poetic Language* (New York: Columbia University Press, 1984).

34. In the past two decades, as previously noted, the new lyric studies and trenchant work in historical poetics have also contributed to the revivification of our sense of these specificities, though it's also true that some classicists, some poets, and even some scholars of poetics never forgot them, even during the supposed hegemony of New Criticism.

35. Mary Douglas, *Purity and Danger: An Analysis of Concepts of Pollution and Taboo* (London: Routledge, 1984), 36.

36. Dorothea Lasky, *Poetry Is Not a Project*, 23.

37. Maureen N. McLane, "Moonrise," in *What You Want* (New York: Farrar, Straus & Giroux, 2023), 100–102.

Bibliography

Abernathy, Robert. "Rhymes, Non-Rhymes and Antirhyme." *To Honor Roman Jakobson* 1 (1967): 1–14.
Abrams, M. H. "The Correspondent Breeze: A Romantic Metaphor." In *English Romantic Poets: Modern Essays in Criticism*, edited by M. H. Abrams, 37–54. Oxford: Oxford University Press, 1960.
Adorno, Theodor. *Minima Moralia. Reflexionen aus dem beschädigten Leben*, edited by Rolf Tiedemann. Frankfurt am Main: Suhrkamp, 1980.
———. *Minima Moralia: Reflections from a Damaged Life*. Translated by E. F. N. Jephcott. London: Verso, 2005.
Albright, Daniel. "Modernist Poetic Form." In *The Cambridge Companion to Twentieth-Century English Poetry*, edited by Neil Corcoran, 24–41. Cambridge: Cambridge University Press, 2007.
Althusser, Louis. *L'avenir dure longtemps; suivi de Les Faits*. Edited by Olivier Corpet and Yann Moulier Boutang. Paris: Stock/IMC, 1992.
———. *The Future Lasts Forever: A Memoir*. Translated by Richard Veasey. New York: New Press, 1992.
———. *Lenin and Philosophy and Other Essays*. New York: Monthly Review Press, 1971.
———. *Philosophy of the Encounter: Later Writings, 1978–1987*. Edited by François Matheron and Oliver Corpet. Translated by G. M. Goshgarian. London: Verso, 2006.
Arendt, Hannah. *The Human Condition*. 2nd ed. Chicago: University of Chicago Press, 2018.
———. *On Revolution*. New York: Viking, 1963.

———. *Thinking without a Banister: Essays in Understanding, 1953–1975*. Edited and with an introduction by Jerome Kohn. New York: Schocken, 2021.
Ashbery, John. *Collected Poems 1956–1987*. Edited by Mark Ford. New York: Library of America, 2008.
Atkinson, David. "Magical Corpses: Ballads, Intertextuality, and the Discovery of Murder." *Journal of Folklore Research* 36, no. 1 (January 1999): 1–29.
Auden, W. H. *Collected Poems*. Edited by Edward Mendelson. New York: Vintage, 1991.
Badiou, Alain. *Being and Event*. Translated by Oliver Feltham. London: Continuum, 2006.
Bakhtin, Mikhail. "Forms of Time and of the Chronotope in the Novel." In *The Dialogic Imagination: Four Essays*, edited by Michael Holquist, translated by Caryl Emerson and Michael Holquist, 84–258. Austin: University of Texas Press, 1981.
Barthes, Roland. *Image-Music-Text*. Translated by Stephen Heath. New York: Hill and Wang, 1977.
———. "An Introduction to the Structural Analysis of Narrative." Translated by Lionel Duisit. *New Literary History* 6, no. 2 (Winter 1975): 237–72.
———. *The Preparation of the Novel: Lecture Courses and Seminars at the Collège de France (1978–1979 and 1979–1980)*. Edited by Nathalie Léger. Translated by Kate Briggs. New York: Columbia University Press, 2011.
———. "The Third Meaning: Notes on Some of Eisenstein's Stills." Translated by Richard Howard. *Artforum* 11, no. 5 (January 1973): 46–50.
Baxandall, Michael. *Painting and Experience in Fifteenth-Century Italy: A Primer in the Social History of Pictorial Styles*. New York: Oxford University Press, 1988.
Bennett, Jane. *Vibrant Matter: A Political Ecology of Things*. Durham, NC: Duke University Press, 2010.
Berlant, Lauren. *Cruel Optimism*. Durham, NC: Duke University Press, 2011.
———. "Genre Flailing." *Capacious: Journal for Emerging Affect Inquiry* 1, no. 2 (2018): 156–62. http://capaciousjournal.com/article/genre-flailing/.
———. "Starved." *South Atlantic Quarterly* 106, no. 3 (Summer 2007): 433–44.
Bernstein, Charles. *A Poetics*. Cambridge, MA: Harvard University Press, 1992.
Blair, Ann. "Note Taking as an Art of Transmission." *Critical Inquiry* 31, no. 1 (2004): 85–107.
———. "The Rise of Note-Taking in Early Modern Europe." *Intellectual History Review* 20, no. 3 (2010): 303–16.
———. *Too Much to Know: Managing Scholarly Information Before the Modern Age*. New Haven, CT: Yale University Press, 2010.
Blake, William. *The Poems of William Blake*. Edited by David V. Erdman. 3rd ed. London: Longman, 2007.
Bök, Christian. "The Xenotext Experiment." Interview by Stephen Voyce. *Postmodern Culture* 17, no. 2. http://pmc.iath.virginia.edu/issue.107/17.2voyce.html.
Bonney, Sean. *Letters against the Firmament*. London: Enitharmon, 2015.

BIBLIOGRAPHY

Boyer, Anne. *Garments against Women*. Boise: Ahsahta, 2015.

———. "'Literature Is against Us': In Conversation with Anne Boyer." Interview by Amy King. Poetry Foundation, August 30, 2015. https://www.poetryfoundation.org/harriet-books/2015/08/literature-is-against-us-in-conversation-with-anne-boyer.

Brogan, T.V.F., S. Cushman, K. S. Chang, R.M.A. Allen, W. L. Hanaway, and C. Scott. "Rhyme." In *The Princeton Encyclopedia of Poetry and Poetics*, 4th ed., edited by Roland Greene, Stephen Cushman, Clare Cavanagh, Jahan Ramazani, and Paul Rouzer, 1182–192. Princeton, NJ: Princeton University Press, 2012.

Bronson, Bertrand Harris. *The Traditional Tunes of the Child Ballads*. 2 vols. Princeton, NJ: Princeton University Press, 2015.

Brooks, Gwendolyn. *The Essential Gwendolyn Brooks*. Edited by Elizabeth Alexander. New York: Library of America, 2005.

Brotchie, Alistair, and Harry Matthews, eds. *Oulipo Compendium*. London: Atlas, 1998.

Buchan-Watts, Sam, and Lavinia Singer, eds. *Try to Be Better*. London: Prototype, 2019.

Bunting, Basil. "The Codex." In *Basil Bunting on Poetry*, edited by Peter Makin, 1–18. Baltimore: Johns Hopkins University Press, 1999.

Bush, Christopher. "Modernism, Orientalism, and East Asia." In *A Handbook of Modernism Studies*, edited by Jean-Michel Rabaté, 192–208. Malden, MA: Wiley, 2013.

Butler, Judith. *Notes toward a Performative Theory of Assembly*. Cambridge, MA: Harvard University Press, 2015.

Caplan, David, ed. *On Rhyme*. Liège: Presses Universitaires de Liège, 2017.

———. *Rhyme's Challenge: Hip Hop, Poetry, and Contemporary Rhyming Culture*. Oxford: Oxford University Press, 2014.

Capildeo, Anthony (Vahni). "Interview with Vahni Capildeo by Zannab Sheikh." *I Don't Call Myself a Poet: Interviews with Contemporary Poets Living & Working in Britain* (blog), August 15, 2012. https://idontcallmyselfapoet.wordpress.com/category/poets-a-e/capildeo-vahni/.

———. *Like a Tree, Walking*. Manchester: Carcanet, 2021.

———. *Measures of Expatriation*. Manchester: Carcanet, 2016.

Carlson, Liane. "What Is Called Thinking in the Anthropocene?" *The Revealer*, August 9, 2019. https://therevealer.org/what-is-called-thinking-in-the-anthropocene/.

Carroll, Lewis. *Jabberwocky and Other Nonsense: Collected Poems*. Edited by Gillian Beer. New York: Penguin Classics, 2014.

Chakrabarty, Dipesh. "The Climate of History: Four Theses," *Critical Inquiry* 35, no. 2 (Winter 2009): 197–222.

———. *The Climate of History in a Planetary Age*. Chicago: University of Chicago Press, 2021.

Chamovitz, David. *What a Plant Knows: A Field Guide to the Senses*. New York: Scientific American / Farrar, Straus & Giroux, 2012.

Chappell, William. *Popular Music of the Olden Time: A Collection of Ancient Songs, Ballads, and Dance Tunes, Illustrative of the National Music of England*. 2 vols. London: Cramer, Beale & Chappell, 1859.

Chaucer, Geoffrey. *The Riverside Chaucer*. Edited by Larry D. Benson. Oxford: Oxford University Press, 1998.

Child, Francis James, ed. *The English and Scottish Popular Ballads*. 5 vols. Boston: Houghton Mifflin, 1884–98.

———. *The English and Scottish Popular Ballads*. Vol. 1, Pt. 1. Cambridge: Cambridge University Press, 2015.

———. *Francis James Child's English and Scottish Popular Ballads*. Edited by George Lyman Kittredge and Helen Child Sargent. Boston: Houghton, Mifflin, 1904.

Chute, Hillary. *Disaster Drawn: Visual Witness, Comics, and Documentary Form*. Cambridge, MA: Harvard University Press, 2016.

———. *Graphic Women: Life Narrative and Contemporary Comics*. New York: Columbia University Press, 2010.

Coleridge, Samuel Taylor. *The Collected Works of Samuel Taylor Coleridge: Poetical Works I; Poems (Reading Text): Part 2*. Edited by J. C. C. Mays. Princeton, NJ: Princeton University Press, 2001.

Coles, Romand, Mark Reinhardt, and George Shulman, eds. *Radical Future Pasts: Untimely Political Theory*. Lexington: University Press of Kentucky, 2014.

Compagnon, Antoine. "Roland Barthes's Novel." Translated by Rosalind Krauss. *October* 112 (Spring 2005): 23–34.

Coste, Claude. "From *Fichier* to *Œuvre*: Barthes and the 'Our Literature' Project." In *Interdisciplinary Barthes*, edited by Diana Knight, 252–75. Oxford: Oxford University Press, 2020.

———. "Roland Barthes's Visits to Greece." Translated by Sam Ferguson. *Barthes Studies* 5 (2019): 4–22.

Crawforth, Hannah. "Queer Echoes: Reading 'The Faerie Queene' with Evie Shockley." *The Spenser Review* 51, nos. 2–3 (Spring–Summer 2021). http://www.english.cam.ac.uk/spenseronline/review/item/51.2.3.

Culler, Jonathan. *Theory of the Lyric*. Cambridge, MA: Harvard University Press, 2015.

Davis, Olena Kalytiak. *The Poem She Didn't Write, and Other Poems*. Port Townsend, WA: Copper Canyon, 2014.

De Beer, Gavin. "An 'Atheist' in the Alps." *Keats–Shelley Memorial Bulletin* 9 (1958): 1–15.

Delany, Samuel. "About 5,750 Words." In *The Jewel-Hinged Jaw: Notes on the Language of Science Fiction*, 2–15. Middletown, CT: Wesleyan University Press, 2009.

Deleuze, Gilles, and Félix Guattari. *A Thousand Plateaus: Capitalism and Schizo-*

phrenia. Translated by Brian Massumi. Minneapolis: University of Minnesota Press, 1987.

De Man, Paul. "Anthropomorphism and Trope in Lyric." In *The Rhetoric of Romanticism*, 239–62. New York: Columbia University Press, 1986.

———. "Lyric and Modernity." In *Blindness and Insight: Essays in the Rhetoric of Contemporary Criticism*, 166–86. Minneapolis: University of Minnesota Press, 1983.

Derksen, Jeff. "Reader's Manual: An Introduction to the Poetics and Contexts of Fred Wah's Early Poetry." In Fred Wah, *Scree: The Collected Earlier Poems, 1962–1991*, 1–16. Vancouver: Talonbooks, 2016.

Dickman, Michael. *Days & Days*. New York: Knopf, 2019.

Di Prima, Diane. *Revolutionary Letters*. San Francisco: City Lights, 2021.

Douglas, Mary. *Purity and Danger: An Analysis of Concepts of Pollution and Taboo*. London: Routledge, 1984.

Dungy, Camille, ed. *Black Nature: Four Centuries of African American Nature Poetry*. Athens: University of Georgia Press, 2009.

Dworkin, Craig, and Kenneth Goldsmith, eds. *Against Expression: An Anthology of Conceptual Writing*. Evanston, IL: Northwestern University Press, 2011.

Edelman, Lee. *No Future: Queer Theory and the Death Drive*. Durham, NC: Duke University Press, 2004.

Eliot, T. S. *On Poetry and Poets*. New York: Farrar, Straus & Cudahy, 1957.

———. *To Criticize the Critic*. New York: Farrar, Straus & Cudahy, 1965.

Éluard, Paul. *Oeuvres completes*, vol. 1. Paris: Gallimard, 1968.

Foster, Tonya. *A Swarm of Bees in High Court*. New York: Belladonna, 2015.

François, Anne-Lise. "'A Little While' More: Further Thoughts on Hartman's Nature as Paraclete." *Essays in Romanticism* 22, no. 2 (2015): 133–49.

Frase, Peter. *Four Futures: Life after Capitalism*. London: Verso, 2016.

Frost, Robert. *Collected Poems, Prose & Plays*. Edited by Richard Poirier and Mark Richardson. New York: Library of America, 1997.

Fukuyama, Francis. "The End of History?" *National Interest* 16 (Summer 1989): 3–18.

Galvin, Rachel. "'This Song Is for My Foe': Olive Senior and Terrance Hayes Rewrite Stevens." In *Poetry and Poetics after Wallace Stevens*, edited by Bart Eeckhout and Lisa Goldfarb, 303–22. London: Bloomsbury, 2016.

Ginsberg, Allen. *Selected Poems, 1947–1995*. New York: Harper Collins, 2001.

Glück, Louise. *The Wild Iris*. Hopewell, NJ: Ecco, 1993.

Godwin, William. *Enquiry Concerning Political Justice and Its Influence on Modern Morals and Happiness*. Edited with an introduction and notes by Isaac Kramnick. New York: Penguin, 1985.

Goldsmith, Kenneth. *Uncreative Writing: Managing Language in the Digital Age*. New York: Columbia University Press, 2011.

Goodman, Kevis. *Pathologies of Motion: Historical Thinking in Medicine, Aesthetics, and Poetics*. New Haven, CT: Yale University Press, 2022.

Goodman, Nelson. "The Problem of Counterfactual Conditionals." *The Journal of Philosophy* 44, no. 5 (February 1947): 113–28.

Gottlieb, Susannah Young-ah. *Auden and the Muse of History*. Stanford, CA: Stanford University Press, 2022.

Graham, W. S. "From a 1949 Notebook: Given to the Late Elizabeth Smart in the 1950s." *Edinburgh Review* 75 (1987): 24–36.

Greene, Roland, Stephen Cushman, Clare Cavanagh, Jahan Ramazani, and Paul Rouzer, eds. *The Princeton Encyclopedia of Poetry and Poetics*. 4th ed, Princeton, NJ: Princeton University Press, 2012.

Grossman, Allen. Commonplace 29, "Scholium on line and breath." "Summa Lyrica: A Primer of the Commonplaces of Speculative Poetics." In *The Sighted Singer: Two Works on Poetry for Readers and Writers*, with Mark Halliday, 205–377. Baltimore: Johns Hopkins University Press, 1991.

Guillory, John. "Mute Inglorious Miltons." In *Cultural Capital*, 85–133. Chicago: University of Chicago Press, 1993.

Hanson, Lenora. *The Romantic Rhetoric of Accumulation*. Stanford, CA: Stanford University Press, 2022.

Harris, Kaplan. "Causes, Movements, Theory: Between Language Poetry and New Narrative." In *A Companion to American Poetry*, edited by Mary McAleer Balkun, Jeffrey Gray, and Paul Jaussen, 146–56. Hoboken, NJ: Wiley Blackwell, 2022.

Hartman, Geoffrey. "'The Nymph Complaining for the Death of Her Faun': A Brief Allegory." *Essays in Criticism* 18, no. 2 (April 1968): 113–35.

———. *Wordsworth's Poetry: 1787–1814*. New Haven, CT: Yale University Press, 1964.

H. D. *Collected Poems 1912–1944*. Edited by Louis L. Martz. New York: New Directions, 1983.

Hass, Robert, trans. and ed. *The Essential Haiku: Versions of Bashō, Buson, & Issa*. New York: Ecco, 1994.

Hayes, Terrance. *Lighthead*. New York; Penguin, 2010.

Hollander, John. "Breaking into Song: Some Notes on Refrain." In *Lyric Poetry: Beyond New Criticism*, edited by Chaviva Hošek and Patricia Parker, 73–89. Ithaca, NY: Cornell University Press, 1985.

———. *Rhyme's Reason: A Guide to English Verse*. 3rd ed. New Haven, CT: Yale University Press, 2001.

Hollier, Denis. "On Literature Considered as a Dead Language." *Modern Language Quarterly* 54, no. 1 (1993): 21–29.

Hong, Cathy Park. "Cathy Park Hong." Interview by Ken Chen. *Bomb*, January 8, 2020. https://bombmagazine.org/articles/cathy-park-hong/.

———. *Dance Dance Revolution*. New York: Norton, 2006.

———. *Engine Empire*. New York: Norton, 2012.

———. *Minor Feelings: An Asian American Reckoning*. New York: One World, 2020.

Howe, Fanny. *Love and I*. Minneapolis: Graywolf, 2019.

Howe, Susan. *My Emily Dickinson*. New York: New Directions, 2017.
Hunter, J. Paul. "Form as Meaning: Pope and the Ideology of the Couplet." *The Eighteenth Century* 37, no. 3 (Fall 1996): 257–70.
———. "The Heroic Couplet: Its Rhyme and Reason." *Ideas from the National Humanities Center* 4, no. 1 (1996): 22–29.
Hunter, Walt. *Forms of a World: Contemporary Poetry and the Making of Globalization*. New York: Fordham University Press, 2019.
Hyland, MC. *The End*. Portland, OR: Sidebrow Books, 2019.
Ives, Lucy. *The Hermit Cave*. Brooklyn: The Song Cave, 2016.
Jabr, Ferris. "The Social Life of Forests." *New York Times Magazine*, December 20, 2020. https://www.nytimes.com/interactive/2020/12/02/magazine/tree-communication-mycorrhiza.html.
Jackson, Virginia. *Dickinson's Misery: A Theory of Lyric Reading*. Princeton, NJ: Princeton University Press, 2005.
Jackson, Virginia, and Yopie Prins, eds. *The Lyric Theory Reader: A Critical Anthology*. Baltimore: Johns Hopkins University Press, 2014.
Jakobson, Roman. "Closing Statement: Linguistics and Poetics." In *Style in Language*, edited by Thomas A. Sebeok, 350–77. Cambridge, MA: MIT Press, 1960.
Jameson, Fredric. "In Hyperspace." Review of *Time Travel: The Popular Philosophy of Narrative*, by David Wittenberg. *London Review of Books* 37, no. 17 (10 September 2015). https://www.lrb.co.uk/the-paper/v37/n17/fredric-jameson/in-hyperspace.
———. *Postmodernism: Or, The Cultural Logic of Late Capitalism*. Durham, NC: Duke University Press, 1991.
Jarcho, Julia. *Writing and the Modern Stage: Theater beyond Drama*. Cambridge: Cambridge University Press, 2017.
Johnson, Barbara. *Persons and Things*. Cambridge, MA: Harvard University Press, 2008.
Johnston, Devin. *Far-Fetched*. New York: Farrar, Straus & Giroux, 2015.
———. *Traveler*. New York: Farrar, Straus & Giroux, 2011.
Kane, Daniel, ed. *What Is Poetry: Conversations with the American Avant-Garde*. New York: Teachers and Writers Books, 2003.
Kapil, Bhanu. *Ban en Banlieue*. New York: Nightboat, 2015.
———. *How to Wash a Heart*. Liverpool: Liverpool University Press, 2020.
Keats, John. *The Letters of John Keats*. Vol. 1, *1814–1818*. Edited by Hyder Edward Rollins. Cambridge: Cambridge University Press, 2011.
Koselleck, Reinhart. *Futures Past: On the Semantics of Historical Time*. Translated by Keith Tribe. New York: Columbia University Press, 2004.
Krauss, Rosalind. "Liar's Paradox." *Artforum* 60, no. 22 (January 2022). https://www.artforum.com/print/202201/rosalind-e-krauss-on-jasper-johns-87451.
Kristeva, Julia. *Desire in Language: A Semiotic Approach to Literature and Art*. New York: Columbia University Press, 1980.

———. *Revolution in Poetic Language*. New York: Columbia University Press, 1984.

Langan, Celeste. "Repetition Run Riot: Refrains, Slogans, and Graffiti." *Wordsworth Circle* 52, no. 2 (Spring 2021): 287–307.

Lasky, Dorothea. *Poetry Is Not a Project*. Brooklyn: Ugly Duckling Presse, 2010.

Latour, Bruno. "An Attempt at a 'Compositionist Manifesto.'" *New Literary History* 41, no. 3 (Summer 2010): 471–90.

———. "Why Has Critique Run Out of Steam? From Matters of Fact to Matters of Concern." *Critical Inquiry* 30, no. 2 (2004): 225–48.

Levin, Richard, and Richard Lewontin. *The Dialectical Biologist*. Cambridge, MA: Harvard University Press, 1985.

Levinson, Marjorie. *Thinking through Poetry: Field Reports on Romantic Lyric*. Oxford: Oxford University Press, 2018.

———. *Wordsworth's Great Period Poems: Four Essays*. Cambridge: Cambridge University Press, 1986.

Lewis, Charlton T., and Charles Short. *A Latin Dictionary: Founded on Andrews' edition of Freund's Latin dictionary. revised, enlarged, and in great part rewritten with many instances of use adduced from Cicero*. Oxford: Clarendon Press, 1879. Archived at http://www.perseus.tufts.edu/hopper/text?doc=Perseus:text:1999.04.0059.

Mabey, Richard. *The Cabaret of Plants: Forty Thousand Years of Plant Life and the Human Imagination*. New York: Norton, 2015.

Mackey, Nathaniel. "Breath and Precarity: The Inaugural Robert Creeley Lecture in Poetry and Poetics." In *Poetics and Precarity: The University at Buffalo Robert Creeley Lectures in Poetry and Poetics*, edited by Myung Mi Kim and Cristanne Miller, 1–30. Albany: State University of New York Press, 2018.

Madrid, Anthony. *I Am Your Slave, Now Do What I Say*. Ann Arbor, MI: Canarium Books, 2012.

———. "Seventeen Quotations with Commentary." In *On Rhyme*, edited by David Caplan, 123–39. Liège: Presses Universitaires de Liège, 2017.

———. *Try Never*. Ann Arbor, MI: Canarium Books, 2017.

———. "Wallace Stevens's Place in the History of English Rhyming: A Talk Given at the 43rd Annual Louisville Conference on Literature and Culture Since 1900." *Prelude* 2 (February 2015). https://preludemag.com/issues/2/wallace-stevenss-place-in-the-history-of-english-rhyming/.

Malthus, Thomas Robert. *An Essay on the Principle of Population*. Edited by Joyce E. Chaplin. New York: Norton, 2018.

Manning, Susan. *The Poetics of Character: Transatlantic Encounters, 1700–1900*. Cambridge: Cambridge University Press, 2013.

Marder, Michael. *Plant-Thinking: A Philosophy of Vegetal Life*. New York: Columbia University Press, 2013.

Marx, Karl. *Capital*. Vol. 1. Translated by Ben Fowkes. London: Penguin, 1990.

———. "The 18th Brumaire of Louis Bonaparte (1852)." *Marx-Engels Archive*. http://www.marxists.org/archive/marx/works/1852/18th-brumaire/ch01.htm.

BIBLIOGRAPHY

Mayer, Mark. "Using the Rotted Names: Wallace Stevens's Racial Ontology as Poetic Key." *Twentieth-Century Literature* 65, no. 3 (September 2019): 217–36.

Mbembe, Achille. "Necropolitics." Translated by Libby Meintjes. *Public Culture* 15, no. 1 (2003): 11–40.

———. *Necropolitics*. Durham, NC: Duke University Press, 2019.

McGann, Jerome. *The Romantic Ideology: A Critical Investigation*. Chicago: University of Chicago Press, 1983.

McKibben, Bill. *The End of Nature*. New York: Random House, 1989.

McLane, Maureen N. *Balladeering, Minstrelsy, and the Making of British Romantic Poetry*. Cambridge: Cambridge University Press, 2008.

———. "Child No. 26 and *Poiesis* Unbound." In *Child's Children: Ballad Study and Its Legacies*, edited by Joseph C. Harris and Barbara Hillers, 140–54. Trier: Wissenschaftlicher Verlag Trier, 2012.

———. "Hoobla-hoo and Hullabaloo: Divagations with Stevens." In *Wallace Stevens, Poetry, and France: "Au pays de la métaphore,"* edited by Juliette Utard, Bart Eeckhout, and Lisa Goldfarb, 81–96. Paris: Éditions Rue d'Ulm, 2018.

———. "Mediating Antiquarians in Britain, 1760–1830: The Invention of Oral Tradition, or, Close-Reading before Coleridge." In *This Is Enlightenment*, edited by Clifford Siskin and William Warner, 247–64. Chicago: University of Chicago Press, 2010.

———. *Romanticism and the Human Sciences: Poetry, Population, and the Discourse of the Species*. Cambridge: Cambridge University Press, 2000.

———. *Same Life*. New York: Farrar, Straus & Giroux, 2008.

———. *Some Say*. New York: Farrar, Straus & Giroux, 2016.

———. *This Blue*. New York: Farrar, Straus & Giroux, 2014.

———. *What You Want*. New York: Farrar, Straus & Giroux, 2023.

———. *World Enough*. New York: Farrar, Straus & Giroux, 2011.

McSweeney, Joyelle. *The Necropastoral: Poetry, Media, Occults*. Ann Arbor: University of Michigan Press, 2014.

Moore, Marianne. *New Collected Poems*. Edited by Heather Cass White. New York: Farrar, Straus & Giroux, 2017.

Morrison, Toni. *Playing in the Dark: Whiteness and the Literary Imagination*. Cambridge, MA: Harvard University Press, 1993.

Morton, Timothy. *The Ecological Thought*. Cambridge, MA: Harvard University Press, 2010.

Moten, Fred. "B 4." *Poetry Magazine*, February 6, 2010. https://www.poetryfoundation.org/harriet/2010/02/b-4.

———. "Refuge, Refuse, Refrain." In *The Universal Machine: Consent Not To Be a Single Being*, 66–139. Durham, NC: Duke University Press, 2018.

———. *The Service Porch*. Tuscon, AZ: Letter Machine Editions, 2016.

———. *The Universal Machine: Consent Not to Be a Single Being*. Durham, NC: Duke University Press, 2018.

Muldoon, Paul. *Hay*. London: Faber and Faber, 1998.

———. *Horse Latitudes*. London: Faber and Faber, 2006.
———. "An Interview with Paul Muldoon." Interview by Lynn Keller. *Contemporary Literature* 35, no. 1 (Spring 1994): 1–29.
———. *Madoc*. London: Faber and Faber, 1990.
———. *Moy Sand and Gravel*. London: Faber and Faber, 2002.
Mullen, Harryette. *Recyclopedia: Trimmings, S*PeRM**K*T, and Muse & Drudge*. Minneapolis: Graywolf, 2006.
———. *Urban Tumbleweed: Notes from a Tanka Diary*. Minneapolis: Graywolf, 2013.
Muñoz, José Esteban. *Cruising Utopia: The Then and There of Queer Futurity*. 10th anniversary ed. New York: New York University Press, 2019.
Myles, Eileen. *I Must Be Living Twice: New and Selected Poems*. New York: Ecco, 2014.
———. *Not Me*. New York: Semiotext(e), 1991.
Nealon, Christopher. *The Matter of Capital: Poetry and Crisis in the American Century*. Cambridge, MA: Harvard University Press, 2011.
———. *The Shore*. Seattle: Wave Books, 2020.
Nelson, Tollof. "Theoretical Apparitions of Haiku: An Intermedial Interrogation of Modernity." *Cinemas: Journal of Film Studies* 10, nos. 2–3 (2000): 185–203.
Nelson, Maggie. *The Argonauts*. Minneapolis: Graywolf, 2015.
Nersessian, Anahid. *The Calamity Form: On Poetry and Social Life*. Chicago: University of Chicago Press, 2020.
———. "Romantic Ecocriticism Lately." *Literature Compass* 15, no. 1 (2018): 1–16.
———. *Utopia, Limited: Romanticism and Adjustment*. Cambridge, MA: Harvard University Press, 2015.
Ngai, Sianne. *Ugly Feelings*. Cambridge, MA: Harvard University Press, 2005.
Niedecker, Lorine. "Five Poems." *Poetry* 106, no. 5 (August 1965): 341–44.
Noel-Tod, Jeremy. "The Quizzical Priest: Inside John Ashbery's Everyday Magical Thinking." Review of Karin Rofmann, *The Songs We Know Best: John Ashbery's Early Life*, *Prospect Magazine*, March 19, 2018. https://www.prospectmagazine.co.uk/magazine/the-quizzical-priest-inside-john-ashberys-everyday-magical-thinking.
Noel, Urayoán. *Transversal*. Tucson: University of Arizona Press, 2021.
O'Neill, Michael. *The All-Sustaining Air: Romantic Legacies and Renewals in British, American, and Irish Poetry Since 1900*. Oxford: Oxford University Press, 2007.
Pepys, Samuel. *The Diary of Samuel Pepys*. Vol. 7, *1666*. Edited by Robert Latham and William Matthews. Berkeley: University of California Press, 1972.
Percy, Thomas. *Reliques of Ancient English Poetry: Consisting of Old Heroic Ballads, Songs, and Other Pieces of Our Earlier Poets (Chiefly of the Lyric Kind.) Together with some few of later Date: Volume the First*. London: J. Dodsley, 1765.
Perloff, Marjorie. "After Free Verse: The New Non-Linear Poetries." In *Poetry on and off the Page*, 141–67. Evanston, IL: Northwestern University Press, 1998.
———. *Unoriginal Genius: Poetry by Other Means in the New Century*. Chicago: University of Chicago Press, 2010.

BIBLIOGRAPHY

Peters, John Durham. *The Marvelous Clouds: Toward a Philosophy of Elemental Media*. Chicago: University of Chicago Press, 2015.

Philip, M. NourbeSe. *Zong!* Middletown, CT: Wesleyan University Press, 2008.

Pollan, Michael. "The Intelligent Plant." *New Yorker* 89, no. 42 (December 23/30, 2013): 92–117.

Posmentier, Sonya. *Cultivation and Catastrophe: The Lyric Ecology of Modern Black Literature*. Baltimore: Johns Hopkins University Press, 2017.

Pound, Ezra. *The Cantos of Ezra Pound*. New York: New Directions, 1971.

———. "How I Began." *T.P.'s Weekly* (June 6, 1913): 707.

———. "In a Station of the Metro," *Poetry* 2, no. 1 (April 1913): 12.

———. *The Literary Essays of Ezra Pound*. Edited by T. S. Eliot. New York: New Directions, 1976.

———. "A Retrospect: A Few Don'ts." In *Pavannes and Divagations*, 95–101. New York: Knopf, 1918.

———. "Vortex." In *Blast* 1, edited by Wyndham Lewis, 153–55. London: John Lane, 1914.

———. "Vorticism." *Fortnightly Review* 96 (September 1, 1914): 461–71.

Preminger, Alex, and T. V. F. Brogan, eds. *The New Princeton Encyclopedia of Poetry and Poetics*. Princeton, NJ: Princeton University Press, 1993.

Prynne, J. H. "Mental Ears and Poetic Work." *Chicago Review* 55, no. 1 (Winter 2010): 126–57.

Ramazani, Jahan. *Poetry and Its Others: News, Prayer, Song, and the Dialogue of Genres*. Chicago: University of Chicago Press, 2013.

———. *Poetry in a Global Age*. Chicago: University of Chicago Press, 2020.

Rancière, Jacques. *Dissensus: On Politics and Aesthetics*. Edited and translated by Steven Corcoran. New York: Continuum, 2010.

———. "Ten Theses on Politics." Translated by Davide Panagia and Rachel Bowlby. *Theory & Event* 5, no. 3 (2001): 1–16.

Rankine, Claudia. *Citizen*. Minneapolis: Graywolf, 2014.

———. "The Poetry of Race." Interview by Charles Monroe-Kane. *To the Best of Our Knowledge* (podcast), February 1, 2015. https://www.ttbook.org/interview/poetry-race.

Rasula, Jed. *This Compost: Ecological Imperatives in American Poetry*. Athens: University of Georgia Press, 2002.

Ravenscroft, Thomas. *Melismata: Musicall Phansies. Fitting the Court, Citie, and Countrey Humours. To 3, 4, and 5. Voyces*. London: Printed by William Stansby for Thomas Adams, 1611.

Reines, Ariana. "The World Is Not Enough." *Artforum International*, January 10, 2020. https://www.artforum.com/slant/ariana-reines-s-full-moon-report-81838.

Robbins, Michael. *Alien vs. Predator*. New York: Penguin, 2012.

———. *The Second Sex*. New York: Penguin, 2014.

Robertson, Lisa. *The Weather*. Vancouver: New Star Books, 2001.

Ronda, Margaret. "Mourning and Melancholia in the Anthropocene." *Post45*, June 10, 2013. https://post45.org/2013/06/mourning-and-melancholia-in-the-anthropocene/.

———. *Remainders: American Poetry at Nature's End*. Stanford, CA: Stanford University Press, 2018.

Ronda, Margaret, and Lindsay Turner. "Poetry's Social Forms," *Post45*, April 22–26, 2019. https://post45.org/sections/contemporaries-essays/poetry-social-forms/.

Ruskin, John. "Of the Pathetic Fallacy." In *Modern Painters*, 3rd ed., 157–72. London: Smith, Elder and Co, 1872.

Sartre, Jean-Paul. *"What Is Literature?" and Other Essays*. Cambridge, MA: Harvard University Press, 1988.

Saussure, Ferdinand. *Course in General Linguistics*. Edited and translated by Roy Harris. London: Bloomsbury Academic, 2013.

Scappettone, Jennifer. "Precarity Shared: Breathing as Tactic in Air's Uneven Commons." In *Poetics and Precarity: The University at Buffalo Robert Creeley Lectures in Poetry and Poetics*, edited by Myung Mi Kim and Cristanne Miller, 41–58. Albany: State University of New York Press, 2018.

Scott, Julius S. *The Common Wind: Afro-American Currents in the Age of the Haitian Revolution*. London: Verso, 2018.

Scott, Walter. *Minstrelsy of the Scottish Border*. 2 vols. London: James Ballantyne, 1802.

———. *The Poetical Works of Walter Scott, Bart*. 12 vols. Edinburgh: Robert Cadell, 1830–1833.

Schlegel, Friedrich von. *Philosophical Fragments*. Translated by Peter Firchow. Minneapolis: University of Minnesota Press, 1991.

Schuyler, James. *Collected Poems*. New York: Farrar, Straus & Giroux, 1993.

Sedgwick, Eve Kosofsky. "A Dialogue on Love." *Critical Inquiry* 24, no. 2 (Winter 1998): 611–31.

———. *A Dialogue on Love*. Boston: Beacon, 2003.

———. *Touching Feeling: Affect, Pedagogy, Performativity*. Durham, NC: Duke University Press, 2003.

Seeger, Charles, ed. "Versions and Variants of the Tunes of 'Barbara Allen.'" *Selected Reports of the Institute of Ethnomusicology* 1, no. 1 (1966): 120–67.

Seidel, Frederick. *Poems 1959–2009*. New York: Farrar, Straus & Giroux, 2010.

———. Translation of Imru al-Qays's "Mu'allaqa." *Poetry* 192, no. 2 (April 2008): 21–25.

Sharpe, Christina. *In the Wake: On Blackness and Being*. Durham, NC: Duke University Press, 2016.

Shelley, Percy Bysshe. *The Complete Poetry of Percy Bysshe Shelley*. Vol. 3. Edited by Donald H. Reiman, Neil Fraistat, and Nora Crook. Baltimore: Johns Hopkins University Press, 2012.

BIBLIOGRAPHY

———. *The Complete Poetry of Percy Bysshe Shelley*. Vol. 7. Edited by Nora Crook. Baltimore: Johns Hopkins University Press, 2021.
———. "A Defence of Poetry." In *Shelley's Poetry and Prose: Authoritative Texts, Criticism*, 2nd ed, edited by Donald H. Reiman and Neil Fraistat, 478–510. New York: Norton, 2002.
———. *Laon and Cyntha*. Edited by Anahid Nersessian. Peterborough, ON: Broadview Editions, 2016.
———. *Shelley's Poetry and Prose*. Edited by Donald H. Reiman and Neil Fraistat. 2nd ed. New York: Norton, 2002.
———. *Shelley's "Prometheus Unbound": A Variorum Edition*. Edited by Lawrence John Zillman. Seattle: University of Washington Press, 1959.
———. "The Triumph of Life." In *The Complete Poetry of Percy Bysshe Shelley*, vol. 7, edited by Nora Crook, 3–31. Baltimore: Johns Hopkins University Press, 2021.
Shockley, Evie. *Renegade Poetics: Black Aesthetics and Formal Innovation in African American Poetry*. Iowa City: University of Iowa Press, 2011.
———. *Semiautomatic*. Middletown, CT: Wesleyan University Press, 2017.
Silliman, Ronald. *The New Sentence*. New York: Roof, 1989.
Simard, Suzanne. *Finding the Mother Tree: Discovering the Wisdom of the Forest*. New York: Knopf, 2021.
Slatkin, Laura M. *The Power of Thetis and Selected Essays*. Cambridge, MA: Harvard University Center for Hellenic Studies, 2011.
Smailbegović, Ada. *The Poetics of Liveliness: Molecules, Fibers, Tissues, Clouds*. New York: Columbia University Press, 2021.
Smith, Barbara Herrnstein. *Poetic Closure: A Study of How Poems End*. Chicago: University of Chicago Press, 1968.
Spahr, Juliana. *That Winter the Wolf Came*. Oakland, CA: Commune Editions, 2015.
———. *This Connection of Everyone with Lungs*. Berkeley: University of California Press, 2006.
Spektor, Regina. *Home, Before and After*. Sire Records, 2022.
Spicer, Jack. *After Lorca*. New York: NYRB/Poets, 2021.
Stein, Gertrude. "Arthur A Grammar." In *How to Write*, 37–101. Craftsbury Common, VT: Sherry Urie, 1977.
———. *Stanzas in Meditation: The Corrected Edition*. Edited by Susannah Hollister and Emily Setina. New Haven, CT: Yale University Press, 2012.
———. *Writings 1903–1932; Q.E.D., Three Lives, Portraits and Other Short Works; The Autobiography of Alice B. Toklas*. Edited by Catharine R. Stimpson and Harriet Chessman. New York: Library of America, 1998.
———. *Writings 1932–1946*. Edited by Catharine R. Stimpson and Harriet Chessman. New York: Library of America, 1998.
Steinman, Lisa M. "Unanticipated Readers." In *Poetry and Poetics after Wallace Stevens*, edited by Bart Eeckhout and Lisa Goldfarb, 288–302. London: Bloomsbury, 2016.

Stephens, Paul. *absence of clutter: minimal writing as art and literature*. Boston: MIT Press, 2020.
Stevens, Wallace. *Collected Poems & Prose*. Edited by Frank Kermode and Joan Richardson. New York: Library of America, 1997.
———. *The Letters of Wallace Stevens*. Edited by Holly Stevens. Berkeley: University of California Press, 1966.
Stewart, Susan. "Notes on Distressed Genres." In *Crimes of Writing: Problems in the Containment of Representation*, 66–101. Oxford: Oxford University Press, 1991.
———. "Rhyme and Freedom." In *The Sound of Poetry/The Poetry of Sound*, edited by Marjorie Perloff and Craig Dworkin, 29–48. Chicago: University of Chicago Press, 2009.
———. *Poetry and the Fate of the Senses*. Chicago: University of Chicago Press, 2003.
———. *The Poet's Freedom: A Notebook on Making*. Chicago: University of Chicago Press, 2011.
Stonecipher, Donna. "Transaction History 3." In *Transaction Histories*, 17–36. Iowa City: University of Iowa Press, 2018.
Teare, Brian. *Doomstead Days*. New York: Nightboat Books, 2019.
Turner, Lindsay. "Poetics and Precarity." Review of *Poetics and Precarity*. Edited by Myung Mi Kim and Cristanne Miller. *ASAP Journal*, February 14, 2019. https://asapjournal.com/poetics-and-precarity-lindsay-turner/.
Ueda, Makoto. *Bashō and His Interpreters: Selected Hokku with Commentary*. Stanford, CA: Stanford University Press, 1992.
———. *Matsuo Bashō*. Tokyo: Kodansha International, 1970.
———. "True Before It Is Made Truth." Interview with Eve Luckring. *Roadrunner* 12–13, nos. 3/1 (December 2012–May 2013): 27–39, 19–31.
Wah, Fred. *Scree: The Collected Earlier Poems, 1962–1991*. Vancouver: Talonbooks, 2015.
Walker, Kara. *A Subtlety: Or the Marvelous Sugar Baby, an Homage to the unpaid and overworked Artisans who have refined our Sweet tastes from the cane fields to the Kitchens of the New World on the Occasion of the demolition of the Domino Sugar Refining Plant*. Installation, Domino Sugar Factory. Brooklyn, NY, May 10–July 6, 2014. https://creativetime.org/projects/karawalker/.
Webster, Gerry, and Brian Goodwin. *Form and Transformation: Generative and Relational Principles in Biology*. Cambridge: Cambridge University Press, 1996.
Weisman, Alan. *The World Without Us*. New York: St. Martin's, 2007.
Weiss, Sasha. "Taylor Mac Wants Theater to Make You Uncomfortable." *New York Times Magazine*, April 2, 2019. https://www.nytimes.com/2019/04/02/magazine/taylor-mac-gary-broadway.html/.
Whitman, Walt. *Poetry and Prose*. Edited by Justin Kaplan. New York: Library of America, 1982.
Williams, Raymond. *Keywords: A Vocabulary of Culture and Society*. London: Routledge, 1976.

Wimsatt, W. K. "One Relation of Rhyme to Reason." In *The Verbal Icon: Studies in the Meaning of Poetry*, 152–66. New York: Noonday Press, 1958.

Wohlleben, Peter. *The Hidden Life of Trees: What They Feel, How They Communicate; Discoveries from a Secret World*. Vancouver: Greystone, 2016.

Wolff, Tristram. *Against the Uprooted Word: Giving Language Time in Transatlantic Romanticism*. Stanford, CA: Stanford University Press, 2022.

Woolf, Virginia. *The Essays of Virginia Woolf*. Vol. 3, *1919–1924*. Edited by Andrew McNeillie. London: Hogarth, 1986.

Wordsworth, William. *Lyrical Ballads, and Other Poems, 1797–1800*. Edited by James Butler and Karen Green. Ithaca, NY: Cornell University Press, 1992.

———. *Poems in Two Volumes, and Other Poems*. Edited by Jared Curtis. Ithaca, NY: Cornell University Press, 1983.

———. *The Thirteen-Book Prelude*. Vol. 1. Edited by Mark L. Reed. Ithaca, NY: Cornell University Press, 1991.

Yanyi. *The Year of Blue Water*. New Haven, CT: Yale University Press, 2019.

Yasuda, Kenneth. *The Japanese Haiku: Its Essential Nature, History, and Possibilities in English, with Selected Examples*. Boston: Tuttle, 2001.

Yeo, Richard. *Notebooks, English Virtuosi, and Early Modern Science*. Chicago: University of Chicago Press, 2014.

Zhirmunsky, Viktor. "Introduction to Rhyme: Its History and Theory." Translated by John Hoffman. *Chicago Review* 57, nos. 3–4 (Winter 2013): 119–27.

Printed in the USA
CPSIA information can be obtained
at www.ICGtesting.com
JSHW052203161123
52090JS00015B/152